Queen Victoria and the
Discovery of the Riviera

1. Queen Victoria in 1897 at Cimiez, above Nice, where, from 1895 to 1899,
she spent five of the nine visits she paid to the Riviera.

Queen Victoria and the Discovery of the Riviera

Michael Nelson

Foreword by
Asa Briggs

I.B.Tauris *Publishers*
LONDON ● NEW YORK

Published in 2001 by I.B.Tauris & Co Ltd
6 Salem Road, London W2 4BU
175 Fifth Avenue, New York NY 10010
www.ibtauris.com

In the United States and Canada distributed by St. Martin's Press
175 Fifth Avenue, New York NY 10010

ISBN 1-86064-646-8

A full CIP record for this book is available from the British Library
A full CIP record for this book is available from the Library of Congress

Library of Congress catalog card: available

Typeset in Perpetua by A. & D. Worthington, Newmarket, Suffolk
Printed and bound in Great Britain by MPG Books Ltd, Bodmin

Contents

Illustrations

Black & white

Foreword

I was glad to be asked to write a foreword to this delightful book, which speaks entirely for itself. Both as a historian of Victorian Britain and as President of the Victorian Society I am interested in any study of the Queen which pushes from Britain across the Channel — or across the Atlantic or to India. The Queen has to be placed in more than a British setting.

I know too that it is the detail of Victorian Britain and of the Queen's own long life, discovered only through research, which is more revealing and significant than any generalizations. Far too many of these are made on the basis of secondary evidence.

The Queen's attitudes towards Germany, which were inextricably bound up with her loving relationship with Albert, the Prince Consort, have often been studied both by biographers and by historians. Her attitudes towards France have now been skilfully and sensitively disentangled by Michael Nelson. She already knew Paris and the north of France before she first travelled to the Riviera in 1882 with no Albert to guide her, and it was in the Riviera that she held important conversations with her last prime minister, Lord Salisbury, between 1896 and 1899. Gladstone, who died in 1898, always preferred Biarritz. Atlantic versus Mediterranean is a major theme in travel history, and the Queen played her part in this. She publicized the Riviera.

Michael Nelson fully appreciates the subtle relationships between the private and the public even in the life of imperial sovereigns, and his highly readable book will interest different kinds of reader. For me it is rich in texture, as, I believe, it will be for them. We begin by accompanying the

'Queen of Balmoral' on a Channel crossing in a yacht called the *Victoria and Albert* before joining her in a special train across France; and we end in Nice, invigorated but not exhausted, ready to accompany her home after her last and longest visit. Appropriately she had left behind a bridge in Nice which she had opened. Bridges symbolize bringing together. Edward VII should not have the only credit for building them.

Asa Briggs

Acknowledgements

This book would not have been possible without the help of the following:

Alison Adams, researcher; Peter Arengo-Jones, author of *Queen Victoria in Switzerland*; Lord Briggs; Emy Chabot, Caretaker, St George's Church, Cannes; Professor Monica Charlot, University of Paris III; Lady Sheila de Bellaigue, Registrar, the Royal Archives; Reverend Ian Barclay, Priest-in-Charge, Holy Trinity Church, Cannes; Laurent Boissin, Assistant, Service Culturel, Hyères; Alain Bottaro, Departmental Archives of the Alpes-Maritimes, Nice; David Chipp, journalist; Robert Elphick, journalist; Professor Jean Esson, University of Nice; Oliver Everett, Librarian and Assistant Keeper, the Royal Archives; Jean Ferrero, Galerie Ferrero, Nice; Professor William Fortescue, University of Kent at Canterbury; John and Pascal Gardiner, owners of the Château de Garibondy, Cannes; Michael Goldman, consultant; Pierre Goujon, architect, Nice; Robin Harcourt Williams, Librarian and Archivist to the Marquess of Salisbury, Hatfield House; Lord Jenkins of Hillhead; Judit Kiraly, author of *Influence Anglo-Saxone sur le développement de la Côte d'Azur, 1800–1940*, doctoral thesis, University of Nice; Jean-Bernard La Croix, Director, Departmental Archives of the Alpes-Maritimes, Nice; Elisabeth Lara, Press Officer, Société d'Economie Mixte pour les Evénements Cannois, Cannes; Professor Michel Lemosse, University of Nice; Reverend Kenneth Letts, Chaplain, Holy Trinity Church, Nice; The Countess of Longford; Canon Richard Marsh, The Archbishop of Canterbury's Secretary for Ecumenical Affairs; Paul Minet, Editor, *Royalty Digest*; Isabelle Nevière, researcher, Nice; Professor Donald Read, University of Kent at

Canterbury; Michael Reupke, journalist; Rainer Rother, Deutsches Historisches Museum, Berlin; Hervé Ruffier, Chef du Service Culturel, Hyères; Dennis Savage, researcher; Professor Ralph Schorr, University of Nice; Gregory Vlamis, author; Professor David Welch, University of Kent at Canterbury; Virginia Youdale, friend of St John's Church, Grasse; Charlotte Zeepvat, Historical Consultant, *Royalty Digest*.

Note on text

The extracts from Queen Victoria's Journals, other material from the
Royal Library and Archives at Windsor Castle and the illustrations are
published by the gracious permission of Her Majesty Queen Elizabeth II.

To Helga,
Patrick, Paul, Shivaun,
Mariana and Sarah

Introduction

In the spring of 1882 Queen Victoria, at the age of 62, arrived for the first time on the French Riviera. That region, which she called a 'paradise of nature', wrought a transformation in the last two decades of her life. She came to the Riviera on nine occasions and spent more time there than in any other part of continental Europe. Half her foreign travel was to France and of that three-quarters was spent on the Riviera. She never travelled outside Europe and never visited any part of her Empire, not even India. 'Oh, if only I were at Nice, I should recover', she said as she was dying.[1]

The Queen usually spent her mornings on the Riviera quietly riding round gardens in her donkey cart, and her afternoons on long carriage trips in the surrounding countryside. But she spent much of her time there with her strange companions, her dour Scottish gillie, John Brown, and, when Brown died, her troublesome Indian secretary, the Munshi, Abdul Karim. The royal household once threatened to go on strike if the Queen brought the Munshi to the Riviera again.

Guests included extraordinary European royalty, such as the reprobate Leopold II, King of the Belgians, who on his deathbed married a former prostitute, and his daughters, Louise and Stephanie, central characters in two of the greatest royal scandals of the nineteenth century, as we shall see.

During Queen Victoria's visits to the Riviera her character appeared to change. According to her entourage, when she arrived on the Riviera she immediately became fresh as a daisy, her face lit up and she beamed at the welcoming officials. She shed many of the inhibitions of her life in England. She behaved as if she was 17, threw flowers at young army officers, enjoyed fireworks like a child and laughed heartily at the local newspapers. There were of course exceptions when she was in mourning, notably during the Cannes visit of 1887 for her son, Prince Leopold, Hyères in

1892 for her grandson, Prince Albert Victor and Cimiez in 1896 for her son-in-law, Prince Henry of Battenberg.

By letting Sarah Bernhardt perform before her she demonstrated that there could be occasions, though maybe rarely, when she would, at least on the Riviera, relax her standards of moral purity. Her reaction to an admonition she received from Alice de Rothschild for stepping on one of her flower beds was evidence that she could even be self-effacing. The Queen's Journals make it apparent that, despite her age, her curiosity was acute and was stimulated by the everyday life of the Riviera.

The Queen's compassionate nature showed itself strongly on the Riviera in her kindness to her staff, however lowly, in her friendliness and gifts to beggars, her welcome to Nice fishwives, her donations to local charities and her messages of commiseration to those in distress.

The visits to the Riviera by Queen Victoria, the monarch of the most powerful empire in the world, were important to the area and to France because they affirmed and strengthened the Riviera's role as the leading holiday centre for the British, for other Europeans and the peoples of the Americas.

The importance of her presence is shown by the increase in visitors during the two decades of her visits, by the concern of the French at the damage which would be done to the tourist industry if she were to cancel her trip in 1899 because of bad relations between France and Britain, by the many hotels, cafés and roads named after her and by the number of statues erected to commemorate her.

Robert Latouche, the principal historian of Nice, considered the 'siren' who enticed sovereigns and princes to Nice 'was a Queen of England; Great Britain was the good fairy which guarded for Nice its prestige with the aristocracy of Europe.'[2]

Queen Victoria did not herself discover the Riviera, of course, but she did affirm its position as an important holiday centre, rather than a centre for convalescence. The French have always been grateful for this, losing no opportunity to commemorate notable anniversaries of her visits. The Queen not only attracted the British to the Riviera, but also other nationalities and, as the 'Grandmother of Europe', the monarchs of other countries. Britain enjoyed a constitutional monarchy, but many countries of continental Europe, ruled by Queen Victoria's relatives, did not. Her contacts with them, many of which she directly or indirectly maintained while she was on the Riviera, were exploited by many of her ministers, especially by Lord Salisbury, who himself holidayed there. Her informal intelligence service, based on this wide cousinage and maintained through extensive letter writing, was in many ways superior to that of the Foreign Office. In particular, the Queen's conversations with Lord Salisbury on the Riviera from 1896 to 1899, when he headed the last administration of her reign, were important in the conduct of British foreign policy through successive crises which might have involved Britain in war.

The Riviera had been a backwater until the British started to settle there in the eighteenth century. At the time of the Queen's death a century and a half later, it was one of the most developed parts of France and Europe.

In the eighteenth century Nice and the Comté de Nice were ruled from Turin by the kings of Sardinia of the House of Savoy. Britain had had an alliance with Sardinia since the seventeenth century as part of its Mediterranean policy following the conquest of Gibraltar and Minorca. Young Britons went to the military academy of Turin. During the War of the Austrian Succession from 1743 to 1748, Britain supported the Austro-Sardinians, and British army officers stayed in Nice in the winter and went back again as visitors after the war.[3] However, the first English people to 'discover' Nice were probably Lord and Lady Cavendish, who visited the city in 1731. Lady Cavendish was heavily pregnant when she arrived there and gave birth to a son, Henry Cavendish, later to be a famous chemist.[4] Appropriately for one born in Nice, he discovered the constitution of water and atmospheric air.

Dr Johnson said that 'The grand object of travelling is to see the shores of the Mediterranean.' He was not, though, thinking of the French shores, but of the Italian. 'A man who has not been in Italy is always conscious of an inferiority, from his not having seen what it is expected a man should see. On those shores were the four great Empires of the world; the Assyrian, the Persian, the Grecian and the Roman.'[5] But the attitude to travel of Johnson and Boswell was becoming outdated. By the end of the eighteenth century Europeans were changing the view of the world which they had learned from the Bible – that man was the centre of the universe. They began to value the natural world and its beauties.[6] 'Within the last thirty years a taste for the picturesque has sprung up and a course of summer travelling is now looked upon to be ... essential', Robert Southey, the poet and man of letters wrote in 1809.[7] Queen Victoria concentrated in her Journals and letters on the natural beauties of the Riviera, not on the remains of the Roman civilizations which lay near the hotels she stayed in above Nice.

There has been much debate about the difference between travel and tourism. Evelyn Waugh said, 'The tourist is the other fellow.'[8] In Old English the word 'travel' was the same as 'travail', meaning work. Travel implied effort, which tourism did not.[9] The coming of the railways in the mid-nineteenth century changed travel into tourism, although the term was much older: the Oxford English Dictionary gives the first use of 'tourist' as 1780. The term quickly became pejorative. As early as 1799 William Wordsworth published a narrative poem, 'The Brothers', in which the priest of Ennerdale saw a stranger lingering over graves in the village churchyard. 'These tourists, heaven preserve us!', he cried.[10] The French drew a further distinction. 'Villégiature' implied rest, luxury, a long-term visit and 'tourisme' movement.[11]

Queen Victoria on the Riviera was clearly a tourist and not a traveller by English language usage. By French usage she was a villégiateuse or a villégiaturiste.

There had been occasional English travellers to Nice in the mid-eighteenth century, including the painter Joshua Reynolds, who, coming from Venice, stayed in Nice in 1752.[12] Arthur Young visited Antibes in September 1789 but, unable to hire a carriage, horse or mule, had had to walk from Cannes. He noted that the previous winter there had been 57 English visitors to only nine French.[13] But Italy, not France, was the principal object of the Grand Tour in the eighteenth century.

Young did not mention American visitors, and there were no doubt few, but in the previous year one of the most distinguished Americans ever to visit the Riviera went there. He was Thomas Jefferson, later to become American President, who visited the Riviera in 1787, when he was minister in Paris. He went to Hyères, Fréjus, Antibes, Nice, Monaco and Menton as part of a tour of the South of France and the north of Italy. 'I have been pleased to find among the people a less degree of physical misery than I had expected,' he wrote to Marquis de Lafayette, from Nice.[14] 'They are generally well clothed and have plenty of food, not animal indeed but vegetable, which is wholesome. Perhaps they are over-worked, the excess of rent required by the landlord obliging them to too many hours of labor, in order to produce that, and wherewith to feed and clothe themselves.' He recommended that Lafayette should investigate as he had done: 'You must be absolutely incognito, you must ferret the people out of their hovels as I have done, look into their kettles, eat their bread, loll on their beds under the pretence of resting yourself, but in fact to find if they are soft.'

In a letter from Nice to William Short, his private secretary, Jefferson compared Nice with Hyères.[15] 'In favor of this place are the circumstances of gay and dissipated society, a handsome city, good accommodations and some commerce. In favour of Hieres [sic] are environs of delicious and extensive plains, a society more contracted and therefore more capable of esteem.'

One of the first visitors to France after travel became possible again following Britain's victory over France in the Seven Years War was Dr Tobias Smollett M.D.[16] In 1763 Smollett, ill with incipient tuberculosis, journeyed to Nice with his wife, his Scottish manservant and two young ladies under the chaperonage of Mrs Smollett. He was seeking a kinder climate than England. When he returned to England he published a book of his experiences, *Travels Through France and Italy*, which was destined to start a revolution in the travel habits of the British. It had great success and was soon republished by pirate publishers in Dublin and in German translations. The consequence was that several members of the British aristocracy followed in his footsteps, including the Duke of York, brother of King George III, the Duke of Gloucester, the Duke of Bedford, the Duchess of Cumberland and the famous dandy, Lord Bessborough.[17]

The British settled in the Croix de Marbre quarter of Nice, which was known as Newborough or Little London. By a strange quirk of history, this development had been made possible by a natural son of James II of England. The son was the Duke of Berwick, who had been brought up in France. At the beginning of the eighteenth century, during the War of the Spanish Succession, the Duke was commanding the French troops and grabbed Nice, for which he was created Maréchal de France. He ordered the ramparts, which enclosed the city, to be destroyed. Thus the burghers could expand to the west, which is where the British established their colony.[18] By 1775 they had an Anglican cemetery and by 1787 110 English families stayed in Nice.[19]

However, the invasion of Nice by French revolutionary troops in 1792 stopped the development of tourism.

British tourism timidly resumed in 1802 following the Peace of Amiens and 15 families wintered in Nice. They were headed by the Duchess of Cumberland, sister-in-law of George III. Napoleon instructed the local Prefect to give a banquet to which 40 leading French citizens and a similar number of English were invited. They drank many toasts. But the resumption of hostilities in June 1803 set tourism back again until the fall of Napoleon in 1814. By the first Treaty of Paris in 1814, Nice reverted to

Sardinia and remained so after Napoleon's defeat at Waterloo in 1815. Gradually the British started to come back and a highlight of their return was the construction of an Anglican church in 1821. King Charles-Félix authorized it on condition it did not look like a church. By 1829, 80–100 families were wintering in Nice.[20]

The percentage of nobles among the visitors was initially high. But a consequence of the Industrial Revolution was that the percentage of bourgeoisie increased and became predominant. Bankers were an important group. As Stendhal had said, 'bankers are the nobility of the bourgeoisie'. A lot of money was needed to spend several months on the Riviera. The season was long, starting in September and finishing at the end of April. But most visitors preferred to arrive in December and start for home at the beginning of April.[21] The minority that travelled grew. In 1866 Anthony Trollope wrote:

> Those who can be allowed to enjoy themselves quietly at home or eat shrimps through their holiday quietly at Ramsgate, are becoming from year to year not fewer in number, but lower down the social scale; so that this imperative duty of travelling abroad – and doing so year after year – becomes much extended, and embraces all of us who are considered anybody by those around us.[22]

The role of the British was underlined in 1834 when the outbreak of cholera in Provence led, by chance, to the establishment of Cannes as a major resort. Lord Brougham, a former Lord Chancellor of England, was on his way to Nice with his sickly daughter and on 28 December 1834 was stopped at the Sardinian frontier because of the outbreak of cholera. He stayed in the little fishing village of Cannes and was so delighted with it that he bought a piece of land and built a villa. This striking representative of early nineteenth-century Britain, a radical, a great lawyer and a utilitarian, had no difficulty in encouraging his friends also to build there and so was founded the large British colony in Cannes.[23]

The main square of Cannes was named after Brougham and a marble statue on the promenade was unveiled in 1879. He was buried in the cemetery. His invention of the brougham, the first four-wheeled carriage intended to be drawn by only one horse, was well known. Every year he left 'Fog-land', as he called England, to pass the winter on the Riviera. His French was not very good and one French wit once said that 'in addition to his other gifts, he must have the gift of unknown tongues'.[24]

The British predominated on the Riviera to such an extent that when the writer Alexandre Dumas asked an innkeeper what the nationality of the guests who were just arriving was, he said that they were all English, but he was not sure if they were Germans or Russians.[25]

The English always predominated, but the Russians' visits increased at a faster rate. (Local sources usually referred to the English and not the British, but no doubt there were Scots, Welsh and Irish there.) In 1850–51 there were 189 English and 52 Russian families in Nice, but by 1856–57 the English had increased to 284 and the Russians to 141.[26] The visits of the Russian Empress-Mother, Alexandra Feodorovna, widow of Nicholas I, in 1856–57 and 1859, were important in attracting other Russians. She installed herself in the vast Villa Bermond, which acquired the name of Parc Impérial.[27] In 1860, 704 foreign families spent at least part of the winter in Nice. They included 252 English, 172 French, 128 Russians, 37 Germans and 22 Americans.[28] Other nationalities were also represented and the Queen of Denmark acquired a villa on the Boulevard Carabacel.[29]

The first waves of visitors either built or rented villas. But by 1847 Nice boasted 30 hotels and, as they became more and more luxurious, visitors started to prefer them to villas. Queen Victoria followed this trend. She stayed in villas for her first two visits to the Riviera and then moved to hotels. Hotel keeping was starting to become a science and in 1874 the architect Edouard Guyer published in Zurich the first analysis of hotel needs, *Das Hotelwesen der Gegenwart* (The Contemporary Organization of Hotels), which he had been working on since 1840. He considered the first duty of a hotelier was to ensure the high quality of the welcome to the traveller arriving with his family and servants. He therefore gave pride of place to an impressive entrance hall.[30]

Piedmont-Sardinia's rulers, the House of Savoy, delighted the British in 1858 by permitting the public celebration of non-Catholic services, and in that year they built a church which looked like a church.[31]

France acquired the Comté de Nice from Piedmont-Sardinia on 24 March 1860, subject to a referendum, which was held on 15 April. According to the official figures 25,743 were in favour and only 160 against. A new department was created, the Alpes-Maritimes, which included Grasse and the surrounding area, which had previously been part of the Department of the Var.[32]

The origins of the change went back to a secret meeting Napoleon III had with Count Camillo di Cavour, Prime Minister of Piedmont-Sardinia, at Plombières in the Vosges on 20 July 1858. Napoleon outlined his plans for a federally united Italy without Austria, which then held Lombardy and Venetia. Piedmont-Sardinia could count on French support in a war. The main French reward would be the eventual acquisition of Savoy. A treaty of alliance between France and Piedmont-Sardinia was signed on 19 January 1859 which provided that Nice, as well as Savoy, would be ceded to France. The idea of a federal Italy was dropped, but France would support Piedmont-Sardinia in the event of war. Cavour and Napoleon did not have to wait long for a *casus belli*. On 19 April Austria issued an ultimatum to Piedmont-Sardinia to disarm, which Cavour rejected on 26 April. On 29 April Austrian forces crossed the Piedmont-Sardinia frontier. The French declared war on 3 May and their army entered Italy. They beat the Austrians at the two famous battles of Magenta and Solferino.

Napoleon made a truce with Francis Joseph, the Austrian Emperor, at Villafranca on 11 July and Austria ceded Parma and Lombardy to France for eventual cession to Piedmont-Sardinia. Napoleon did not immediately demand from Piedmont-Sardinia his reward of Nice and Savoy because the Austrians still held Venetia. But when central Italian states moved to join the Kingdom of Sardinia, Cavour offered Nice and Savoy to Napoleon, subject to a referendum, if he would accept the adhesion of the Italian states to the Kingdom, which he did.[33] Thus Nice became part of the French Riviera and the momentous return to 'natural frontiers' was marked by a celebratory visit to Nice of Napoleon III and Empress Eugénie in the autumn of 1860.

Bad or non-existent roads had always been the greatest barrier to the development in tourism on the Riviera. On the west were the mountains of the Esterel, which were difficult to cross and which also carried the risk of encounters with bandits. Once at the border with Nice, the barrier of the River Var was often overcome only by being ferried on the shoulders of the locals. The sea route had the danger of pirates. It took 16 days of continuous and uncomfortable travel to reach Nice from London.[34]

'All the inns of this country are execrable', claimed Dr Smollett. He particularly objected to the state of the toilets, which he called 'conveniences' and 'temples of Cloacina'. The cantankerous doctor also considered dealing with a Frenchman a burden: 'He will even affirm that his endeavours to corrupt your wife, or deflower your daughter, were the most genuine proofs he could give of his particular regard for your family', he complained, presumably based on some experience during his long journey through France.[35]

Improvements to the roads by Napoleon for military reasons cut the journey to under two weeks early in the nineteenth century.[36] Nice was

connected to Menton and the Italian Riviera only by a mule track laid by
the Romans as part of the Via Aurelia. Napoleon improved things somewhat by cutting a carriage-way eastwards from Nice – the Grande
Corniche.[37]

On 10 April 1863 the railway from Paris first reached Cannes and the
journey time was only 21 hours 28 minutes. In October 1864 it reached
Nice and in 1869 Menton.[38] 'Railways have all but annihilated space',
enthused Dr James Henry Bennett, who had first visited the Riviera before
trains served the area. 'A traveller may leave London Bridge station at
7.40 on Monday morning by mail train for Paris, and be at Nice or Mentone for supper the following day, Tuesday.'[39] By the time of Queen
Victoria's first visit by train to the Riviera in 1882 it was estimated that 20
million people in the world were travelling by train, of which nearly
three-quarters were in Europe.[40]

Not that all was sweetness and light. Henry Alford, Dean of Canterbury, attacked the Paris–Nice Express in 1870 as:

> a wretched imposture, of which any civilised nation ought to be ashamed. ...
> What would the English public think of a train so ordered that ... by its car-
> rying only first-class passengers, it compels invalids and delicate ladies to be
> shut up with brutal drunken men, offending (to say nothing of other annoy-
> ances) their ears with profane and foul language during the whole night and
> day of the journey?[41]

Most European trains were unheated until the 1870s, although hot-water
footstools were offered to first-class passengers on French trains. Few
trains had toilets, so there was a great rush for the station conveniences at
any stop. Only the principal stations had buffets and the food was not very
good. Dining cars were not introduced until 1883.[42] But even in the 1898
edition of his guide to south-eastern France, Baedeker was counselling
travellers to bring their own food and consume it at leisure in the railway
carriage.[43] The Compagnie Internationale des Wagons-Lits was founded to
provide sleeping cars in 1872.[44]

The impact of the railways on the numbers of visitors who stayed in the
area was considerable. At the start of the 1860s about 4000 visitors stayed
in Nice.[45] By 1879 the number had at least trebled to between 12,000 and
15,000. But by the end of the roughly two decades of Queen Victoria's
visits to the Riviera, the number of visits had increased six to eightfold, to
about 100,000.

The census for the Alpes-Maritimes of March 1886 showed 43,770
foreigners resident in the department. Ten years later the number had

increased by two-thirds to 72,265. In 1886 there were only 870 English, Scottish and Irish but by 1896 the number of British had quadrupled to 3509.[46]

How much of the colossal increase in British visitors was due to the Queen's visits is impossible to say. But that it was considerable is clearly shown by the great concern evinced in 1899 when the Fashoda Incident in the Sudan, when a party of Frenchmen took over a fort which the British considered in their sphere of influence and which represented a serious conflict between Britain and France, looked like leading to a cancellation of the Queen's visit.

The local government were very conscious of the transformation tourism had wrought on the economy of the Riviera, and Nice in particular, compared with the rest of France. In the half century between 1861 and 1911 the population of France grew by only 5.9 per cent. The population of the Department of the Alpes-Maritimes grew by 83 per cent.[47] But Nice, which had 44,091 inhabitants in 1861[48], had grown to 142,940 in 1911, an increase of 225 per cent.

An intriguing statistic which was used in France as an indicator of wealth of a town was the number of doors and windows per inhabitant. The national average was 1.5 but Nice stood at nearly double that at 2.64.[49]

A month before Queen Victoria arrived on the Riviera for the first time in March 1882 a local newspaper, La Colonie Etrangère, said, 'We need visitors, more visitors and still more visitors.' Earlier Abbot Bonifassi compared the new culture of tourism with the old one of agriculture: 'It is real income and equivalent to a good olive oil year.'[50] Before tourism the only important industries in a stagnating Nice were the manufacture of sail-cloth, soap, candles, leather goods and liquor. The people were mostly engaged in processing the agricultural produce of the hinterland – grain, wine, olive oil, fruit and silk cocoons. Nice had to import grain and wine and its only exports were olive oil, cocoons, linen and hemp.[51]

The great French historian of the Mediterranean, Fernand Braudel, said of the mountains which ring the Mediterranean:

> Life there is possible, but not easy. On the slopes where farm animals can hardly be used at all, the work is difficult. The stony fields must be cleared by hand, the earth has to be prevented from slipping down the hill, and if necessary must be carried up to the hilltop and banked up with dry stone walls. It is painful work and never-ending.[52]

Even the produce of the fertile plain between the Alps and the sea had the problems of transport. Turin was the administrative and political capital of Piedmont-Sardinia, but in the winter even mule carts found getting there very difficult. The position of Nice worsened after the Congress of Vienna in 1815, when Piedmont-Sardinia was given the port of Genoa. Piedmont-Sardinia abandoned the use of the port of Nice. Tourism was the salvation.[53] C. James Haug, a scholar specializing in tourism, claims that Nice was the first major city of the modern Western world to become dependent on an economy based on tourism.[54]

Queen Victoria was welcomed to the Riviera with brass bands and cheering crowds in the street. But not all French citizens appreciated the benefits they derived from the British visitors. *La Revue de Cannes* reported that on several occasions in Le Cannet urchins of 12 to 14 years insulted foreigners and tried to tear their clothes, jumping up at their faces and trying to grab their watches and earrings, shouting out that they were attacking them because they were foreigners. The journalist wrote:

> It is impossible to explain the anger of these children other than by the stupid feeling of hatred and jealousy which they heard their families expressing against foreigners. Several foreigners have expressed their indignation to me that they could not only not go along paths in the country, but could not even walk along the main street without being insulted and pursued by stone-throwing, and surprisingly enough they had seen the children being incited by grown-ups.[55]

Queen Victoria was famous for her generosity to beggars while she was on the Riviera, but the generosity of foreigners was not always appreciated. The *Journal de Nice* reported that on 4 January 1866 a little girl of 12 was persistently demanding alms of passers-by. A policeman tried to arrest her, but had to give up because of the shouts of the crowd. But a few years later the same thing happened and, not very logically, it was the foreigners who, by giving alms, showed themselves in flagrant opposition to French law, which wanted, at all costs, to eliminate begging. Sometimes the locals wanted neither the foreigners nor their money, the newspaper concluded.[56]

One of the main reasons why Queen Victoria and other foreigners visited the Riviera was medical. She was there to be with her son, Prince Leopold, the Duke of Albany, who suffered from haemophilia.

The president of the society of medical men practising in Menton was Dr James Henry Bennet. He had done much to publicize Menton as a health resort, having gone there in 1859 'to die in a quiet corner ... like a wounded denizen of the forest', he said. He had contracted tuberculosis, but to his surprise, his condition soon improved. He thought the reason was the effects of the winter sunshine. The next year he decided to go further south to Italy but he concluded that was a bad move because 'the unhygienic state of the large towns of that classical land partly undid the good previously obtained.' In 1861 he made Menton his permanent winter home. His routine was soon to be to practise as a doctor in Menton in the winter, to take a holiday in April and May, when he studied the Mediterranean climate and vegetation, and to resume his medical practice in England in the summer.[57]

Bennet decided as a result of his careful meteorological records what many later travellers also discovered as they sheltered from the rain in the cafés on the Promenade des Anglais in Nice. The Riviera is not a land of perpetual spring or eternal summer. But he did state that there was a greater probability of tuberculosis being arrested, of life being prolonged and even of a cure being eventually effected if the patient could winter in the south. The proof was that he was surrounded in Menton by 'a phalanx of cured and arrested consumption cases'.

In 1861 he published the first edition of his book *Winter and Spring on the Shores of the Mediterranean*, in which he described the benefits of the town for the invalid. At that time it was a quiet little Italian town on the sunny shore of the Riviera, with two or three small hotels, principally used by passing travellers, and half a dozen recently erected villas. By his 1875 edition he was describing it as 'a well-known and frequented winter resort, with thirty hotels, four times that number of villas, and a mixed foreign population of about sixteen hundred'.[58] With some prescience he wrote:

> The opening of the railway from Paris to Nice and Genoa has rendered the lovely Riviera very easy of access, even to confirmed invalids, and I believe that the time is fast approaching when tens of thousands from the north of Europe will adopt the habits of the swallow, and transform every town and village on its coast into sunny winter retreats. I may remark that it is the first point of the Mediterranean shore where birds of passage from the north make a halt for the winter.[59]

The Queen was no doubt influenced in her decision to go to the Riviera by Bennet's conclusion that 'our beloved country is "merrie" in winter, only for the hale and strong, who can defy and enjoy the cutting winds, the rain, the snow, and the frost of a northern land.'[60]

Bennet published a German translation of his book in 1863, which brought in a flood of Germans. In 1870 an edition appeared in New York and he reported, 'Our American cousins are finding their way to Menton in increasing numbers.'[61]

The motivations of the Americans in visiting the Riviera were generally different from those of Europeans. In 1879 the American writer Henry James wrote:

> One might enumerate the items of high civilisation, as it exists in other countries, which are absent from the texture of American life, until it should become a wonder to know what was left. No State, in the European sense of the word, and indeed barely a specific national name. No sovereign, no court, no personal loyalty, no aristocracy, no church, no clergy, no army, no diplomatic service, no country gentlemen, no palaces, no castles ... no museums, no pictures.[62]

To be associated with these elements of 'high civilisation' was undoubtedly the reason why many Americans went to Europe. On the Riviera there were few cultural attractions and it must have been a combination of the weather and the desire to be where European royalty and aristocracy went that drew Americans there. Writing in 1865, Robert Tomes said, 'It is not easy to analyze the vague and confused motives which induce our wealthy people to travel abroad. Many of them go for no better reason than because traveling costs money, and being more or less exclusive, is approved by fashion.'[63]

But some Americans went to Europe to save money. The American novelist, Edith Wharton, recounted how the depreciation in the American currency at the close of the Civil War so reduced her father's income that, in common with many friends and relations, he let his town and country houses and went to live in Europe for six years.[64] In 1880, when she was 18, the family went back again. Edith Wharton went to Cannes and later described life there:

> The small and intimate society we frequented was made up of French and English families, mostly connected by old friendship, and some by blood. Our amusements were simple and informal, as social pleasures were in those days, and picnics on the shore, or among the red rocks and pine forests of the Esterel, lawn tennis parties and small dinners, united the same young people day after day, under the guardianship of a pleasant group of their elders.[65]

In 1887 the Americans moved a step ahead of the British when James Gordon Bennett Jr., who had a house in Beaulieu, founded the *Paris*

Herald, an off-shoot of the *New York Herald*, which visitors to Nice could peruse in a *Herald* reading room there. Not until 1906 did the British get an affiliate of a London newspaper, when the *Daily Mail* started a Continental edition.

The Queen's return to the Riviera in 1887 after an absence of five years epitomized the transformation of Riviera tourism. She did not return for medical reasons. Her invalid son, Prince Leopold, had slipped in the Cercle Nautique yacht club in Cannes in 1884 and had died. When she returned to the Riviera she went for a holiday. The Queen was among the first Europeans to show that it was possible to visit the Riviera for relaxation and not for a cure. In the very year of the Queen's return, Dr J.A. Lindsay, a specialist in consumption, wrote that he detected a decline in the popularity of the Mediterranean resorts 'in the presence of the modern drift of medical opinion in favour of the view that they afford on the whole less favourable results in consumption than the mountain sanatoria [and] the dry inland resorts'.[66]

The Riviera resorts were victims of their own success. 'Large centres of population are uniformly and radically ineligible as sanatoria for consumption,' wrote Lindsay. 'The evidence that the disease is essentially one of civilised life in large communities is overwhelming.'[67] But the main Riviera sanatoria of Nice and Cannes had become large cities precisely because of the influx of invalids with consumption. Even Menton became crowded in the season.

Immorality was a further important reason for condemnation of the Riviera health resorts. 'Where climate supplies constant stimulation for the senses passion will predominate over reason; and where the passions are indulged, the range of existence will be curtailed.' Thus warned Dr James Johnson in 1830.[68] Dr Lindsay weighed in again with: 'Undue excitement, heated and crowded rooms, over-exertion and late hours – the usual accompaniments of life at the fashionable sanatoria are ... in the last degree noxious to the sufferer from pulmonary disease.'[69] The Ex-Lord Provost of Edinburgh, William Chambers, had a wealth of cautionary tales from his stay in Menton. A young gentleman of fortune with his lungs much gone, contrary to advice, attended a dancing party. He collapsed, was carried out, and died in the passage. 'In that Dance of Death he had finished the last atom of lung ... gaily ending his days in the revelry of a waltz,' intoned the ex-Provost. Ladies brought enormous boxfuls of fashionable attire and wanted to show it off somehow. One young lady, considered to be the reigning beauty, had had only one lung 'which it was alleged she was doing all in her power to get rid of'.[70]

But despite the attractions of Switzerland compared with the climatological and moral disadvantages of the Riviera, at the end of the century the total population of Davos, the most popular mountain resort, was only 13,000, compared with the increase in population in Nice in the winter of 80,000 and a total population of 170,000.[71] The Riviera continued to be supreme in Europe because it replaced its role as a convalescent centre with that of a holiday region, greatly increasing the number of visitors in the process. Lindsay believed the resorts of the Riviera were surviving only by virtue of 'their long-famous name, the ample and often luxurious accommodation, and the patronage of wealth and fashion'.[72]

The Queen Empress was the summit of that patronage.

CHAPTER 1

Prologue: The Queen's delight with France

Victoria paid her first visit to France, which was also her first visit abroad, in 1843. Her consort, Prince Albert, accompanied her. King Louis-Philippe invited Victoria and Albert to visit him and his queen at the Château d'Eu. His relations with the British royal family were close, partly because of inter-marriage, but also because he was eternally grateful that Victoria's father, the Duke of Kent, had in 1796 lent him £200 when, as the Duc d'Orléans, he had been near destitute in Halifax, Nova Scotia. The loan enabled him to go to Philadelphia, where he became a teacher.

Louis-Philippe, King of the French rather than King of France, had come to power in the July Revolution of 1830. The Citizen King, as he was known, was a strange portly figure with a pear-shaped head, who walked the streets of Paris with an umbrella under his arm. His authoritarianism, which contrasted with the role of his guest, Queen Victoria, who reigned but did not rule, led to his eventual downfall. Beset by rebellions and attempts on his life, he resorted increasingly to repressive measures. The February Revolution forced him to abdicate in 1848. He settled in England, where he died in 1850.

The British royals sailed on the new royal yacht, *Victoria and Albert*, and landed at Le Tréport in the Seine-Maritime on 2 September. 'I feel so gay and happy with these dear people,' the Queen wrote of the French royal family in her Journal, 'The people are very respectable-looking and very civil, crying "Vive la Reine d'Angleterre!"', she enthused. She and Albert spent five joyful days sightseeing, shopping, picnicking and dining.[1]

The Queen's name was French, and there had been a right royal row when William IV became king in 1830 and tried to get the foreign-sounding name of his heiress presumptive changed to something more befitting an English queen. King George IV, who was Prince Regent at the

time, had chosen the name, Victoria herself was attached to it, and her
mother, the Duchess of Kent, refused any change, despite the offer from
the King of a huge financial bribe. There was support for 'Victoria' in
London newspapers, who thought it sounded regal. The name 'Victoria'
remained.[2]

Twelve years after the first visit the royal couple visited Paris. On 18
August 1855 they were welcomed by the Emperor Napoleon III and
Empress Eugénie, who had visited the Queen in England in April that
year. This was the first visit to Paris by an English monarch since the
English boy king, Henry VI, had been crowned there as King of France on
16 December 1431. 'I am <u>delighted, enchanted, amused</u>, and <u>interested</u>
and think I never saw anything more <u>beautiful</u> and gay than Paris – or
more splendid than all the Palaces,' she gushed in a letter to her uncle,
Leopold I, the King of the Belgians.[3]

The heat always bothered the Queen: 'The heat is very great, but the
weather splendid, and although the sun may be hotter, the air is certainly
<u>lighter</u> than ours – and I have no headache.'[4]

The highlight of the visit was the Grand Ball in the Hall of Mirrors at
Versailles. Thousands of torches were reflected in the mirrors; in the
centre was an Arc de Triomphe, crowned with the arms of France and
England and 200 musicians played. At 10 pm fireworks burst across the
sky and the finale represented the walls and turrets of Windsor Castle.
The French Emperor swept on to the floor with the Queen of England to
open the ball.[5]

Lord Clarendon, talking in the terminology of the middle of the nineteenth century, described Napoleon III's 'making love' to Victoria.[6] The
Queen said she had formed a '<u>great</u> affection for the Emperor'.[7]

The French did not think much of Victoria's haute couture. She wore a
plain straw bonnet and carried a brilliant green parasol. She had a massive
handbag with a white poodle embroidered on it, which made her look
even shorter and dumpier than she was.[8]

The visit made a great impression on the Queen and memories of it
must have flooded back when she considered visiting France 26 years
later.

It also made a great impression on the 13-year-old Prince of Wales,
who so fell in love with it that he asked the Empress if he and his sister,
the Princess Royal, could stay on in France a little longer. Charles Greville
recorded:

The Empress said she was afraid this would not be possible, as the Queen and the Prince would not be able to do without them; to which the boy replied: 'Not do without us. I don't fancy that for there are six more of us at home and they don't want us.'[9]

The Prince of Wales returned to France at the earliest opportunity and it became the foreign country he most loved.

The usual pattern of royal family holidays was visits to Windsor, Osborne on the Isle of Wight and Balmoral in Scotland. Much of England the royal family never visited and there the Queen was known as 'The Great Unseen'. She only knew the north of Wales and for nearly 40 years did not visit Ireland. More important to her were visits to relatives in Germany and Belgium.

In the quarter of a century following the exciting trip to Paris in 1855, Victoria stayed in Germany eight times, Belgium three times and Switzerland and Italy once each. But apart from brief visits to Cherbourg and transits through Paris, she did not visit France, which was curious, given her great enthusiasms of 1855. The natural place to have gone to would have been the Riviera, which was becoming fashionable with the English. Perhaps the reason she did not go to the Riviera was her disapproval of the pleasure-seeking life in Cannes of her son, the Prince of Wales, and the hedonism of Monte Carlo.

It was the Italian visit that drew the Queen at last to the Riviera. In 1878 she spent a month in the spring and two months in the autumn at Balmoral. She said she felt 'unusually depressed and weak'. On 14 December, the anniversary of the death of Prince Albert in 1861, her second daughter, Princess Alice, Grand Duchess of Hesse and the Rhine, died. Victoria decided that she could not 'stand another summer and autumn in total seclusion'. She therefore accepted the offer from an Englishman, Charles Henfrey, who had made his fortune building railways in India and Italy, to borrow his villa at Baveno, on Lake Maggiore in Northern Italy. She stayed there, at the Villa Clara, from 28 March to 23 April 1879.

She would not have agreed with the description of the house by Richard Bagot in *The Italian Lakes* (1905) that it was 'a replica of the Wimbledon or Putney residence of a retired tradesman'. She found the villa comfortable and charming. She sat on the open loggia looking out towards Lake Maggiore sketching and painting, 'trying to catch the effect of the ever-changing lights on the lovely scenery'.[10]

John Brown, the Queen's Scottish servant, could not understand her desire for a change of air and surroundings. He was bored and made himself intensely disagreeable. Henry Ponsonby, the Queen's Private

Secretary, wrote of driving to a lovely place, but the Queen did not get out of the carriage. 'We believe it was because Brown would not allow her to get out. He is surly beyond measure and today we could see him all the way – a beautiful drive – with his eyes fixed on the horses' tails and refusing to look up.' He tried hard to make the visit a failure, trying to arrange that the Queen did not go out driving before 4 pm, so missing the best part of the day and making long trips impossible.[11]

The Queen loved the holiday in Charles Henfrey's house so much that she gladly accepted the offer of his house at Menton on the French Riviera, where she holidayed with a miserable John Brown in 1882.[12]

CHAPTER 2

1882: Menton. The first visit to the paradise of nature

A t exactly 10.20 am – five minutes late – on a raw and foggy Tuesday, 14 March 1882, the sun just beginning to penetrate the mist, the Queen's special train steamed out of Windsor station en route for her first visit to the French Riviera. She was 62 and ready for a new adventure.

The Queen had driven from the Castle in a closed carriage with a pair of grays, the equerries, Sir Carstairs McNeill and Captain Edwards, riding on horseback beside. *The Times*, which covered the departure in meticulous detail, considered it important to note that this had not been usual at Windsor, except on State or semi-State occasions, for a long time. The public were not allowed in the railway station but gathered on the Castle Hill and in the High Street and loudly cheered. The windows of the carriage were lowered and the Queen graciously acknowledged the salutations.[1]

The Queen travelled in her own saloon carriage, but the train was under the direction of the chief officials of the Great Western Railway. Such senior control of the train was partly necessary because the monarch was terrified of railway accidents. She well remembered the death of Dr Baly, the royal physician, in a derailment between the London suburbs of Wimbledon and Malden in 1861. The doctor fell through the carriage floor and was mangled by the wheels.[2] The Queen never crossed the Channel on Fridays. Despite the fact that she laid down strict speed limits for train journeys, the train arrived at Portsmouth 30 minutes ahead of schedule at 12.30 pm.[3]

The royal household had a curious idea of security. She travelled incognito as the Countess of Balmoral, but her journey was reported in *The Times* on the day of her departure and her baggage was labelled 'Queen of England'.[4] The Quai d'Orsay assured the British Ambassador that there

would be no customs inspection of the baggage of the Queen or her suite.[5]
Travelling incognito was also a device to indicate to foreign states that she
was journeying unofficially, thus avoiding endless ceremonial. It clearly
became fashionable to travel under a pseudonym. In 1899 the Duchess of
Aosta travelled from Italy under the name of the Countess of Cisterna, to
call on the Queen in Cimiez and also dine with her.[6]

The crossing was in the yacht, the *Victoria and Albert*, escorted by
torpedo boats. When she first went abroad, the Queen travelled via
Boulogne on the ordinary channel steamer, but now that she was so lame
that she had difficulty in walking, she always insisted that a covered gangway was rigged up so that the crowd could not see her being carried on
board in her chair, although the gangway was so steep that no one would
have expected an old lady to walk up it.[7] It was by now a fine day and the
crossing was smooth, the sea like a pond.[8] The royal party spent the night
on board in the French port of Cherbourg. On the pier was a beautiful red
velvet and gold lace tent for the Queen to sit in and a guard of honour of
the French army. A host of generals, admirals and officials were drawn up
near the tent hoping to be presented. The band played and the crowd
cheered.[9]

A special train left Cherbourg at 10 am for Menton.[10] Two of the seven
coaches in the royal train were the Queen's private property. They consisted of her drawing room and sleeping car and were kept at the Gare du
Nord in Brussels because they had been built and furnished in Belgium.
The drawing room and a small compartment, used by John Brown on the
trip to Menton, made up the day car. A corridor led to the sleeping car,
which consisted of a dressing room, bedroom and a compartment for light
luggage where the maids slept on sofas. The Queen slept on the larger bed
in the sleeping compartment and Princess Beatrice on the smaller.

The drawing room walls were hung with silk – blue for the dado and
pearl grey above, brocaded in pale yellow, with the shamrock, rose and
thistle. There were four lights in the padded ceiling. A dark Indian carpet
covered the floor and the curtains were blue and white. A sofa, two
armchairs and footstools in the style of Louis XVI were covered in blue
silk, with yellow fringes and tassels. Between the windows was a beech-
wood table. Xavier Paoli, the French official in charge of royal security,
thought it presented:

> in its somewhat antiquated splendour, the exact appearance of an old-
> fashioned apartment in a provincial town. Everything about it was heavy,
> large and comfortable. I used to feel as if I was travelling in a steam bath-

chair; and I must confess that in this rolling palace, the journey never appeared either very long or very tiring.[11]

The dressing room motif was Japanese, and protective bamboo hung round the walls. The wash stand was covered in dark red morocco leather. All the items in the toilet service, including the basin, were made of white metal.[12]

So that the Queen's sleep should not be disturbed, there were no brakes on the six wheels and the carriage was perfectly swung.[13] The saloons were largely based on British design, similar to those on the London and North Western Railway, which she used to travel to Balmoral.[14]

The biographer of Sir James Reid, the Queen's doctor, drew on his papers to describe the train journey across France:

> The saloon carriages in which the Queen and her entourage travelled from Cherbourg to Menton were her own property and the passengers on the royal train numbered between sixty and a hundred. Her slow progress along the Continental lines was a spectacle. The speed of the train was limited to thirty-five miles per hour by day and twenty-five by night. It was halted between eight and nine in the morning so that the Queen could dress in comfort, and stops were made for meals. Gentlemen requiring hot water for shaving sent word ahead and a jug awaited them at a convenient station. The Queen even brought food packed in special containers from Windsor but on the whole the French menus were preferred by the more discerning of the Suite.[15]

The food included Irish stew, which was kept lukewarm in red flannel cushions. Marie Adeane, a maid of honour, later to become on marriage Marie Mallet, complained that the stew 'could not be compared with the excellent dinner provided on the train that goes round Paris'.[16] Although restaurant cars were introduced in 1883, the Queen did not attach one to the train to and from the Riviera.

The members of the Suite listed by *The Times* were Princess Beatrice, Major-General Sir Henry Ponsonby, Lord Bridport, equerry, Lady Churchill, lady-in-waiting, the Hon. Victoria Baillie, lady-in-waiting and the Queen's doctor, Dr Reid, whose name *The Times* spelt incorrectly.[17]

Colonel Carrington, an equerry, tried to cut down on the vast number of servants who went to the Riviera. He submitted a list of their names to the Queen, which she went through carefully. She then declared she could not do without any of them.[18]

The train transited Paris and stopped briefly in Marseilles on the morning of 16 March. Quoting a Reuters telegram, *The Times* said those on the platform included Mr Walhouse Mark, son of the British Consul in

Marseilles, but we are not told what more important engagement than welcoming his monarch occupied the Consul himself. Also present were some of the directors of the railway and several police inspectors.[19] The train also stopped at Cannes station, where, the Court Circular reported, the Marquis Camden had the honour of presenting a bouquet to Her Majesty.[20] Impressions of Marseilles comprised the very first entry of the holiday in the Queen's Journal:

> We reached Marseilles at 10. It is overhung by hills, but it was very hazy and the number of manufactories with high smoking chimneys, makes the atmosphere quite thick. The station seems an enormous one. Many fine gardens, with all sorts of exotic plants.[21]

The train arrived at 4.23 pm in the afternoon of Thursday 16 March, a journey of 18 hours. It stopped at a temporary station opposite the Chalet des Rosiers, where the Queen was to stay. *The Times* said the journey had been accomplished without the slightest hitch and the Queen and Princess Beatrice appeared on their arrival to be in excellent health and but little fatigued. There was no official reception, but a nameless English Vice-Consul received the royal party. There was still no mention of the mysterious absence of the Consul. The Municipality sent a large bouquet.[22]

The Queen's Journal reported on the arrival at length:

> Got into the carriage and drove a short distance to the Châlet des Rosiers, a small villa in the Swiss style, something like the Villa Hohenlohe. [The house in Baden-Baden, Germany, left to her in 1872 by her half sister, Feodora, daughter of the first husband of Queen Victoria's mother, Emich Charles, Prince of Leiningen.] Mr Henfrey was at the door, with 2 little girls, daughters of a cousin, who presented bouquets. Mr Henfrey said he felt quite nervous at the idea of our coming to his 'humble habitation', as he described the house. It is very prettily situated, out of the town, well above the sea, with Mentone to the right, close under the mountains, and near a fine valley covered with olive woods. We went first into the Drawingroom, a nice sized room, opening on to a balcony and then went upstairs, to our quite small rooms, which are pleasantly and conveniently arranged. The gentlemen all live in an Hotel, close by, and only a few of the servants are in the house. Dreadfully hot and tired. Took tea and rested. Much unpacking! Dined à 4, in a nice little Diningroom, which opens into the Drawingroom, then sat out on the balcony, the night quite splendid, – many stars, not a sound to be heard. We might have been at Osborne or Balmoral, so quiet it was, only an occasional train, rushing past below, but it does not disturb one.[23]

But she was disturbed by mosquitoes. 'Had a dreadful night on account of mosquitoes,' she told her Journal on 30 March.[24] The Queen would have disagreed with the statement of John Murray, the publisher of travel guides, in his 1848 guide to France that mosquitoes appeared from May to September only. She would, however, have agreed with his exquisite description of the suffering:

> The sufferer awakes in the middle of the night in a state of fever, and adieu to all further prospect of rest. The pain inflicted by the bites is bad enough, but it is the air of triumph with which the enemy blows his trumpet, the tingling, agonising buzzing which fills the air, gradually advancing nearer and nearer, announcing the certainty of fresh attack, which carries the irritation to the highest pitch.[25]

The Chalet des Rosiers was smaller than that at Baveno. It had recently been completed in railway architecture style, with pierced and fretted valances and balcony balustrades. The Queen acquired three watercolours of the chalet and its surroundings, which were placed in the Royal Collection at Windsor.[26]

Ponsonby, the Queen's Private Secretary, Bridport and Reid stayed in the Hôtel des Anglais. Reid wrote home:

> Our Hotel is a capital one, and from my bedroom window I could throw a stone into the Mediterranean. Our bedrooms are all in line, and we have a very nice sitting room and dining room. We have all gone in for white umbrellas to keep off the sun, that being most indispensable in the heat of the day.[27]

His duties were light: 'I go to the Châlet twice a day, and am free all the rest of the day; so it is very nice for me. Bridport is also pretty idle, so we loaf about a good deal together.'

His loafing was interrupted a few times. Once he got an urgent message from the Queen: 'The stopping having quite suddenly come out of the Queen's tooth, she wishes him to bring up something to stop it with <u>if possible</u> this evening before dinner.' He stopped it 'with complete and permanent success'. On another occasion the problem was a sore throat. She complained in a note to Reid:

> In spraying her throat with tannin before dinner, the Queen found it made the part near the right ear burn, and it is sore. She wishes to know if she had better not spray with cold water instead? The throat does not hurt at all in swallowing but the ear still aches a little. Should the poultice be <u>only linseed</u>.[28]

The British fleet was visiting the ports of the Mediterranean, but the ironclad *Inflexible* did not arrive off Menton until 18 March, two days after the monarch's arrival, which was odd if it was meant to protect her. It stayed until the end of her visit.[29] Princess Beatrice visited the warship and also borrowed Her Majesty's gunboat *Cygnet* one afternoon to go shopping in Nice.[30]

In addition to the battleship, The British Ambassador, Lord Lyons, was on hand. He told his superiors that he would have with him Mr Sheffield, one of the second secretaries at the Embassy, and cyphers and decyphers O, U and N.[31]

Reporting from Menton, which was then spelt Mentone, was from a number of sources. *The Times* had a column under the heading THE QUEEN on most days, which included the Court Circular, which was believed to have been often written by the Queen herself. There were also the reports of its own correspondent, and Reuters and, curiously enough, *The British Medical Journal* and *The Lancet*, which *The Times* sometimes quoted. The reason was that, as a health centre, Menton had many British doctors. *The Times* reported, '*The British Medical Journal* states that the municipal authorities at Mentone have had under their official notice and have taken into serious consideration, all the hygiene recommendations of the society of medical men practising in that town and promised to carry them out as far as lies in their power.' The report does not say what the recommendations were. Sir William Jenner, famous for his work on typhus and typhoid fevers, had also been involved.[32]

Prince Leopold, Duke of Albany, arrived on 19 March. He did not have tuberculosis, but, as James Henry Bennet, the doctor who lived for part of the year on the Riviera, said, sufferers from other afflictions also benefited from the Menton winter, so the doctors had decided that a sufferer from haemophilia might also gain advantage from a visit.[33] Three days after his arrival he had a slight fall when he slipped on some orange peel and had to be confined to his rooms.[34] There were frequent reports on his condition and by 31 March Reuters reported, 'Prince Leopold is better.'[35]

The Lancet reported on 13 April that the Prince was progressing very favourably. The swelling of the knee was subsiding rapidly, the daily diminution being a quarter of an inch in circumference. He drove out twice a day and was in excellent health and spirits, the medical journal reported. He left for Paris that day.[36]

On Good Friday, 7 April the Queen had written in her Journal:

Dear Leopold's birthday, his 29th. How thankful we must be that he has been preserved to us. How often has his poor young life hung on a thread, and how many bad and wearisome illnesses has he not recovered from! Though the idea of his marrying makes me anxious, still, as he has found a girl so charming, ready to accept and love him, in spite of his ailments, I hope he may be happy and carefully watched over.[37]

In fact it was not Prince Leopold who had found his bride-to-be, but the Queen. In view of his health, she could not imagine anyone suitable would have him. But it suddenly struck her that he should go and look at Princess Helena of Waldeck. She accepted him and they were married in St George's Chapel, Windsor, on 27 April 1882. Ten months later, to the Queen's surprise, the Duchess of Albany produced a granddaughter. 'I can scarcely believe that dear Leopold has got a child', said the Queen.[38]

There were other European royals on the Riviera. Victoria gave breakfast to King Albert and Queen Caroline of Saxony. Duke Ernst and the Duchess of Saxe-Coburg stayed for luncheon. The Duke was Prince Albert's elder brother. Her grandson, Prince Henry of Prussia, the son of her daughter Victoria and Prince Friedrich of Prussia, called on her.

The Queen spent most of her time riding about the countryside in her carriage or pony and trap, usually with her daughter Princess Beatrice and her ladies-in-waiting. She wrote frequently and enthusiastically about her adventures in her Journal:

A most splendid morning and day. But we have never, excepting for a few hours, been without sun, and it certainly has a very invigorating exhilarating effect on mind and body. Drove with Beatrice, Jane C. [Churchill] and Lady Bridport, again on the Italian Ride. ... We went to the point, where there is such a lovely view of Bordighera. In the distance, we saw a balloon ascend from Mentone and watched it sailing along in the air; when after ½ an hour, we looked for it again, Beatrice suddenly discovered it in the sea! Knowing that 2 people were in it, we were much alarmed, as we soon saw it disappear altogether. On getting home, we were quite relieved to hear that the occupants of the balloon had been saved by a boat, which had been out on the look out.[39]

She went out for a walk one day with Lady Jane Churchill and met their washerwoman, who was so overcome with seeing her that she knelt down in the road.

The trap met lots of people, which she fully reported on:

Frequently met carriages, and donkeys, of which here are endless numbers, laden with grass and fodder, often with a barrel on either side, led by a woman. The children often throw, or offer us little bunches of wild flowers. An old woman who passed us on her donkey said 'Bonjour Madame la Reine èt votre compagnie'. They speak very bad French.[40]

The Magnat Artistic Pottery Works appealed to her and she bought several objects when she visited it.[41] She even invited the owner to the house, complimented him on his work and 'made further considerable purchases from him'.[42]

She did not walk much, but she went on foot one day to visit Prince Leopold in the nearby Hôtel Bellevue.[43]

The weather was unusually fine. Typical temperatures were 61 degrees fahrenheit maximum and 46 degrees minimum. The usual gales and rain did not occur and there was rain and hail on only one night. *The British Medical Journal* explained the weather:

> The fine clear weather on the Genoese Riviera is almost invariably with north-east or north-west winds, which blow over the mountains into the sea, miles from land, leaving the sheltered coastline steeped in sunshine. When the wind is in the south, if slight, the sky becomes more or less covered with fleecy clouds; if strong, the clouds darken, collect on the mountains and rain falls. South winds coming from the sea are necessarily moisture laden, which explains this fact.[44]

There were relatively few private gardens in Menton because the local inhabitants were deterred by the high cost of watering from growing flowers other than those that could be sold to scent factories. Bennet wrote that 'they cannot understand anyone making a mere flower garden for pleasure on the mountain side, a mile or two from town'. They were considered all but demented. But Bennet made a garden, aided by an intelligent peasant called Antoine, whom he raised, as he said, 'to the dignity of a head-gardener'.[45] Bennet made available to the Queen his garden of eight acres, equipped with a fern grotto to sit in, and she and Beatrice spent many hours there walking and sketching.[46] None of the sketches are in the Royal Archives.[47] The garden was in Italy, about a mile from the town, but such was the flexibility of frontiers that no one commented on the fact that they had to cross the border each time they visited it. It was on the side of a mountain 300 feet above sea level and consisted of terraces rising one above the other, planted with olives, oranges, lemons and flora of the southern hemisphere.[48]

The Palazzo Orengo in the gardens of La Mortola, meaning Myrtle, across the border in Italy and now called the Villa Hanbury, was the most important garden the Queen visited and sketched in. Sir Thomas Hanbury was a member of a leading English Quaker family, part-owners of the pharmaceutical company, Allen & Hanbury. Hanbury had made a fortune in the Far East as a cloth merchant, buying silk for sale in Europe. He had acquired a great reputation for honesty during the Taiping rebellion when the Chinese made their property over to him in the belief that there would be no threat to an Englishman's property. He handed it all back when the troubles ended. In 1867 he returned to Europe to buy property and find a wife.[49] He bought La Mortola and began to plant a garden of 18 hectares.[50] The next year he found a wife, Katharine Aldam Pease, and later returned to China.

This is Charles Quest-Ritson's description of the gardens in *The English Garden Abroad*:

> No visitor to La Mortola ever forgets his first sight of it. One of the great experiences of a garden lover's life is to pass through the gates of Villa Hanbury and discover the garden spread out below, a great wooded hillside dropping first steeply, then gently down 259 steps to the rocky shore beneath, an enchanted landscape of palms, cypresses, olives, cycads and Judas trees that stretches to the pines by the edge of the sea.

> The garden displays itself openly and immediately as you enter its portals. As you descend towards the palazzo, the views and prospects come and go, but the distant perspective is lost, so that it is the memory of that splendid first overview which urges exploration in all directions at once. That, and the vistas and plants encountered on the descent. Sometimes you drop quickly from one level to the next; sometimes you pass slowly from one end of a terrace to the other, making a leisurely progress. The central structure of the garden is the long straight avenue that always frames a distant view of the sea (all paths ultimately lead down to it) while the botanical and horticultural effects are spread upon the terraces, bidding the visitor to dally among the flowers and take note of their beauty and their names. No other garden offers such equality between the whole and its parts, between the design and the planting.[51]

Thomas Hanbury worked on the gardens with his elder brother, Daniel, a distinguished pharmacist and botanist. Their plan was to engage in scientific experiments in acclimatization and to put together a collection that was useful and instructive. Their main achievement was in importing plants from the Orient. The head gardener was for a time Ludwig Winter, a young German who had once worked in the gardens of the Tuileries, but was sacked by the Empress Eugénie for singing 'La Marseillaise'. Lady Hanbury gave the Villa Hanbury to the Italian state in 1960 and after a period of neglect the house and gardens were restored by the local office of the Arts Ministry.[52] It is now run by Genoa University.

Winston Churchill was wheeled up and down the steep slopes in Queen Victoria's special chair when he visited there in the 1950s.[53] [54] The other places the Queen visited were La Turbie and the monastery at Laghetto.

A friend of Hanbury had been Edward Lear, the poet and artist, who built a house in San Remo in 1871, the Villa Emily. Hanbury and Lear ceased to be friends when Hanbury built a hotel between the Villa Emily and the sea, blocking Lear's view. Lear had to sell and in 1881 built another property, the Villa Tennyson. It had to be identical to the Villa Emily, otherwise Foss, Lear's famous cat, would not have liked it.

There was a rumour that the monarch would visit Lear's new house and garden. In 1846, following the publication of *Illustrated Excursions in Italy*, Lear had been invited by the Queen to give her 12 lessons in drawing. She had been very proud that the artist had been very pleased with her drawing. Giorgio Kocali, Lear's long-time servant, worked day and night baking macaroons because it was well known that the Queen ate macaroons continually and made her Suite do the same. Lord Spencer, the President of the Council, who was in attendance on Victoria, came to lunch and more than 100 'owly fools' waited outside to greet her, but she never came.[55] The story was that she could not come because of the protocol that would have been involved with the Italian government. But that was clearly not the case since she had already visited other gardens across the border in Italy.

Lear was no doubt disappointed because he was proud of his garden, but he wrote to a friend, 'I dislike contact with Royalty as you know, being a dirty landscape-painter apt only to speak his thoughts and not to conceal them.'[56] The following year he described the garden the monarch would have seen: 'And my garden is now admirably beautiful, & and were it not for the Slugs and Snails would be inimitable. But these melancholy mucilaginous Molluscs have eaten up all my Highercynths & also my Lower=cynths.' He was particularly proud of his roses, as is seen by these verses which he penned in 1885:

And this is certain; if so be
You could just now my garden see,
The aspic of my flowers so bright
Would make you shudder with delight.

And if you voz to see my roziz
As is a boon to all men's noziz, –
You'd fall upon your back and scream –
O Lawk! O cricky! It's a dream![57]

But there was a consolation for the absence of the Queen. While he was dining one evening he saw a little woman looking at him through the dining room door. In due course the man with her opened the door and addressed him: 'My wife wishes to know if you are Mr Lear, and she would be glad to make your acquaintance again – the Princess Royal of England.' The man was her husband, Friedrich, the Crown Prince of Prussia.[58] Some years earlier, when Lear had met the Princess Royal and Princess Alice of Hesse and the Rhine on the Riviera, he had commented that in a lower rank they might have been called flippant and common.[59] Lear was more complimentary later in 1882 when he met the Princess Royal again. 'Distinctly Princess Victoria is the most absolute duck of a Princess imaginable, so natural and unaffected, with a real simplicity one feels is not an affectation of simplicity,' he wrote in his diary.[60]

The Queen disapproved of nearby Monte Carlo. Indeed, at the instigation of her daughter, Vicky, she spoke about its evils to Lord Lyons, the British Ambassador to France, in the hope that he might raise it with the French government, which the Crown Princess seemed to think could do something about the wickedness. But Lord Lyons declined to do so because he was afraid that actual meddling would not do. What was worse, Vicky said that the owner of the Chalet des Rosiers where the Queen was staying was a member of the 'committee', by which she presumably meant the joint stock company that owned the gambling concession.[61]

The Queen took a drive to Monte Carlo one afternoon, but did not, of course, visit the casino. Her comments were:

Monte Carlo is a very clean looking place, with many Hotels and Villas, the Casino with its gambling rooms, is an immense building with splendid gardens, and terraces going down to the sea. ...

One saw very nasty disreputable looking people walking about at Monte Carlo, though many respectable people go there also for their health. The harm this attractive gambling establishment does, cannot be overestimated. The old Prince of Monaco, derives his income from it and therefore does not wish to stop it, though efforts are being made to do so.[62]

It is curious that there is only the passing reference to Charles III, Prince of Monaco, whose territory she was on. Her failure to involve the ruler in her visit was a breach of protocol, whatever her views on the immorality of Monte Carlo. The Queen had met Prince Charles and Princess Antoinette at the great ball held in the Queen's honour when she visited France in 1855. That meeting and the regal splendour of the occasion set Antoinette dreaming that her son, Albert, heir to the Monégasque throne, would marry into the British royal family. In 1866 Princess Antoinette's mother-in-law, Princess Caroline, had tried through the Empress Eugénie to get Albert considered as a possible husband for Queen Victoria's cousin, Princess Mary Adelaide of Cambridge, a large lady, 15 years older than the 18-year-old Albert.[63] But Queen Victoria was not having that. Princess Mary married Francis, Duke of Teck. They produced May, who married the future King George V.

The Queen would clearly have agreed with the French saying that Nice, Cannes and Monte Carlo were the World, the Flesh and the Devil.[64]

The luscious and flamboyant casino she admired had been designed by Charles Garnier and been opened only three years before in 1879. In 1856, motivated by the success of the gambling resort at Baden-Baden in Germany, and in an attempt to compensate for his difficulty in collecting taxes and to recoup his family's losses in the French Revolution, Prince Charles had granted a 30-year casino monopoly to two French entrepreneurs. They planned to build gaming rooms and a hotel and introduce other amenities to attract visitors. They also envisaged a steamer service between Monaco and Nice. The project was described as a spa, for reasons of respectability.

The roulette wheel was spun for the first time on 14 December 1856, but the concessionaires lacked capital, could not realize their plans and the casino floundered. The concession changed hands a number of times, but there was little progress and the Prince's finances continued in a parlous state. Worse happened in 1861 when, under the treaty signed between France and Austria, Monaco lost about four-fifths of its territory, including Menton, and was reduced to 0.73 square miles (1.89 square kilometres). That same year Charles had the concession given to François Blanc, who had made such a success of the Homburg casino in Germany. He improved access by road and steamship, built the casino and a hotel and laid out the gardens which Victoria so liked. One of the shareholders later became Pope Leo XIII.[65]

Public gambling had become illegal in France in 1857. Not until 1907, under pressure from cities such as Nice and Cannes, jealous of the success of Monte Carlo, were baccarat and chemin-de-fer legalized. Roulette had to wait until 1933. (Britain had to wait until 1960 in the reign of Queen Victoria's great-great-granddaughter, Elizabeth II, for casinos to be legalized.)

The British Medical Journal, in a dispatch which dealt with the sanitary arrangements at the royal residence, reported that a large bouquet of exotic flowers which had been sent to the Chalet des Rosiers by the authorities of the gambling house at Monte Carlo was at once and peremptorily refused.[66]

The Queen's disapproval of Monte Carlo was echoed by the London Society for the Abolition of the Monte Carlo Casino. The Society also had a Paris branch. She no doubt read some of the attacks on casinos in general by such writers as the novelist William Makepeace Thackeray, in his book *The Kickleburys on the Rhine*, and specifically on Monte Carlo by John Addington Symonds, the author of *History of the Italian Renaissance* and one of the earliest English visitors to Monaco. He wrote:

> There is a large house of sin blazing with gas lamps by night, flaming and shining by the shore, like pandemonium or the habitation of some romantic witch. ... Splendid women with bold eyes and golden hair and marble columns of Imperial throats are there to laugh, to sing songs, to tempt. ... The croupiers are either fat, sensual cormorants or sallow, lean cheeked vultures, or suspicious foxes. Compare them with Coutts men.[67]

The comparison with the frock-coated gentlemen of Coutts, the Queen's own bankers, would have been very telling.

Doctors condemned the Monte Carlo casino as a threat to health. Dr Burney Yeo warned of 'the dangerous seductions of the gaming tables'.[68] Dr Bennet was also against Monaco. 'I cannot but think that the immediate proximity of a gaming table, in the absence of all other occupations, is dangerous to many who would never positively seek its excitements and risk,' he wrote.[69] Dr Edward Sparks said its noxious influence was infecting even Nice, Menton and San Remo, both in the class of unwelcome visitors which it attracted and in the ruin it brought upon respectable families.[70]

Blanc made so much money out of the casino that he was able to subsidize the Battle of the Flowers in Nice, which Victoria so much enjoyed.[71]

The casino was attacked in the Press of the area, inspired by the Church of England's Bishop of Gibraltar, in whose see the Riviera towns came, and by the City of Nice. The bishop was furious that he had been refused permission to establish an Anglican church in the principality and denounced it: 'Is it right for Christian men and women ever to enter a place where they are sure to rub shoulders with the swindler, the harlot and the thief, whose chambers are built with the wages of iniquity, and whose riches are the price of blood?'[72]

The historian J.R. Green wrote a more sober description:

> The salon itself, the terrible 'Hell', which one has pictured with all sorts of Dantesque accompaniments, is a pleasant room, gaily painted, with cosies all round it and a huge mass of gorgeous flowers in the centre. Nothing can be more unlike one's preconceived ideas than the gambling itself, or the aspect of the gamblers around the tables. Of the wild excitement, the frenzy of gain, the outbursts of despair one has come prepared to witness, there is not a sign.[73]

The Niçois attacked the Monte Carlo casino because of their plan to establish a rival gambling house on the Promenade des Anglais. They spread lurid stories about the many suicides of those who had lost their fortunes in Monte Carlo. 'The suicides are carefully wrapped, put in cases and sent out of the principality by ordinary mail', a Nice newspaper later reported. Other reports said the corpses were stuffed into grand pianos or sunk out at sea. It was rumoured in turn that to inflate the suicide statistics the Niçois took the bodies of people who had died of natural causes, fired revolvers into their heads and smuggled them into Monaco at the dead of night.[74]

The Queen did not stop Prince Leopold going into the den of iniquity. He went there with Dr Reid, Dr Arnold Royle, his own doctor, Sir Henry Ponsonby and Lord Bridport, who was the grandson of Admiral Nelson. Dr Reid described their visit: 'The place was quite crowded at the different tables, and a very motley crew the people are, all nations, ages and classes being represented, and half the players being women!'[75]

Already the Riviera was acquiring the reputation that Somerset Maugham later described as a sunny place for shady people. Menton had several brothels by the time of the 1882 visit. In 1898 Oscar Wilde came across accommodating local boys who were transformed into what he described as the noble army of the boulevard. 'The fishing population of the Riviera have the same morals as the Neapolitans,' he said.[76]

Despite these temptations, a well-known saying became current: Cannes is for living, Monte Carlo is for gambling and Menton for dying. The authors of *Monte Carlo and How To Do It*, which was published in 1891, described Menton's residents and visitors as 'being of a bronchial nature, suggestive of Bournemouth, apt to cough and spit in a manner that does not act as a gin-and-bitters to your next meal.' They added, 'We will have but a brief stay at Menton.'[77]

The entertainment for the royal party was more restrained in Menton than it would have been in Monte Carlo. The Queen's Journal of Good Friday, 7 April 1882 recorded:

> We had to dine early, in time to see a religious procession, which was to take place at 9. We saw it from the windows of the Vice Consul's house, which is in the principal street. Soon we heard the sounds of distant music. Priests and Penitents carrying lanterns appeared and acolytes in white and red with censors. Then came the band playing a somewhat profane march, and after that, preceded by the chief Clergy, a ghastly looking, life sized figure of Our Saviour was carried by, under a black canopy, with numbers of lamps on either side, followed by a great crowd, who had come out of the Cathedral. The procession went down a small side street, and we watched it disappearing on to the Place where the figure was placed on a Catafalque. After that it was taken back to the church. We waited a little in M. Palmaro's house, and then returned to the Châlet.[78]

Divine service had been performed at the Chalet earlier in the day by the Reverend Canon Anson, and the royal household attended service each Sunday.[79] The Queen did not go to the church in Menton. The Anglican church of St John is still there today on the Avenue Carnot, staffed by a Priest-in-Charge. The town, which was gaily decorated, held a fete in honour of the British monarch. She watched it from the balcony of the Chalet and the illuminations were magnificent.[80] The return match, which the Queen did not attend, was on HMS *Inflexible*. Many English and local residents of Menton watched the dancing, a display of torpedo practice and other amusements.[81]

There was not much contact with the locals. Sir Henry Ponsonby gave a lunch for the general in command of the military division in Nice, with his staff, the Mayor of Menton and the Prefect of the Alpes-Maritimes. They were then presented to the Queen and, as the Reuters report put it, had the honour of inscribing their names in Her Majesty's visiting book.[82] The chief of the Menton municipal band composed a cantata in her honour and the Queen in turn presented him with a diamond breast pin.[83]

There is no mention of John Brown in Victoria's Menton Journals. Perhaps it was because he clearly so disliked the place. He was not pleased by the attention of the locals, although that was not surprising given that he not only wore a kilt, but also a topee.[84]

Brown was particularly worried about the threat from Fenian Irish revolutionaries. The local police were making much of reports that three Irishmen were on their way from Paris to Menton, Brown told the Queen. The British police who accompanied the Queen thought it was a hoax. Nevertheless special precautions were taken. The Queen herself was not nervous, but she worried about Brown. She clearly liked writing letters, because, although he was on call a few hundred yards away, she wrote about it to Sir Henry Ponsonby on 20 March 1882:

> The Queen thanks Sir Henry Ponsonby for his kind letter which has much re-assured her tho' she cannot say she felt so much alarmed but it gave her a great shock as she was forgetting the 2nd of March & she trusts Sir Henry will also reassure Brown who was in such a state heightened by his increasing ha-tred of being 'abroad' which blinds his admiration of the country even.

> The Queen thinks that one principal cause of this (w^h was not the case in Switzerland) is that he can communicate with no one when out, not keep anyone off the carriage nor the coachmen either.[85]

(The seventh attempt on the monarch's life had been on 2 March 1882, when Roderick MacLean shot at her and missed as she left her train at Windsor. He was set upon by boys from Eton College armed with um-brellas.)

John Brown's state of mind was also affected by erysipelas, a disease of inflammation of the skin or subcutaneous cellular tissue, which caused him much pain and from which he died a year later, on 27 March 1883.

Affairs of state took up part of the Queen's day: 'I heard from Mr Gladstone that there have been great delays and trouble in the Hse of C as usual, at which he seems much annoyed.'[86] He was having to hold off introducing a Local Government Bill because of obstruction from the opposition.[87]

The Queen had not lost her well-known interest in handsome men, which had contributed to her being called 'Mrs Brown'. Her Journal of 5 April, 1882 said:

> Out driving with Beatrice and the 2 ladies. ... In one place, we saw sheep climbing amongst the rocks. The shepherds are very picturesque looking, wearing knee breeches, sort of white stockings and leggings, and a large black felt hat. Some are very handsome boys. They have no dogs with them.[88]

The Queen's last duty before she left was, as was her wont, to plant two trees in the garden to commemorate her visit.[89] To the sound of a royal salute from the *Inflexible* the holiday came to an end. The Queen and her courtiers left Menton at 10 am on the morning of 12 April. They arrived in Cherbourg at 6.30 pm the following evening.[90]

The Queen's Journal entry on the train between Cannes and Toulon on 12 April 1882 reads:

> Alas! already far away from beloved and beautiful Mentone! It is too sad to watch the beautiful mountains and vegetation (though the latter not yet) disappearing. But I must be grateful to have been permitted to spend 4 weeks in that lovely and far famed Riviera.[91]

The fourteenth of April was Princess Beatrice's birthday and the royal party was awakened on board the royal yacht *Victoria and Albert* by the band of the 25th Regiment of the French Army. The selection of music included the march 'Salut à la Princesse' (dedicated to HRH Princess Beatrice) and the waltz 'Souvenir de Cherbourg' (dedicated to Her Majesty the Queen of England), both by J. Meyer.[92]

The crossing from Cherbourg to Portsmouth on 14 April increased her regrets at having to leave. She wrote (on board ship, after breakfast):

> It was fine but still blew hard. I wished not to go, but a lugger, which just came in, reported no bad <u>sea</u>. The 'Enchantress' which had been outside, reported the same, so Capt: Thornton advised our starting for fear of its getting worse, and so I unwillingly consented. We were off at 10. I went down at once to my cabin and remained there. We rolled a good deal, and instead of getting better it got worse as we neared England. I was not ill, but felt very nervous, as I always do. At 3.35 we arrived at Portsmouth and landed at 5.[93]

The Queen arrived back at Windsor Castle shortly before 7 pm.

The Lancet expressed its relief on her return that she had improved in health despite the misgivings it had earlier expressed about the defective sanitary conditions.[94]

The visit, chargeable to the Lord Chamberlain's Department, had cost, excluding food and drink, £915.8.0.[95] [96]

Today the Chalet des Rosiers is converted into six apartments and part of the garden is now incorporated into the Exotic Botanical Garden of Val Rahmeh.[97] On 10 April 1939 a statue of Queen Victoria was unveiled in Menton. When the Germans seized Menton in the Second World War they threw the statue in the sea. It was replaced in 1960.

CHAPTER 3

1887: Cannes. A pilgrimage to mourn the death of son Leopold

The Queen went to Menton in 1882 because of the sickness of her son Leopold, Duke of Albany. She went to Cannes in 1887 because of his death. She wanted to see the Church of St George, built in his memory, and the Villa Nevada, where he had died three years earlier.

Leopold's visit to Cannes in 1884 was induced by illness; he was suffering from painful swelling of the smaller joints. He had planned to take with him his wife, Helena, who was pregnant, but she fell sick and was unable to accompany him. He arrived towards the end of February and stayed with his friend and former equerry, Captain Perceval, and his aunt Marie at the Villa Nevada on a hill to the west of Cannes.[1]

Thursday 27 March 1884 was a heavy day for Prince Leopold. He had been at a ball at Mont Fleuri, which went on until 4 am. He had a few hours sleep, took a bath, wrote some letters in his room at the Cercle Nautique, the yacht club, and went out to lunch with friends.[2] In the afternoon he planned to go to a Battle of the Flowers. First he wanted a shave and went back to the Cercle Nautique where, hurrying to his room, he slipped on the tiled floor of the hall and hit his right knee hard against the bottom step. He was in intense pain and taken back to the Villa Nevada. He nevertheless summoned the strength to write to his wife, who was expecting to see him back in England in a few days:

> such a pain it was. I at once thought – as I lay on the ground – of my sweet Nellie, & the idea of your making yourself unhappy made me burst into tears!
>
> Darling, you shall know the truth every day – I do not mind the pain (I have very little this moment) but the idea of you unhappy – perhaps crying – at Claremont [their country seat] joined to my horrible disappointment at not coming home – makes me howl. Oh! Death w^d be preferable to this – Darling, we must not shut our eyes – I may be 3 or 4 weeks longer without being

able to move. ...

Darling the morphia is struggling <u>so</u> with me that I can not <u>possibly</u> write more.[3]

In the early hours of the next morning, 28 March, he had convulsions and died. Some time before he had been with Captain Perceval, looking out to sea from the balcony of his room and told him, 'Perceval, I would rather die here than anywhere else in the world.'[4]

Neither the French nor the British death certificates gave a cause of death, but speculation ranged from epilepsy to haemorrhage. He was both a mild epileptic and a haemophiliac.[5] Two distinguished doctors, D.M. Potts and W.T.W. Potts, who believe the cause of Leopold's death was haemophilia, in 1995 published a book, *Queen Victoria's Gene*. They claimed that, since no member of the royal family before his generation had suffered from this very visible condition, the haemophilia of Leopold and other descendants of Queen Victoria meant that either one of Victoria's parents had suffered a random 1 in 25 to 50,000 mutation of the genes, or that she was the illegitimate child of a haemophiliac man.[6] It is fortunate for the contemporary image of the monarch that such a thesis was not advanced during her lifetime.

Leopold was so taken by the Cannes area that when he died he was negotiating to buy 5000 square metres of land at Juan les Pins. The price was to be FF5 a square metre.[7]

The Queen recorded in her Journal:

Another blow has fallen upon me and all of us today. My beloved Leopold, that bright clever son, who had so many times recovered from such fearfull illnesses, and from various small accidents has been taken from us! To lose another dear child, far from me, and one who was so gifted, and such a help to me, is too dreadful.

Am utterly crushed. How dear he was to me, how I had watched over him!

I am a poor desolate old woman, and my cup of sorrow overflows. Oh! God, in His mercy spare my other dear children.[8]

The Prince of Wales brought Leopold's body back to Windsor.

The February before the Queen's visit, the Prince of Wales had laid a dedication stone on a memorial to Leopold, a fountain topped by a statue of St George, by Paul Liénard. It had been funded by subscription from the residents of Cannes, 'who without distinction of nationality or religion wanted to render a last hommage to the young prince', as the inscription says. The previous year the Prince of Wales had laid a foundation stone for St George's Church, the other memorial. Leopold's widow, Helena, wanted to place a bust of the Prince in the south-east chapel, but the Queen vetoed it and insisted instead that a copy of the tomb statue from Windsor be placed in the church.[9] A plaque in memory of Helena is set alongside it. In 1974 St George's was sold to the Catholic Church for FF300,000 and it flourishes today.[10]

In 1891 the Duchess of Albany and her children visited the Villa Nevada where her husband had died. The family acquired it in 1893 and the Duchess often went there.[11] After the Second World War Alice, the daughter of Leopold and Helena, sold the Villa Nevada to a London banker. Today it is still the residence of a single family.[12] Above it still lies the Villa Edelweiss, where the Queen stayed.[13]

When she arrived in Cannes the Queen would have well remembered how, on the advice of doctors following a serious illness, she had sent Leopold there in 1861 when he was eight, and that while he was there Prince Albert died. Leopold was sent in the care of a German doctor and tutor, Theodore Guenther, accompanied by Sir Edward Bowater, a veteran of Waterloo, his wife and 19-year-old daughter, Louisa. They stayed in the Château Leader, a fine villa with a view of the Mediterranean and also the mountains, to the west of Cannes. The homesick young prince spent his time at his lessons, playing chess with Louisa, riding donkeys and playing croquet, which had not before been seen in Cannes and which was his passion. Thomas Robinson Woolfield, a friend of Lord Brougham's, had laid out the croquet lawn for Leopold in the garden of his Villa Victoria.[14] In 1874 croquet became less popular and Woolfield replaced it with a tennis lawn, the first in Cannes. Woolfield's gardener was John Taylor, who in 1864 founded the first English estate agency on the Riviera.

The last letter Albert wrote before he died was to Leopold. Soon after he received it, not only did the child have to bear the news of his father's death, but Sir Edward Bowater also died. A letter from Leopold's mother was typically macabre. She sent him 'a Locket with beloved Papa's hair & a photograph – w^h I wish you to wear <u>attached</u> to a string or chain round your neck & a <u>dear</u> pocket handkerchief of beloved Papa's, which you ought to keep constantly with you.'[15]

While she was visiting the Villa Nevada the Queen must have reflected on the bad relations which had existed between herself and her son in the months before he died, and which had, curiously enough, emanated from Cannes in the previous year – another good reason to be unhappy with the place. Leopold had tried to be appointed Governor-General of Canada and had written to his mother from Cannes, where he was on holiday, pleading to be appointed. His timing, however, was all wrong, he went about it the wrong way and the Queen was appalled. The government was against his appointment and there was a great fuss about his bid both in Parliament and in the Press and he did not get the job. *Reynolds' Newspaper* said he was a feeble-minded individual, covered in sores, who would not even have been able to find Canada on a map.[16]

Leopold's next attempt to find an appointment came in January 1884 when he tried to become Governor of Victoria in Australia. He again upset his mother by talking to ministers before consulting her. Her message to him was that he had caused her deep pain and that she had been made quite ill by this new and totally unexpected shock.[17] This time the government was in favour of the appointment but the Queen blocked it, at least for the time being.[18]

After the Cannes visit Leopold was due to go to Darmstadt in Germany for the wedding of a niece and had asked not to be put in the same building as his mother as they had not spoken for three months. He wrote to his brother-in-law, Louis, Grand Duke of Hesse and the Rhine, 'Don't say anything when you write to Windsor about the squabbles between myself and the Queen – I'll tell you about it when I come to Darmstadt. But it is very serious this time, and no joke.'[19]

Leopold never lost the love of Cannes which he had acquired during his five months there as a child and on visits in 1876 and, with his wife, in 1883. The Prince of Wales liked it very much, as he told his mother after she had reproved him for the 'round of gaieties' which he indulged in there.[20] Cannes was also much favoured by the British aristocracy (one diarist listed as early as the mid-1850s the houses of the Duchess of Gordon, the Duchess of Manchester, Lord Brougham, Lord Londesborough and Lady Oxford).[21] But it clearly did not appeal to the Queen, who spent only four nights there. She had held off her departure from Windsor until 29 March so that she could mark the third anniversary of the death of Leopold on the previous day by visiting his tomb in the Albert Chapel, where she laid chaplets and crosses of flowers.[22] Auguries for Cannes were not helped by the breakdown of the train when one of the wheels of the sleeping compartment became red hot as it travelled only a quarter of the way from Paris to Marseilles. The Queen declined to change the carriage that night because Princess Beatrice had already gone to bed, so they arrived late in Cannes on 1 April, the whole journey having taken 72 hours.

The *Times* correspondent reported that no military escort had been provided for the arrival, as the Queen wished to be perfectly quiet – 'a very natural wish when we remember the melancholy recollections which her first visit to Cannes must necessarily evoke'. He ascribed the silence of the French on her arrival to ignorance and that of the British to discretion. 'The French do not know what it is to cheer a Sovereign, and the English had the good taste to respect the Queen's wish for privacy, and were content to bare their heads as she drove past.'[23]

However, the French did know that when the Duke of Edinburgh arrived with a squadron consisting of the dreadnoughts *Thunderer*, *Agamemnon* and *Colossus* he should have saluted the French flag and soil. He excused himself by explaining that he did not have a saluting battery.[24] What he did have was electric light and when the Queen departed it was flashed from the ships along the route of the royal train.[25]

The gloom continued when Mr Augustus Savile, who was lending the Queen his house, fell critically ill and could not receive the royal party when it arrived. The Queen called on him at a nearby house which he had moved to and he died soon after she left Cannes. The Villa Edelweiss was very small, although it had beautiful gardens with red and white camellias in full flower.[26] The weather was cold and there was no sun.

The house was one of the highest in Cannes, so from the bow window of her room the Queen looked out over the other houses to the sea and the islands. Napoleon had landed in Cannes when he escaped from Elba in 1815. Many of the houses she saw were occupied by her subjects.

Margaret Maria Brewster rented the Château St Marguerite about two miles from Cannes and her *Letters from Cannes and Nice*, which she published in 1857, are the best description of what life was like for the foreigner. She rented the house for FF2500 (£100)[27] for the season, from 1 November to 1 June. She bemoaned the rising prices and that you had to take the house for the full season.[28] But she was fortunate to have a good man-of-all-work, Giuseppe Odoni, because she did not think much of most domestics in Cannes:

> Domestic service is one of the weak points of Cannes, – the native female servants are stupid, idle, ignorant, and far from cleanly, yet their wages are very high, from twenty to thirty francs [£0.80 to £1.19][29] a month, besides wine and coffee; most of them are bad cooks, none of them can wait at table, and they do not market well; the consequence is that most people complain

of the badness of food here; it is dear, but when well chosen and kept a proper time, it is excellent.[30]

St George's Church, Leopold's memorial, was the fourth English Protestant church to be built in Cannes. Thomas Woolfield, to whom the Queen owed a debt for his entertainment of Leopold as a child, had in 1855 built Christ Church, which was the first to be opened on the French Riviera. Trinity Church opened in 1864 and St Paul's in 1869. The French authorities in Cannes were not as indulgent towards Protestants as were the Sardinians in Nice and they expelled from the country a Protestant evangelist, Monsieur Charbonny. The persecution upset the local population because they thought it would deter foreigners from settling there and prevent Cannes becoming an important resort like Nice.

In 1846 Thomas Woolfield, who had first visited Cannes in 1838, bought no less than two properties, the Villa Victoria and the Château St Georges. For his devotions he rented the ground floor of a house at the end of the promenade on the beach, fitted it up as a little chapel and appointed a Monsieur Boucher as minister to conduct French services. As soon as the minister gave out the number of the first hymn on the first Sunday the Commissaire of Police, in full dress, marched in with two gendarmes, declared the service an illegal assembly and closed it. But two weeks later, Woolfield and Boucher having convinced the authorities that they had acted legally, the same gendarmes escorted the congregation into the chapel. 'Since that first disappointment, no hostility has ever been shown at Cannes, by any of the authorities, to Protestant worship', Woolfield recorded. When he moved into his house Woolfield started English services in the afternoon in the drawing room, but he still went to the French service in the morning. When English friends left Cannes, Woolfield recounted that they told him, 'If only there was an English church at Cannes, we should not run away from you', so he built one.[31]

Among Woolfield's other achievements were the importation in 1862 of the Australian eucalyptus with seeds from the Royal Botanic Gardens in Sydney (the eucalyptus being little known on the Riviera) and the introduction of sweet potatoes and gooseberries.

The croquet lawn, which Woolfield had laid out for Prince Leopold, was much appreciated by the Prince's nephews, Prince Wilhelm and Prince Henry, the children of his sister, Victoria, the Crown Princess of Prussia, when they spent six months at the Grand Hôtel and at the Villa Gabrielle in 1869. The Crown Princess always described Woolfield as 'the oldest inhabitant and real founder of Cannes'. Croquet was the particular favourite of Prince Wilhelm, later Kaiser Wilhelm II, and he wrote to his English grandmother about Cannes. Brougham, and presumably Woolfield too, used to import fresh turf by boat from England every year. Prince Albert of Prussia spent the season of 1869–70 in Cannes and frequently attended Woolfield's Christ Church, where, as one might expect of one with his background, his favourite hymn was 'The Son of God goes forth to war'.[32]

Fifty years before Brougham and Woolfield discovered Cannes, a Swiss, Jean-Jacques Sulzer, who went to the Riviera from 1775–76, expressed his surprise that the English had not discovered it. 'I am really amazed that among the English who go to Nice for the winter, no one has thought of stopping in Cannes, where the winter is also very mild, for lemons and oranges are abundant', he wrote in his *Voyage de Berlin à Nice (aller et retour)*.[33]

However, when the English did discover Cannes there was no lack of critics of the town and what had been perpetrated there. Walburga, Lady Paget, who in the 1890s used to visit the Château de Garibondy, wrote in December 1895:

Cannes I think detestable; it is a long string of very ugly villas built by millionaires. They all spend enormous sums in keeping up a subtropical vegetation, beds of specimen flowers, artificial lawns which have to be resown every year. Everything about these gardens reeks of money. The best of them attain a theatrical effect with huge palms and roses climbing to their top, shrubs with big flowers, fountains, stone balustrades, and bit of blue sea or blue mountain in the distance. There are no drives or walks or resources of any kind within the reach of a moderate income.[34]

Prosper Mérimée, the author of *Carmen*, who was an inspector of historic monuments, complained that the English had 'settled here as if in conquered territory. ... They have built fifty villas or chateaux, each more extraordinary than the last, and deserve to be impaled upon the architecture they have brought to this area.'[35]

Mérimée was acquainted with his neighbour, Edward Lear, who shared his sentiments and who wrote in 1870 that, 'could Cannes have been saved from the VULGAR – it might really have been Paradise.'[36] Lear was particularly influenced by his difficulty in selling his paintings there and the philistinism of some of the residents who came to his studio. 'What books did you copy all these drawings from?', asked one lady. 'O don't look at the drawings – only come & see the view from the window,' cried another.[37]

Lear had the consolation of the company of John Addington Symonds and his family, including his 2½-year-old daughter Janet. 'Mr Lear ... makes rhymes for her and illustrates them; one about "the owl and the pussy-cat, who went to sea in a pea-green boat" is notable', Symonds wrote to a friend.[38] Symonds also disliked Cannes, so they could grumble together and Lear could write nonsense verse about the place:[39]

> Edwardus: What makes you look so black, so glum, so cross?
> ... Is it neuralgia, headache or remorse?
> Johannes: What makes you look as cross, or even more so?
> ... Less like a man than is a broken Torso?
> Edwardus: Why did I leave my native land, to find
> ... Sharp hailstones, snow and most disgusting wind?
> Johannes: What boots it that we orange trees or lemons see,
> ... If we must suffer from such vile inclemency
> Edwardus: Why did I take the lodgings I have got,
> ... Where all I don't want is:– all I want not?

Soon after she arrived in Cannes on 1 April 1887 the Queen walked down to the Villa Nevada, which was just below the Villa Edelweiss, and the next day visited St George's Church.[40] She did not think much of the service on Palm Sunday, which was very dreary, with no music and 'the poor Bishop of Gibraltar's voice was so weak, that it was barely intelligible.'[41]

The only Anglican church which still operates in Cannes according to the Anglican rite is Holy Trinity, which originally opened on 19 December 1874 in succession to Trinity Church. That in turn was replaced by a new church in September 1973.[42]

Other than the visits to the Villa Nevada and St George's Church, the only event which the Queen put in her Journal was also sad:

> A poor blind man, sang in the garden, after dinner, which he did most beautifully accompanying himself on a portable harmonium. He sang some operatic airs and some other things really charmingly, with a voice and in an excellent style. We enquired about him, he had been an 'élève du Conservatoire', and blind since he had been 3 months old; – that he had won 3 prizes, and had bought the instrument he played on. It is shocking to think of his wandering about out of doors in this way, when he evidently is a well educated man.[43]

She visited the Villa Nevada once more before her departure on 5 April.[44] She never stayed in Cannes again.

It is reasonable to assume that initially she shunned Cannes because it was the favourite resort of the Prince of Wales and because she so disapproved of his behaviour there. After Leopold's death it brought back unhappy memories.

The Queen had been convinced that Bertie, the Prince of Wales, had caused Albert's death. In his twentieth year he was doing military training in the Curragh camp near Dublin. One night, after a party, his fellow officers in the Grenadier Guards put an actress named Nelly Clifden in his bed. His father eventually found out and wrote upbraiding his son. Bertie expressed contrition, Albert forgave him and went to visit him at Cambridge. He returned exhausted from that visit, contracted typhoid fever and died.

'I never can or shall look at him without a shudder', Victoria wrote of Bertie on 26 December 1861.[45] However, by 18 June of the following year she seems to have stopped shuddering when she looked at him because she then recorded that 'He is much improved and is ready to do everything I wish, and we get on very well.'[46]

Xavier Paoli considered that, like his mother, the Prince contributed to the prosperity of the Riviera. He wrote in his memoirs:

> He was in a certain sense, King of the Côte d'Azur, where nothing was decided in the matter of festivities without his approval and consent. He made Cannes his headquarters and the Cercle Nautique his favourite residence; but his kingdom of fashion and pleasure extended beyond Nice, as far as Mentone; and all those winter-resorts competed for the honour of his visits. As a matter of fact, he contributed largely towards developing their prosperity by attracting an enormous British colony in that direction.

Paoli noted that he never stayed in the same town as his mother.[47]

The Prince of Wales travelled incognito with his arrivals unannounced when he travelled in France. His alias was Baron Renfrew. His first visit to Cannes seems to have been in 1872, when he stayed at the Hôtel Gray d'Albion, on his way to Italy with the Princess of Wales. When he arrived in Cannes incognito in January 1883 the *Times* correspondent said he was staying at the Hôtel Pavillon, but the visit had been kept very quiet. 'There is much curiosity as to the purpose of the visit, but I have obtained no satisfactory answer to the question', he reported.[48] Reuters reported that he had visited the Comte de Paris and Princess Clémentine of Saxe-Coburg-Gotha and that Mr Gladstone was to give a big dinner in his honour.[49] He attended a ball at the Cercle Nautique where there were some 500 guests, and a bazaar organized in aid of a charity.[50] But the correspondents did not venture to suggest that those engagements were the purpose of the visit. What they, of course, knew, but did not report, was that at least one important purpose of the visit was the Prince's quest for mistresses.

One lady whom he pursued was an American beauty, Miss Chamberlayne, from Cleveland, Ohio, who was doing a Grand Tour of Europe with her parents. He had met them at Homburg in Germany and followed them to Cannes. He could never see Miss Chamberlayne alone so he entertained her parents as well.[51] Princess Alexandra called her 'Miss Chamberpots'.[52]

The future King started a more significant relationship in Cannes when Baroness de Stoeckl introduced him to Mrs George Keppel. She recounted in her memoirs:

> Staying at Villa Kazbeck was Mrs. George Keppel. She was entertaining, handsome and very refreshing. It was decided she might amuse the Prince, so my husband [Sasha – Baron Alexander de Stoeckl] was told to arrange a small luncheon party – just the Grand Duke Michel and Countess Torby [the morganatic wife of the Grand Duke], Mrs. Keppel, Sasha and myself. He saw her then for the first time and from that day started their friendship.[53]

That meeting took place in the 1870s and they probably did not meet again until 1898. But Alice Keppel then became one of the most important of the mistresses of the Prince and later King.

Continental tourist guides were confused by the amours of the British royalty. Alice Keppel and her husband George settled in Tuscany, where guides would tell tourists that George Keppel, Alice's husband, was the last lover of Queen Victoria.[54]

The reputation of the Prince of Wales as an eager participant in the Battle of the Flowers, which he regarded as 'capital fun', led to French and German caricatures depicting him as a field-marshal whose experience of war was limited to the annual Battle of the Flowers on the Riviera. This stung him into pleading with the Queen and government to allow him to serve in the British invasion of Egypt in 1882. His pleas were ignored.[55]

In 1883 the Prince of Wales had his own Nice carnival float. Gladstone was on the official stand.[56] In the carnivals the middle-aged Prince surprised the French by appearing costumed and masked – on one occasion in Cannes as a devil – like a young man.[57]

His reputation soared as a result of his behaviour when an earthquake hit the Riviera on 23 February 1887. The earthquake struck at 5.37 am and the Prince stayed in bed, refusing to go down to the gardens of the hotel. Nine thousand persons left Nice and Cannes, but the Prince stayed on for several days so as not to induce panic.[58]

Yvette Guilbert, the singer, proudly recounted in her memoirs how delighted the Prince had been when he learned that she had been bribed with £600 to break a contract in Paris in order to sing before him in Cannes. She also told the story of how La Goulue, the dancer, had greeted his appearance at the Moulin Rouge in Paris with a shout of 'Ullo Wales' to which he responded with champagne for all the dancers and members of the orchestra.[59]

Monte Carlo and its casino were an attraction to the Prince. Frank Harris, the fin de siècle bon vivant and writer, described meeting the Prince in the casino. The Prince got him to put some bets on for him as Harris was having a run of luck. He spent the rest of the night telling the Prince risqué stories.[60]

However, his activities were not all frivolous and when he laid the foundation stone of a new jetty in Cannes on 10 March 1898 he made a speech calling for better relations with France.[61]

Sport was important to him. The popularity of tennis on the Riviera can be attributed to the Prince who started playing it in Cannes in 1883, giving it great prestige.[62] The Prince had joined the Royal Yacht Squadron and had a great interest in yachting on the Riviera. From 1894 to 1897 he sailed his yacht *Britannia* in the Mediterranean and usually won the regattas which took place from Cannes, Nice, Monaco, Hyères and Marseilles.[63]

The French generally admired the Prince. Paoli described him as:

a powerfully built, broad-shouldered man, with an expansive face tapering into a short beard. His features were open and prepossessing. His gait was supple and his bearing one of supreme ease under the faultless cut of his navy-blue serge suit. Everything about him pointed to a love of sober elegance and subtle refinement in dress: his skillfully-tied sailor's knot; his rich silk handkerchief. ... But what struck me most of all was the clearness of the blue-grey eyes, which were very prominent under their heavy lids.[64]

When he became King he told Paoli, 'I no longer go to Cannes and Nice, because you meet too many princes there. I should be obliged to spend all my time in paying and receiving visits, whereas I come to the Continent to rest.'[65] So he went to Biarritz instead.

He was reported as saying that he went to the Riviera as if he were visiting a club. It was a country of good company where everyone found his level, like at a garden party.[66]

The clubbism which the Prince of Wales so liked came out well in one of the early headlines of the *Paris Herald*:

Southern Sunshine
Opening of the Season at all the Famous resorts
Monarchs Galore[67]

The Prince told his mother, 'I like Cannes excessively, especially for its climate and scenery, just the same as you do Aix.'[68] After only four days in Cannes, it was for Aix-les-Bains in Savoy, which, as her son said, she liked, that the Queen departed by the overnight train on 5 April.[69]

The choice of the resort was once again dictated by sickness. Princess Beatrice suffered from rheumatism, took a cure at Aix-les-Bains in 1883 and persuaded her mother to accompany her two years later. They stayed in the Maison Mottet, an annexe of the Hôtel de l'Europe, on each visit.

The Queen knew all about the earthquake of 23 February, when her son had acquitted himself with such British sang froid, and she began to worry about earthquakes. Ponsonby wrote:

> She told me that on the previous night about 12 o'clock she had heard noises below her room and, not being sure whether it was the regular rumblings of an earthquake or what, she sent for Hyman the Footman in waiting who had the audacity to say 'I think it must be Sir Henry.' It is true I do live just under the Queen and it is true I went to bed early, but I don't believe it was my snoring. However the anecdote has caused great hilarity in our circles, in which I do not join.[70]

The highlight of the stay was the visit to the Monastery of the Grande Chartreuse, the mother house of the Carthusians, a tough drive up into the mountains towards Grenoble. The Empress Eugénie was the first Roman Catholic woman to be allowed to enter the monastery and Queen Victoria and Princess Beatrice were the first Protestant women to go inside.

The Journal recorded:

> Aix-les-Bains, April 23 – This was the day for our long-planned and wished-for expedition to the Grande Chartreuse. It was a splendid day. The scenery of the Gorge frequently reminded me of the St. Gothard, and is very grand. We passed the distillery of the celebrated and excellent liqueur, called Chartreuse, made by the monks, who alone possess the secret. It is made of herbs and flowers gathered by them in the country round.

> The Monastery nestles in among the high mountains. As we approached, we could see a monk standing under the doorway, who approached our carriage

in his white habit and cowl and bare shaven head, a fine-looking man, the Procureur, who wished us la bienvenue. Just inside the Monastery the Grand Prieur Général received us, a stout, burly, rosy-cheeked man, wearing spectacles. The interior struck one as very cold.

... We were shown where the cells were, and told I should see a young compatriote, an Englishman who had been there for some time. The Grand Prieur unlocked the cell, which is composed of two small rooms, and the young inmate immediately appeared, kneeling down and kissing my hand, and saying, 'I am proud to be a subject of Your Majesty'. ... I remarked how young he looked, and he answered, 'I am 23', and that he had been five years in the Grande Chartreuse, having entered at 18!! I asked if he was contented, and he replied without hesitation, 'I am very happy'. He is very good-looking and tall, with rather a delicate complexion and a beautiful, saintly, almost rapt expression.

... As I felt very tired, I asked not to go up any more stairs, and we turned back and went down again. The Général ... walked across with us to the Hôtellerie des Dames, only a few hundred yards, where the ladies who wish to see the fine scenery and position often come up to spend a night or two. Here two very friendly Sisters, sort of Soeurs de Charité, welcomed us.

Refreshments were prepared in a big room, and here the Général took leave of us, but the Procureur remained. He offered me wine, but I asked for some of their liqueur, and by mistake he gave me some of the strongest.[71]

Dr Reid asked one of the Fathers an odd question during the visit: 'Is it true that you have a monk here who was a Russian general and murdered three wives?' 'I can't say about the murders', the monk replied, 'but as he has never married he can't have murdered his wives.'[72]

An important acquisition was a donkey. For some time the Queen had been finding difficulty in walking and needed some way to get around gardens. The solution was a donkey and she saw one she liked one afternoon while she was out in her carriage. He was harnessed to a peasant's cart. The Queen bargained with the peasant herself. When he told her he had paid FF100 she doubled the price to FF200 (£8)[73] and the donkey was hers. She named him Jacquot and he served her well for many years.[74] He was eventually replaced by a pure white donkey, which Lord Wolseley had brought from Egypt. In July 1899 Lord Kitchener was charged with finding 'the finest female white donkey procurable in Egypt' as a mate for it.[75]

The royal party left Aix for home on 28 April. The cost of the holiday at £718.9.0[76] was a little less than in Menton.[77]

Some years later the town placed a bronze bust of Queen Victoria in the Place du Revard above a flower bed in the shape of a crown. Members of the French Resistance took it away and hid it in 1943. It was put back after the Liberation.

Less than two months after the departure from Aix the Queen celebrated her Golden Jubilee. On 20 June 1887 she had been 'Fifty Years a Queen'.

CHAPTER 4

1891: Grasse. The Rothschild gardens and Duleep Singh's confession

In 1888 the Queen took her spring holiday in Florence, travelling back via Austria and Berlin, where she visited her son-in-law, Kaiser Friedrich III, who was dying.

She visited France again in 1889 when she stayed in Biarritz and became the first British monarch to visit Spain when she went over the border to San Sebastian for the day to meet Maria Christina, the Queen Regent. The Empress Eugénie had recommended Biarritz and the Queen liked it. But she was less fortunate in her choice of a house to stay in than she had been in the Chalet des Rosiers in Menton and the Villa Edelweiss in Cannes. The house itself, the Villa Rochefoucauld-le Pavillon, was fine, picturesque and with excellent views. The problem was that the wife of the Comte de la Rochefoucauld was a divorced woman. Guilty or innocent, divorced ladies were never received at the British Court or at British embassies. The Comtesse was told she would not be received by the Queen, but when on 7 March the Queen arrived at the house she hid behind a door, leapt out and thrust a bouquet of flowers at the amazed Queen, who was furious. On 30 March the Queen wrote on black-edged writing paper that the La Rochefoucaulds were quite intolerable and that on no account would she receive her.[1]

In 1890 she went to Aix-les-Bains and on to Darmstadt in Germany. On 10 May she had appointed E. Dosse as 'Director of Her Majesty's Continental Journeys'. The courier Kanné, who had accompanied the Queen on all her Continental journeys since 1857, had died in April 1888. The extent of the Queen's travels clearly now demanded a high-sounding title for the organizer of them.[2]

The return to the Riviera, after an absence of four years, came in 1891. She arrived on 25 March. She was attended by the usual vast entourage. Apart from the luggage on the train, 76 boxes and horses and carriages were sent on ahead. 'Our horses have changed their minds and will now arrive at Boulogne at 2 p.m. on the 11th,' Ponsonby reported.[3]

Since her previous visit, the Riviera had acquired another name. On 15 November 1888 the Académie Française opened its annual meeting by awarding a prize to Stéphen Liégard for his book *La Côte d'Azur*.[4] The French language acquired a new phrase and the Riviera a new standing. The Queen never used the new phrase in her Journals. For her the area she loved so much was always the Riviera.

On the occasion of the 1891 visit she moved away from the sea and stayed in Grasse. This attractive medieval town sits in the foothills of the Alps, 250 metres above sea-level with a stunning view over the limestone terraces which rise up from the Bay of Cannes 15 kilometres away.

A curious fashion of the sixteenth century led to its role as the perfume centre of France or, as the locals would claim, of the world. One of its principal industries had been leather glove-making; it was particularly successful because the gloves were made supple and waterproof through the secret practice of passing the leather through a powder of myrtle and pistachio.[5] In the sixteenth century scented gloves became the fashion. Thus was born the perfume industry.

Princess Louise, the Queen's daughter, and her husband, the Marquess of Lorne, had stayed in Grasse in the previous year and had recommended it to the Queen. It had the attraction of a healthy climate, the Grand Hôtel, which had opened in 1882, and the magnificent gardens which Baroness Rothschild had recently laid out at her Villa Victoria. The Queen took the whole of the hotel.

An advertisement of 1887 described it as a first-class hotel, facing full south, in an exceptionally fine position and commanding magnificent and unrivalled views of the Valley of Grasse, the Estérel Mountains and the Sea. It boasted dining, reading, smoking and billiard rooms, hot and cold baths, a lawn-tennis court and a gymnasium. English church services were held in the hotel. The weekly journal *Le Commerce* of 22 February 1891 reported that two officers of the royal household had signed a contract with Monsieur Rost, the director, renting the whole of the Grand Hôtel for one month. 'This has to be a jumping off point for a new era for our winter resort', the newspaper gloated.[6] The commercial consequences of the visit were not lost on the citizens of Grasse and one of them wrote to the newspaper on 22 March:

> Seduced already by an example which has come from so high, notable English people are coming who until now knew Grasse only by name. This is why a feeling of heartfelt gratitude mixes in our hearts to the unanimous respect we feel for the sovereign of a great nation with which our country is happy to maintain cordial relations of friendship.[7]

The town showed its appreciation by naming a street after her. The newspaper breathlessly reported:

> Day and night, workmen are busy with the final alterations to the beautiful establishment on the Avenue Thiers. Paper-hangers, painters and decorators are putting the finishing touches to their work. ... The Queen's apartments consist of a bedroom with two dressing rooms on the first floor facing North; a boudoir and two drawing rooms facing South, one large and one small; a dining room where the royal table can seat six or seven persons. ... Should Her Majesty wish to give banquets, as is very probable, the large dining-room would be made available for this purpose. ... Mr Rost has risen magnificently to the occasion.[8]

The hotel is now a block of apartments called La Résidence du Grand Palais and it carries a plaque over the door recording the Queen's visit.[9]

The lasting importance of the visit to Grasse is shown by the publication by the town council of a book about her stay for the centenary in 1991, which they also had translated into English.[10]

The gardens of Alice de Rothschild's Villa Victoria were clearly the main reason why the Queen chose Grasse for her 1891 holiday over competing and more lively resorts. She had visited Alice de Rothschild at Waddesdon Manor, near Aylesbury, on 14 March 1890. Waddesdon Manor was the extraordinary creation of Alice's brother, Ferdinand, who had bought 1000 hectares of land from the Duke of Marlborough and spent ten years laying out the magnificent gardens. Alice was chatelaine, learned her gardening there and was famous for her roses, which she bought by the thousand. Alice was born in Frankfurt in 1845. She caught smallpox, which pitted her face, which she always covered with a veil – she was known as 'the lady with the veil' – and she never married. Her passion was gardening. Alice considered the coast vulgar and in 1887 she spent the winter at the Grand Hôtel in Grasse and started to buy land on which in 1888 she started building the Villa Victoria and, without any professional advice, laying out the garden, which Vivian Russell, the gardening expert, has described in her book *Gardens of the Riviera* as 'perhaps the most ostentatious garden ever seen'. At its most extensive it covered 135 hectares and Alice employed 50 full-time gardeners, seasonally supplemented with 30 to 40. They wore the blue and yellow of the Rothschilds (which were also the colours of the tiles of the teahouse) and their rank was marked by the colour of their hats. One visitor was quoted as saying that every 20 metres stood a gardener waiting for a leaf to fall so that he could pick it up. The garden contained 55,000 daisies, 25,000 pansies, 10,000 wallflowers, 5000 forget-me-nots and 23,000 bulbs, including tulips and narcissi.[11]

Vivian Russell describes the garden as follows:

Alice bought a hundred hectares of terraced hillside and immediately proceeded to landscape the ancient terraces into rolling parkland, where she planted citrus trees by the hundred, arranged in groups to make them appear more natural and 'integrate' with the landscape.

Hers was the ultimate 'exotic' garden for August Hare, Maupassant and Mérimée to complain about. It contained an enormous collection of ornamental plants: palms twenty metres high, *Yucca folifera* ten metres high, bamboos with thick trunks, a 'debauchery' of agaves and flaming aloes.

Along the public highway that bisects the estate, mimosas of every species had been grafted on to small trees for a shrubby effect, and flowering was continuous from November to May. Alice advised her gardeners to plant yellow and white between clashing colours – a spectacle that would make even a municipal gardener blush, but with bedding and borders overflowing with fifty-five thousand daisies, twenty-five thousand stocks and five thousand myosotis, perhaps no one would notice.

There was a rock-garden, a winter flowering grotto, and a spectacular three-kilometre drive designed with hairpin bends; around every corner lay a surprise, the planting becoming progressively wilder and the panorama extending itself further and further, the higher one climbed. At the entrance were a few dozen specimens of palms, agaves and aloes, then a thirty-metre retaining wall planted with perennials; around the next bend, lawns carpeted with spring bulbs, followed by a wood underplanted with lavender, rosemary and citronella; higher still, a cascade and a miniature lake with a wild-looking rockery beneath; and finally, at the top – what else but a Tea Pavilion.[12]

Alice de Rothschild spent six months a year at the Villa Victoria, arriving at Cannes station in great splendour from London. The staff lined up to meet her at the Villa as she marched up the red carpet. The tour of the gardens was conducted by the head gardener, Monsieur Gaucher, who had always to wear a bowler hat. One day she came across Monsieur Gaucher in shirt-sleeves without his bowler hat on, trimming a bush. 'It's your head I pay, not your hands. Leave that work to your men,' she reproved him.[13] His son, Marcel, who also worked for the Rothschilds when he grew up, recalled in his memoirs that Alice only once spoke to him. The great lady regarded the presence of children in a garden as undesirable as cats and dogs. She wore only grey and was like a starched silhouette. Her skirt was floor-length and her face was hidden under a mauve veil and straw hat almost like a bee keeper's.[14]

Lady Battersea, then Mrs Flower, a Rothschild cousin, described a typical visit to the gardens with the Queen:

> We had a delicious morning, with air like crystal; part of it I spent on the mountain side, panting after H.M's donkey chair. Off goes the donkey at a good firm pace, led by the groom, Randall. H.M. in a grey shawl, with a mushroom hat, a large white sunshade, sits comfortably installed in a donkey chair. ...
>
> Alice is continuing her road as a surprise to the Queen; but Her Majesty's keen eyes discovered signs and tokens of the new road and she was informed of Alice's plans. I told Her Majesty that it was a state secret, and begged of her not to appear as if she knew anything about it when Alice will conduct her for the first time on the road, which is being levelled, widened, and straightened by about 50 stalwart Provencal peasants. 'It is a secret, a secret', said H.M. with a smile and a twinkle, like a child who thinks that the great fun of a secret is in divulging it.[15]

Probably the only reprimand the Queen ever received in her adult life came from Alice de Rothschild. Marcel Gaucher recalled the famous story:

> As tradition demanded the Queen planted a tree. Everything went according to a minutely laid down drill when suddenly, in order to look more closely at a rare plant, the Queen stepped on a lawn and across a flower-bed, inadvertently crushing several plants. The baroness could not contain herself and roughly told the sovereign in effect to 'Get out'. If the story is untrue it is at least probable.[16]

Thereafter the Queen always referred to her as 'The All-Powerful One'.[17]

Alice de Rothschild also terrorized her staff. One day she came across a shrub covered in insects. 'I demand that this man who has not done his job is fired', she exclaimed. 'But it is the first time', Gaucher's father pleaded. 'Until now I have never had anything to reproach him with. Also he has a wife and children.' 'Very well, keep him, but I never want to see him again. Move him to a part of the garden away from where I usually walk.'[18]

This was an odd decision because most of the employees had to disappear anyway when the hour of her daily walk came.

Despite the autocratic rule, a period working at the Villa Victoria was much sought after by trainee gardeners, and in addition to young Frenchmen came Swiss, English, Germans, Austrians and Dutch.[19]

She had strong management theories. She told Gaucher, 'Reflect carefully before giving an order. Above all never give the impression of hesitating and never go back on your decision because, if you do, you will lose all authority. Never forget that orders and counter orders engender disorder.'[20]

On leaving Grasse, Victoria gave Alice de Rothschild an enamel bracelet with a picture of herself on it, set in diamonds. She was intensely delighted with it, the Queen reported.[21]

Alice de Rothschild died in 1922. Edmond de Rothshchild gave the property to the municipality of Grasse, who carved it up into hundreds of plots, on which were built luxurious villas and a camping site. Only the Rothschild villa, the Villa Victoria, and the teahouse remain today. The Villa Victoria is now a block of apartments called the Palais Provençal.[22] The teahouse remains as a fine villa with the blue and yellow rooftiles in the Rothschild colours in perfect condition.[23]

There had been some suggestion in the British Press that Grasse was unsuitable for the Queen because it was unhealthy. *Le Commerce* of 8 April explained the conditions in Grasse, and also had a dig at competing resorts:

> The sanitary conditions in the old part of town are naturally not altogether satisfactory. But the Queen will run no greater risks from that part of Grasse whilst residing at the Grand Hôtel, than she does from the borough of Westminster when she is living at Buckingham Palace.

> The old quarters of towns such as Hyères, Fréjus, Cannes, Nice, Eze, Roquebrune and San Remo all have several points in common: in particular narrow, ill-paved and smelly streets.

> In one respect Grasse is superior to its neighbours: all waste is used as fertiliser, instead of being allowed to pollute the sea coast as is the case in the so-called hygienic towns along the Riviera.

> The land around Grasse is highly cultivated and sewage is transformed into

violets, roses, jasmine and orange blossom.[24]

But the calumnies about Grasse continued to reverberate and Marie Adeane reported on 25 April that there was a tremendous row and that the Queen was very angry about the paragraphs which had appeared in the *St James Gazette* saying that Grasse was unhealthy and that if she had escaped, her entourage had greatly suffered. Marie thought the drainage was first rate.[25] With no reference to questions of the freedom of the Press, the next day she told her fiancé:

> The 'Times' correspondent has been interviewed today and ordered to write an article refuting the St. James Gazette paragraph which originally came from 'The Lancet'. He says 'The Lancet' always abuses the Riviera and cracks up Bournemouth and Torquay, and no doubt got its information from Cannes where envy reigns supreme owing to the Queen's preference for humble Grasse. ...
>
> We all feel better, but the gentlemen complain bitterly of the dullness of the place and indeed it is too dull for words.[26]

The Queen was furious with the *Times* correspondent, 'a sharp little man who wears a pince-nez', because she considered that his reports on her were unauthorized and inexact. He was outraged and replied that *The Times* paid £50[27] a week for its information. It is not clear who pocketed the £50. He considered the Court Circular 'meagre, uninteresting and most incorrect'. 'This makes matters worse as the Queen always corrects the Court Circular with her own hand,' Marie Adeane wrote.[28]

The Queen must also have been annoyed by the story of the correspondent of *The Times* that she had gone by special train to Cannes mainly to visit the Grand Duke and Duchess of Mecklenburg-Schwerin, but that they were out.[29]

When they were not out, the Queen probably saw more of the Mecklenburg-Schwerins on the Riviera than any couple outside her family circle. Friedrich Franz had one of the largest private fortunes in Europe. His wife, Anastasia, a granddaughter of Tsar Nicholas I, who had been brought up in the Caucasus, was of outstanding appearance, tall, slim, dark-haired and with delicate skin and green eyes. They spent much of the year away from their seat at Schwerin in north Germany at Cannes, where they owned the Villa Wenden, the first house in Cannes to have electricity.[30] Anastasia spent large sums of money at the tables in Monte Carlo, while her husband stayed in Cannes because of ill health.[31]

The Queen had better fortune three days after she had tried to see the Mecklenburg-Schwerins. She paid a visit to the Château de Garibondy to call on Lady Alfred Paget, who was in, and where she was able to plant a tree.[32] The fine yew still stands in the gardens of the property with an appropriate plaque. Today the chateau, still owned by English people, is rented out to participants at the Cannes Film Festival each year. Other places the Queen visited included the Château de Gourdon, the Pont du Loup, Cabris and the Château de Sartoux.

In his corrective story about sanitation and health the correspondent of *The Times* claimed that the members of the household had all suffered from ennui and did not display a great amount of enthusiasm at the idea of the Queen coming to Grasse another year.[33]

The Queen clearly did not suffer from boredom. She started most days with her Hindustani lessons. She had state papers to deal with, which two Queen's messengers a week brought from London.[34] She had her daily drives and in the evenings Princess Beatrice and others would sometimes play the piano, with the Queen beating time with her crochet hook. On one occasion she visited the Chiris perfumery and was given a bottle of perfume called 'Queen's Bouquet' in her honour.[35] The carpet of flowers on which she walked in the perfumery were thereafter called 'Violette Victoria'.[36] She reported that Princess Louise and Princess Beatrice went to see the paintings of Fragonard, a son of Grasse, which they said were beautiful, but oddly did not go herself.[37] A highlight was the Battle of the Flowers, given in Her Majesty's honour:

> I feel I can hardly describe the gay fête, which took place this afternoon at 3. It was what they call a 'Bataille de Fleurs', of which I have so often heard and read accounts, but of course never seen. It is pretty and curious. We were all there excepting poor Liko [Prince Henry of Battenberg, husband of Princess Beatrice], who could see nothing, as his windows look out the other way (he had measles!). We were on a balcony covered with an awning, just over the entrance. The procession was headed by mounted Jeux d'Armes, followed by Buglers in the dress of Louis XV, and the Band of the Chasseurs playing a march. Then came endless people in every conceivable costume seated in cars all decked with flowers and emblems, saluting and throwing flowers up at our balcony as they passed. We also threw flowers, of which we had baskets full ready prepared, but it was almost impossible to hit any one. The procession was a very long one. It was a very original and amusing sight. Unfortunately there was a very high wind, but we were tolerably sheltered by screens.[38]

Constance Battersea added in her reminiscences that some daring masque-raders, disguised as pierrots, climbed up to the balcony, holding out money boxes. The Queen pelted them with flowers, but Sir Henry Pon-sonby gave them some money. The Queen demanded more and more flowers, so her staff had to resort to the trick of having the flowers picked up from the street and thrown down again.[39]

The only thing about Grasse that seemed to upset the Queen was cru-elty to horses and mules. She proposed that the president of the Cannes branch of the Society for the Prevention of Cruelty to Animals should send an inspector to Grasse to punish the offenders.[40] She sent the Menton branch £5[41] because she had heard that that branch was becoming more effective.[42]

The Queen's doctor, James Reid, had his hands full in dealing with sickness during the stay in Grasse. There was the smallpox scare, which meant he had to vaccinate everyone. 'All the Suite and ten of the servants have been ill', he wrote. The chief cook had diphtheria, the Queen had a bad cold, Prince Henry had measles and Reid himself had a sore throat and a cold. 'Our party have all taken a dislike to Grasse in consequence of every one being ill,' he complained.[43]

The Queen's tranquil stay in Grasse was interrupted by a strange mix of visitors. Guests included His Serene Highness Prince Albert I of Mon-aco and Princess Alice, surprising given the way the Queen had snubbed his predecessor in 1882 and how disapproving she had been of Monte Carlo.[44]

Having failed to get Princess Mary Adelaide as his wife, following Queen Victoria's opposition, Albert had married the wealthy Mary Victo-ria, who was remotely related to the Queen through her mother, Marie Amelie, who had been married to a Scot, William Douglas-Hamilton, 11th Duke of Hamilton and 8th Duke of Brandon.[45] Mary was a cousin of Napoleon III and the marriage had been arranged by the Empress Eugénie. One Scottish newspaper had enthused over the marriage. 'The daughter of our Scotch Duke will become a sovereign princess,' it boasted.[46] But not for long. The marriage did not last. It was annulled by the Pope on 28 July 1880 and Albert married Alice, Duchess of Richelieu, whom he had met while studying oceanography in Paris, away from the watchful eye of Princess Mary.[47] Alice had the distinction of having been admired by Marcel Proust and was used as the model for the Princesse de Luxem-bourg in *A la Recherche du Temps Perdu*.[48]

Marie Adeane was very rude about Dom Pedro II, the former Emperor of Brazil, who had abdicated in 1889 after a revolution and had fled to Europe. He died soon after his visit to the Queen:

> The Emperor is a most extraordinary looking old man with a piercing voice, very squeaky and quite cracked, an intelligent face entirely spoilt by the most appalling 'râtelier' [set of false teeth] I have ever seen. I expected every moment to see his teeth upon the floor. His Suite consisted of a middle-aged Comtesse and two men exactly like monkeys. The Brazilians must indeed be an ugly people.[49]

Bismarck had called Coburg 'the stud-farm of Europe'. He might well have added 'and South America'. Pedro's two daughters were married to Coburgs, who were therefore related to the Queen.[50] The Queen echoed Bismarck's comment on the fecundity of the Coburgs after the birth of her fourteenth grand-child: 'it seems to me to go on like the rabbits in Windsor Park!'[51]

Tucked away in the Grasse Court Circular of 16 April was this seemingly innocent announcement:

> Her Imperial Highness the Archduchess Stephanie of Austria and Their Royal Highnesses Prince and Princess Philip of Saxe Coburg Gotha visited the Queen and remained to luncheon.

The Queen's guests were participants in two of the most extraordinary royal scandals of nineteenth-century Europe, one of which had been played out in Austria two years earlier, the other of which was to take place, for much of the time in Nice, six years later.

The Archduchess Stephanie, a daughter of Leopold II, King of the Belgians, and daughter-in-law of Francis Joseph, Emperor of Austria, had made a good match by marrying Crown Prince Rudolf, heir to the imperial throne. But on 30 January 1889 he had shot himself at the imperial hunting lodge at Mayerling in a suicide pact with his mistress, the 17-year-old Baroness Maria Vetsera, whom he had murdered the previous day. The Mayerling affair was one of the great romantic scandals of the nineteenth century and was the subject of a ballet, books and films.

Stephanie received a farewell letter, undated:[52]

Dear Stephanie,

You are freed henceforth from the torment of my presence. Be happy, in your own way. Be good to the poor little girl who is the only thing I leave behind. ...

I face death calmly, death alone can save my good name.

With warmest love from

Your affectionate Rudolf

Even before their first night together on 5 October 1881 Rudolf seemed to have realized he had made a mistake, saying little to his new bride on their honeymoon journey. Her mother, Queen Marie-Henriette, had been shocked and disgusted by her own wedding night with Leopold and even prayed that death might release her from the marriage.[53] Nevertheless she had done nothing to prepare her daughter Louise for her sexual initiation. She knew what a trauma Louise had gone through, but still did nothing to prepare Stephanie. 'What a night', Stephanie wrote in her memoirs. 'What torments, what horror! I had not had the ghost of a notion what lay before me, but had been led to the altar as an ignorant child. My illusions, my youthful dreams, were shattered. I thought I should die of my disillusionment. I was cold as ice, my teeth were chattering, and I shivered with terror. ... One thought dominated my mind. To get away!'[54]

Queen Victoria had met Rudolf. In 1877, just before Christmas, Rudolf had accompanied his mother, the Empress of Austria, to England. He made a good impression on both the Queen and the Prince of Wales, although the Queen thought he looked a little overgrown and not very robust.[55] Ten years later he went to London to represent Austria-Hungary at the Queen's Jubilee. He wrote to Stephanie: 'The old Queen came today, was most friendly and bestowed on me the Order of the Garter, pinning it on herself, and fondling me as she did so, so that I could hardly refrain from laughing.'[56]

Stephanie had visited Queen Victoria when she was six and the Queen instructed that she should wear her hair unbound, which was the English fashion for young girls. 'I was tall for my age, with lovely hair, falling in golden tresses down my little back, almost to the ground,' Stephanie wrote in her memoirs. When she walked round Windsor she claims that all the passers-by stopped and stared at her. Thereafter her hair was kept enveloped in a net, to curb her vanity.[57]

Stephanie regarded herself as Queen Victoria's favourite niece, although she was in fact a cousin and not a niece, and soon after the Mayerling tragedy the Queen hastened to invite her to move to Windsor and become a member of her household. Stephanie would have liked to have accepted this 'compassionate and sympathetic gesture'. 'But, for reasons of etiquette and prestige, the Court of Vienna regarded my acceptance of the invitation as impossible,' she wrote.[58]

When the news of the deaths had come through to England Lord Salisbury had thought the Crown Prince had been murdered, but the Queen, always well informed on royal matters, assured him that Rudolf had fired the fatal shots.[59] Stephanie eventually married Count Elmer Lonyay, a Hungarian who, although a count, was regarded as a commoner. Emperor Francis Joseph gave his permission, but King Leopold was furious and withheld his. Nevertheless Stephanie went ahead with the marriage and her father refused to have anything more to do with her.[60] Marie Adeane described her on her visit to Grasse as tall and handsome, with golden hair and a brilliant complexion, but not looking at all interesting. 'She steadily refused to wear mourning for her husband (no wonder) so there is a great coolness between her and the Empress of Austria,' she wrote.[61]

Two other guests were of very dubious character. Marie Adeane reported in a letter to her fiancé:

> The old Duke of Saxe-Coburg Gotha has been here today with his wife. He is the Prince Consort's only brother and an awful looking man, the Queen dislikes him particularly. He is always writing anonymous pamphlets against the Queen and the Empress Frederick, which naturally creates a deal of annoyance in the family.[62]

Duke Ernst was a licentious contrast to his brother Albert. He contracted venereal disease before he was married. Albert was horrified:

> To marry would be as immoral as dangerous. ... If the worst should happen, you would deprive your wife of her health and honour, and should you have a family, you would give your children a life full of suffering ... and your country a sick heir. For God's sake do not trifle with matters which are so sacred.[63]

He had not heeded his brother's words and the lady who accompanied him on his visit to his sister-in-law in Grasse in 1891 was Princess Alexandrina of Baden, whom he had married in 1842, the year after he had received his brother's missive. They did not have children, but not for want of trying. Alexandrina had several miscarriages. She was devoted to him and believed him when he told her that the young ladies he visited in a small house in the palace park were secretaries and translators. She frequently referred to him as 'der liebe, gute Ernst'.[64] The Queen had not received him in England for years; no wonder his visit to her holidaying in Grasse was so unwelcome.

The other dubious visitor was Maharajah Duleep Singh. The Journal of
31 March recorded:

Louise [Marchioness of Lorne] came to luncheon, after which I saw in the
small Drawingroom below the poor misguided Maharajah Duleep Singh, who
had asked to see me, having some months ago humbly begged forgiveness for
his faults and rebellion. He is nearly paralysed down his left side. He was in
European clothes, with nothing on his head, and when I gave him my hand he
kissed it and said 'Pray excuse my kneeling'. His 2nd son Frederick, who has a
very amiable countenance came over from Nice with him. I made the poor
broken down Maharajah take a seat and almost immediately afterwards he
broke into a most violent fit of weeping. I took and stroked his hand, and he
became calmer and said 'Pray excuse me and forgive my grievous faults' to
which I replied 'that is all forgiven and past'. He complained of his health and
said he was a poor broken down man. After a few minutes talk about his sons
and daughters, I wished him goodbye and went up stairs again, very thankful
that this painful interview was well over. He was to have some refreshments
and then drive back to Nice.[65]

Marie Adeane's comment was, 'I believe he is a monster of the deepest
dye and is treated far better than he deserves.'[66]

Duleep Singh was born on 4 September 1838, the son of Jindan Kour,
daughter of a doorkeeper in the palace of Runjit Singh, Sikh Maharajah of
the Punjab in Lahore. The ageing Runjit Singh recognized him as his fourth
son. On the death of Runjit Singh in the year after his birth, Duleep
Singh's mother started to intrigue for him to succeed Runjit Singh. On 18
September 1843, at the age of five, he was proclaimed Maharajah in
Lahore.

The victory of the British in the first Sikh war in 1846 resulted in the
young Maharajah becoming a ward of the government of British India,
whose Resident at Lahore ruled in his name. When the British won the
second Sikh war in 1849 at the fierce Battle of Gujrat, they deposed the
Maharajah and annexed his kingdom. He was given a pension of the
equivalent of £10,000[67] a year, became a Christian and elected to live in
England.[68]

On 1 July 1854 the 15-year-old boy met the Queen. She recorded the
meeting in her Journal:

After luncheon, to which Mama [Duchess of Kent] came, we received the
young Maharajah Duleep Singh, the son of Runjeet Singh, who was deposed
by us after the annexation of the Punjaub. He has been carefully brought up,
chiefly in the hills, and was baptised last year, so that he is a Christian. He is

extremely handsome and speaks English perfectly, and has a pretty graceful and dignified manner. He was beautifully dressed and covered with diamonds. The 'Koh-i-Noor' belonged to, and was once worn by him. I always feel so much for these poor deposed Indian Princes.[69]

Within a week the Queen had invited him to dinner; she commissioned Winterhalter to paint him and invited him to Osborne, her Italianate palace on the Isle of Wight, to meet the family. When she met him in Grasse she must have recalled how he had been particularly popular with little Prince Leopold, whom he carried round on his back so that he would not fall and could keep up with the other royal children, and who died just near Grasse in Cannes.[70] She had been very concerned with the Maharajah's reaction to cold weather when she first met him in England and wanted him to wear woollen underclothes. 'Indeed, Ma'am I cannot bear the feel of flannel next to my skin', he told the maternal monarch. 'It makes me long to scratch and you would not want to see me scratching myself in your presence.'[71]

Encouraged no doubt by the Queen's attentions, Duleep Singh took on more and more the life of the English gentleman, acquiring country seats for entertaining and hunting. The most notable was Elveden Hall in Suffolk, where he entertained the Prince of Wales at shooting parties and where he became known as the Black Prince. He overspent his allowance and engaged in a long hassle with the India Board over his income and his financial future.

The Queen approved of his marriage to Bamba, a Christian, whom, when she was 15, he had picked from a mission school in Cairo, and was godmother to their first child, Victor. But Duleep Singh soon followed the example of the wild life of Prince of Wales. He became a frequent visitor to the Alhambra Theatre, where he would arrive in the dressing room with a piece of jewellery and ask the ladies of the chorus, 'What nice little girl is going to have this?' Despite his financial problems, he set up a member of the chorus, Polly Ash, in an apartment in Covent Garden and bestowed an annuity on her. He gambled and often visited Paris to play the tables and to dally with other courtesans.[72]

Soon he was declaring that he had been deprived of the kingdom of the Punjab with its vast revenues and the Koh-i-noor diamond. The Maharajah plotted to get his kingdom back from the Queen Empress, tried to return to the Punjab and was detained in Aden, where he returned to the Sikh religion. He settled in Paris, where he described himself as 'Sovereign of the Sikh Nation and proud implacable foe of England'. From Paris he visited Moscow where he posed as an Irish rebel, to try to get the Russians to intervene in the Punjab. The Maharenee died in 1887 and in 1889 he married his mistress, Miss Ada Douglas Wetherill. As the years went by and his plans came to nothing, he became poorer and poorer and was laid low by a stroke. At last he asked the Queen for a pardon. 'I believe many feel with me that the former Govt. are very gtly to blame for what has happened & therefore we shd. be merciful', wrote the Queen.[73] (The former government was Gladstone's third ministry.) The Salisbury government, in the person of Viscount Cross, Secretary for India, transmitted the Queen's pardon on 1 August 1890.[74] Seven months later the Queen received Duleep Singh in Grasse. Sir Henry Ponsonby, the Queen's Private Secretary, and Lord Henniker, an old friend of the Maharajah's from his early days in England, contrived for him to be in Nice while the Queen was in Grasse.[75] Duleep Singh had first visited Nice soon after he had first arrived in England, when he was sent on an educational tour of Europe. The tour had its curious moments. In Rome Pope Pius IX made a special benediction as he passed by in his carriage. Duleep Singh thought he had only made 'snooks' at him.[76]

The Queen's magnanimity on the occasion of the Grasse visit was soured because Duleep Singh was offended that she had not received the new Maharanee, his former mistress. He wrote to the Prince of Wales, who had met her in Paris, to complain. The Queen's objection to meeting her was that she had lived with the Maharajah while his wife was still alive. 'The Queen has the strong impression that this Maharani has not been correct. Her being an actress wd. not raise any objections', was her comment.[77]

Duleep Singh died in Paris of an apoplectic fit on 22 October 1893. He was buried at Elveden Hall. The Queen wrote to her godchild, his son Victor:

> I need hardly say how I like to <u>dwell</u> on former years when I knew your dear Father so well, and saw him so often, & we were all so fond of him. He was so handsome & so charming! But I will <u>not</u> dwell on the few years which followed and which were so painful. It is however a great comfort & satisfaction to me that I saw the Maharajah Duleep Singh two years ago at Grasse, & that all was made up between us.[78]

Duleep Singh's three daughters continued to live in England and on their deaths left much of their money to such good causes as the Battersea Dogs' Home.[79] There appear to be no descendants.[80]

In the spring of 1999 the Victoria and Albert Museum put on an exhibition of 'The Arts of the Sikh Kingdoms', which prominently featured Duleep Singh.

On 29 July 1999 Queen Victoria's great-great-great-grandson, Prince Charles, unveiled a bronze statue to Duleep Singh on a small wooded island in Thetford, Norfolk. Just over a century after his death, the 500,000-strong Sikh community in Britain raised £100,000 to restore him to 'his rightful place in history', as Harbinder Singh, director of the appeal, said. 'He has been neglected in the past and the Sikh community has not always been aware of his contribution. He symbolises Sikh sovereignty and the Sikh presence in this country. While it is true that Britain annexed the Punjab, we are trying to put a positive interpretation on history. What happened was well documented and cannot be changed.' With great tact Harbinger Singh's speech did not mention the return of the Koh-i-noor diamond, the Sikh religion's most treasured relic which is today the centrepiece of the coronation crown of the Queen Mother.[81]

There was more unhappiness during the stay in Grasse. Elizabeth Reynolds, the Queen's personal housemaid, died of blood poisoning to her hand. For six days the Journal contained only entries about Elizabeth, showing the Queen's great compassion and devotion to her staff. On 8 April she recorded her death:

> I went in again to see poor Elizabeth with Louise and Beatrice. She recognised me and tried to smile, but could not speak. Drove in the afternoon with Beatrice and Marie A.[Adeane], going half way along the road to Cannes. A splendid afternoon. In coming home, heard that all was over with poor Elizabeth, that she had passed away quietly and almost imperceptibly. Two nurses were with her besides Dr Reid, and my other housemaid, who was sent for from Windsor. Later went with Jane C. [Churchill] to see her lying peacefully with such a happy look on her face, so different to this morning. Her hands were folded with flowers in them and flowers were laid all round her. Her fine hair was hanging loose about her head. One could but say, as I did, 'she is at rest,' after such a sad time of suffering and struggling for life. The nurses both said it was a terrible and most unusual case.[82]

Since the loss of Albert, death had obsessed the Queen, and the detailed funeral and burial arrangements for Elizabeth consumed her attention for days. She wrote to Dr Reid:

> I hope you will never often think me fastidious, but I have in my drive this afternoon to Peymeiran twice passed the cemetery, and I cannot bear the thought that my poor Elizabeth should be put for two whole nights in that

dreary place out by herself all alone – so far away. And I must ask that she be taken to the Church nearby. The objection to the funeral being there in the middle of the day should be abolished by her being taken quite quietly, say at 6 or even 5 in the morning to the cemetery and then let her funeral be at any hour there, at 10.30 or 11 or 12, or when most convenient, but I cannot let her be taken there tonight. No, my whole soul and body revolt against it.[83]

The first funeral service took place at 10 pm on the same evening in the large dining room of the Grand Hôtel in the presence of the Queen, the royal family and the Suite, all in evening dress, and servants who were sobbing. The coffin, which was not screwed down, was covered with a black and white pall and flowers. Dr Reid thought it 'rather a weird business'. The body was removed to the English Church at 1.30 am and two days later it was taken to the cemetery of Saint Brigitte where there was yet another service.[84]

The Queen had earlier driven to the cemetery and chose a quiet sunny spot for the grave. She made a sketch of what she wanted placed over it – a simple white cross, with a little railing round it – and bought the plot.[85]

Marie Adeane thought it very curious to see how the Queen took the keenest interest in death and all its horrors. She complained that the whole talk of the Suite had been of coffins and winding sheets. 'Of course I admire the Queen for taking such a lively interest in her servants, but it is overdone in this sort of way and is very trying for the Household', she wrote to her mother.[86]

As if she had not had enough of cemeteries, four days later the Queen went to a cemetery near Cannes to see the graves of people she had known.[87]

A week later an officer of the 23rd Chasseurs des Alpes died and the Queen insisted on going to see the funeral procession. 'The Queen really enjoys these melancholy entertainments', said Marie Adeane.[88] But it did not meet the Queen's high standards for such events. 'It was a long impressive cortège, but the absence of muffled drums and the Band playing no real funeral march, lessened the solemnity and effect of the whole,' was the verdict of the Queen.[89]

The English church of St John had been finished just three weeks before the Queen arrived in Grasse. She thought it very pretty and went there for the Good Friday service on 27 March. The singing was not bad, she thought, but the way the lady played the harmonium left a lot to be desired.[90] St John's, very English looking, half timbered with a steeple, had been built by the Société Civile St John's Church by John Lord Bowes,

Isabelle Bowes, his sister, and Charles Booker. John Bowes bought the land for FF6000 (£240).[91] In 1907 the owners sold it to the United Society for the Propagation of the Gospel for FF20,000 (£800).[92] The church, which contains three stained glass windows given by the Queen, is now called the Chapelle Anglaise or the Chapelle Victoria. In 1970 the owners gave it to the French Reformed Church, who had been using it since 1945, on condition that the Anglican Church could continue to hold services there.[93] It is supervised from Holy Trinity Church in Cannes, but there is now need for few Anglican services.[94]

Easter Saturday was the anniversary of the death of Prince Leopold. There was a service at St George's Church attended by the widow and her children. The Queen did not attend but drove over in the afternoon and for an hour visited the Villa Nevada, where he had died.[95] On 22 April the Queen drove to the church from Grasse and spent some time in the Albany Chapel which contained the sculpture of Leopold which she had arranged should be copied from Windsor.[96]

Marie Adeane was one of the most interesting members of the royal household to accompany the Queen to the Riviera. When she was appointed a maid of honour, she was receiving congratulations at a party and her host said, 'What an interesting journal you can keep!' When Marie told him that journal-keeping was forbidden, he said he thought she should keep one all the same. 'Then', replied Marie, 'whatever you were you would not be a maid of honour.'[97] Nevertheless, she used the device of keeping a journal by sending voluminous letters to her mother and fiancé and still retained her honour. Her letters are full of colour and give us an excellent insight into the spirit of the Queen, whom she greatly loved.

Arrival in Grasse: 'the Queen was less tired than any of us, looked as fresh as a daisy and beamed upon all the Grasse officials who met her at the Station.'[98]

Drive to Pont du Loup: 'she enjoys everything as if she were 17 instead of 72.'[99]

Local newspapers: 'Last night she was laughing heartily at the extremely comic account of our arrival in the local newspaper.'[100]

Princess Beatrice's birthday banquet: 'and finally some very good fireworks in the garden which the Queen enjoyed like a child.'[101]

Talking to Marie: 'the Queen could not have been kinder or more affectionate had I been her own child and this great sympathy is what endears her to all who come within its scope for it is thoroughly genuine.'[102]

Marie, among other members of the household, had to write descriptions of their expeditions for the Queen's Memorandum Book. Marie found them a strain: 'Messages arrive from the Queen, "Why do you not mention the old woman on a mule or the brown goat with the tuft on its head", and I rack my poor brains in vain and feel desperate.'[103] Marie took the Queen's admonishment to heart and the next day, having racked her brains, introduced some colour into her entry:

> This afternoon as the Queen was starting for a drive, Her Majesty noticed a group of sisters of charity standing in front of the hotel. Their dress was very curious and consisted of a sort of double cap of white linen and a short black cloak and hood, over a black petticoat, over their breasts they had large crosses of red and blue cloth.[104]

Before she left Grasse for England on 28 April, having extended her stay because she was enjoying herself so much, the Queen went to the cemetery and placed some flowers on Elizabeth's grave. 'So sad to leave her earthly remains amongst strangers, in a foreign land. It is a neglected dreary churchyard.'[105] Today Elizabeth's grave is neglected, with the lettering indecipherable.

At £2330.5.9[106] the Grasse trip was a lot more expensive than Menton and Cannes and Aix because of the cost of the hotel. The details were:

Rent	1780	0	0	
Preparation of hotel	152	6	0	
Piano hire	10	6	0	
Linens	38	10	11	
Hire of extra servants	25	0	0	
Travelling allowances	8	18	6	
Carriage of goods	315	3	10	[107]

The Queen bought a magnificent she-ass at Châteauneuf-de-Grasse just before she left, but it must have been paid for out of some other appropriation than the above. 'The beast was immediately harnessed to the donkey chair and will make life correspondingly easier for Pierrot, the Queen's Scottish donkey', Le Commerce reported.[108] Jacquot did not get a mention.

CHAPTER 5

1892: Hyères. The royal resort

Overhanging the Queen's visit to Hyères in March 1892 was deep mourning. Prince Albert Victor, known in the family as Eddy, elder son of the Prince of Wales and eventual heir to the throne, had died on 14 January of influenza and pneumonia. To compound her grief, just as she was about to leave for the Riviera, her son-in-law, Louis, Grand Duke of Hesse and the Rhine, had died on 13 March.

The Queen postponed her departure from Windsor by two days so that she could hold a special funeral service for the Grand Duke; she arrived in Hyères on 21 March. Surprisingly, in view of the mourning, the railway station at Hyères was gaily decorated and illuminated. But 'owing to recent events and by her Majesty's express request, no Naval and Military honours were paid on the journey, nor was the Queen anywhere received by the local officials.'[1]

The Queen drove directly to the Hôtel Costebelle, where she liked the rooms very much. She wrote in her Journal that her sitting room was a large one with five windows and just opposite was a nice dressing room opening into a good-sized bedroom. There was a small drawing room, which opened into a fairly large dining room – all on the same floor.[2]

The municipality of Hyères were so eager to make the Queen welcome that they built a new road over the Col de Serre specially for her.[3]

Hyères was the most southerly point and the oldest winter resort on the Riviera. The Queen would have felt at home because it had for some centuries been the royal resort of French kings. It was shaped like an amphitheatre, protected from the north winds, and since the thirteenth century kings and queens of France had visited it and had benefited from its mild climate. Louis IX had landed there in 1254, when it was still a seaport, on his way back from the Seventh Crusade. Louis XIV had visited it in 1660 and Napoleon in 1793.[4] Queen Victoria's uncle, Frederick, Duke of York and Albany, had stayed there in the season 1788–89.[5] The local inhabitants had long had a reputation for their affable nature. In 1807 one traveller wrote that they had the interest and the desire to satisfy the tastes of visitors and also 'dealt with the capricious fantasies of invalids; in a word, they are as mild as the climate they live in'.[6] In the eighteenth century it was considered the only rival to Madeira for those with respiratory illnesses.

Hyères was cosmopolitan and as early as 1835 a writer of a history of the town listed as foreign residents Germans, English, Belgians, Spaniards, Italians, Romanians, Russians, Poles and Swiss. The English, Russians and, surprisingly, Poles, were the largest groups.[7]

In the early part of the nineteenth century Hyères benefited from the difficulty of reaching Cannes by coach and by the fact that Nice was not French. The town suffered for a period after the railway from Marseilles to Cannes and Nice bypassed Hyères, but the setback was corrected when the spur of the Marseilles–Cannes railway line, on which Queen Victoria was to arrive, was opened in 1875. In the 1881 edition of his *Handbook for Travellers in France* John Murray reported that many English had settled in Costebelle to the south of the town and built villas. 'Costebelle is a charming spot, 2 m. nearer the sea than Hyères, amidst the pinewoods and will probably prove the most attractive quarter of Hyères,' he wrote. There was a daily bus service to Hyères.

In Hyères itself there were two English physicians, Dr Griffith and Dr Biden. Mr R.J. Corbett ran an eponymous English bank and cashed cheques and circular notes of English and American banks. He was very obliging to strangers. The Cabinet de Lecture on the Place des Palmiers had a library and a reading room. Pure water had been laid on for the town and the authorities had become more careful in securing cleanliness and drainage. The prices of provisions were not so high as at Cannes or Nice and vegetables were abundant and cheap. Pattieson's was a good shop for groceries and English stores. Apartments ranged from FF600 to FF4000 (£24 to £160)[8] for the season from 15 October to 15 May. Ground floors had to be avoided for reasons Murray did not disclose; and the advice of an English resident should be obtained before selecting an apartment. There were two public lawn-tennis grounds, and musical and theatrical entertainments were given during the season.

There was a daily service by diligence, a large four-wheeled closed stagecoach, by a beautiful road to St Tropez, 32 miles away; the journey took seven hours. St Tropez was described as a small seaport of 3739 inhabitants, beautifully situated in the gulf of the same name.

The British Mediterranean naval squadron sometimes used the anchorage in the roadstead formed by the Levant islands of the Iles d'Hyères which lay to the east of Hyères.

The Rev. P. Singer was the chaplain of the English church, which Murray did not name, on the Boulevard des Palmiers.[9] Hyères had a long history of Protestantism, which dated from 1562 when Protestants there first met together in secret to read their bibles. The Edict of Nantes of 1598 allowed them to come into the open, but the Revocation in 1685 again forced them underground. Only in 1788 was an edict of tolerance again promulgated. The first Protestant cemetery was established in Hyères in 1806.

Charles Cook, an English Wesleyan preacher, came to Hyères in 1819 and met the local Protestants, who had rarely had a visit from a preacher of any nationality. The visit was part of his 40-year campaign to revive Protestantism in France and to introduce Methodism. His efforts and those of others, including the Swiss, had an effect. In 1815 there were some 100 Protestants in the Var, of whom 60 were in Hyères, but by 1862 there were 1000, of whom 154 were in Hyères. The Protestants were often men of substance and one, M. Peyron, owned the Hôtel Costebelle, where the Queen stayed. *Le Guide des étrangers à Hyères*, which was published between 1865 and 1869, gives a list of foreigners during the winter season of 1865 and mentions two English Protestant ministers, Mr Forbes and his family domiciled locally, and Mr and Mrs Jebb domiciled in London. A Protestant church was opened in 1853 on the Avenue des Iles d'Or, which the different nationalities shared, with the Anglicans taking the 11 am and 3 pm slots for their services.[10] The English built a church for their exclusive use in 1867 and this was replaced by the much larger fine neo-Gothic church of St Paul's which was consecrated in 1884.[11]

'I was only happy once, and that was at Hyères', wrote Robert Louis Stevenson, its most famous resident. His first visit to the Riviera as a married man was for health reasons and was in the same year as that of the Queen in 1882. He moved to Hyères from Nice in 1883 with his wife and stepson and lived in a villa, 'La Solitude', above the old town and below a ruined castle. He described the villa as 'Eden and Beulah and the Delectable Mountains and Eldorado and the Hesperidean Isles.'[12] It was a small Swiss chalet of bricks and wood, with gables and balconies, which had been designed for a Paris exhibition in 1878. The garden contained roses, aloes, fig-marigolds and olive trees where nightingales nested.

The house and Hyères suited Stevenson well and he started to work hard, finishing his novel *Prince Otto* and working on *A Child's Garden of Verses*. He also started *The Black Arrow*. *Treasure Island* was published while he was there and he received £100 and, as he put it, his first breath of popular applause. He suffered from ophthalmia, rheumatism and sciatica and was confined to bed for a long time following an almost fatal haemorrhage. The writer could not use his right hand but continued writing in a darkened room with his left hand. When he recovered he grew a little imperial on his chin and walked around Hyères in a straw hat and black cape: his wife decided he was beginning to be quite good looking again. But the invalid fell ill once more, this time with pneumonia. Cholera broke out in Hyères and the family went back to England. 'Would to God I had died in Hyères', Stevenson declared on his first journey to Samoa.[13]

Given her great obsession with death, the Queen would have been interested in the funeral practices of Hyères. Fanny Stevenson reported on a typhus outbreak when:

all day the death-bells rang, and we could hear the chanting whilst the wretched villagers carried about their dead lying bare to the sun on their coffin-lids, so spreading the contagion through the streets. During the night a peasant-man died in a house in our garden, and in the morning the corpse, hideously swollen in the stomach, was lying on its coffin-lid at our gates.[14]

Stevenson's time on the Riviera drew him to the conclusion that the relative merits and defects of the English and French made a balance, as he explained in a letter[15]:

The English	The French
hypocrites	free from hypocrisy
good, stout reliable friends	incapable of friendship
dishonest to the root	fairly honest
fairly decent to women	rather indecent to women

The historian J.R. Green also lived in Hyères. He died in Menton in 1883 and his tombstone in the cemetery there carries the words, 'He died learning'.[16]

The most important issue pre-occupying the Queen and her household in Hyères was the consequences of the death of Prince Albert Victor. In the month before he died he had become engaged to Princess Victoria Mary of Teck, known as May, whose mother was Princess Mary Adelaide, sister of the Duke of Cambridge. 'We have seen a great deal of May', the

Queen told her daughter, Victoria, in the previous October, 'and I cannot say enough good about her. May is a particularly nice girl, so quiet and yet so cheerful.'[17] She later wrote to the Archbishop of Canterbury that the Princess was very charming 'with much sense and amiability, and very unfrivolous, so that I have every hope that the young couple will set an example of a steady quiet life, which, alas, is not the fashion in these days.'[18] Nevertheless the Queen later admitted that May had never been in love with poor Eddy.[19]

Speculation was rife in England that May would marry Prince George, eventual heir to the throne, and the correspondent of *The Times* pursued the story in the corridors of the Hôtel Costebelle. He cornered Henry Ponsonby and told him:

'It is assumed that Prince George and Princess May will, of course marry as they are always together.' Ponsonby did not reply, so the correspondent used the old journalist's trick of pretending to know something when he did not.

'Oh yes, I know you can't say anything but we know the Prince of Wales is for it and the Queen dead against it.'

Ponsonby fell into the trap: 'That's not true', he snapped back. He then had to explain that Her Majesty had not yet expressed any opinion.

'Oh, no of course not – much too soon – but we more than suspect.' The correspondent had his story.[20]

It was not that simple. George wanted to marry his cousin Marie, known as Missy, daughter of Prince Alfred of Edinburgh. But at the beginning of June her engagement was suddenly announced to Ferdinand, heir to the Romanian throne. So George did marry May. The engagement was announced on 3 May 1893 and the future king and queen of England married on 6 July.[21]

Another preoccupation of the Queen in Hyères was constitutional. The King of Greece had recently dismissed his government for 'leading the country to bankruptcy'. She discussed with Ponsonby whether he had the right to do so. She felt he had, 'but whether it is wise to exercise this right must depend on circumstances', she told him.[22]

There were a number of Liberals staying in Hyères who had differing views on the subject, but did not have the opportunity to discuss them with the monarch. To Ponsonby's horror, the sub-Prefect of Hyères wanted to show the Queen the beautiful garden of Sir Charles Dilke, former Liberal MP for Chelsea and former Under-Secretary at the Foreign Office.[23] He was one of the principal critics of the monarchy. In 1871, at the age of 28, he had delivered a speech at Newcastle-upon-Tyne under the title 'Representation and Royalty' in which he estimated that the 'waste, corruption and inefficiency' of the monarchy was costing the nation a million pounds a year. The Queen was furious and sent Gladstone a letter complaining of Dilke's 'gross misstatements and fabrications, injurious to the credit of the Queen and injurious to the Monarchy'. The Times called the allegations 'recklessness bordering on criminality'. As a child, Dilke had been walking with his father, who was a friend of the Prince of Wales, in Hyde Park when the Queen passed by. She stopped and stroked his head. 'I suppose I stroked it the wrong way', she said when, as a grown man, he started to attack her.[24]

Dilke's villa, 'La Sainte Campagne', which he rented in 1876 and bought in 1877, was on Cap Brun, near Toulon. It had a fine view and good garden, but the house itself was modest and would not have greatly impressed the monarch. However, if she had been able to overcome her hostility to her former minister, she would have found his knowledge of the area fascinating. 'He knows our country and our legends better than we know them ourselves', M. Noel Blache, a neighbour and President of the Conseil-Général of the Department of the Var, said of 'Sir Dilke'. Dilke would not have disagreed. 'It is my boast, probably vain, to have invented the Mountains of the Moors', he wrote.[25] An indication of the way the Riviera became so much a part of the life of the English upper classes is the facility with which Dilke travelled along the coast to Cannes on several occasions to both dine and attend church with Gladstone when he was resting there in January 1883.

Another Liberal who visited the Riviera, George Childers, used to sport a primrose because it was the Queen's favourite flower and he hoped that by wearing it he would stop it becoming a Conservative emblem.[26]

The Queen did not visit Dilke's garden. But she spent most of her time in the gardens of the hotel and in visiting other gardens. The problem with the hotel garden was that the mosquitoes and other insects were troublesome and they had to burn pastilles. (Flies were a bother at dinner and one of the Indian servants had to sweep a gold whisk of cowstail over the monarch's head. It seemed to work because Ponsonby said the flies went to his dining room instead.)[27]

The Times reported that all the proprietors of villas in the neighbourhood had placed their grounds at her disposal. Some of them had gone to the expense of repairing their pathways and making them smooth for the passage of the small donkey carriage.[28] 'Really the gardens here are quite a paradise', was her judgement.[29]

The most interesting house she visited was one with an aquarium:

> At 11, drove with Beatrice and Jane C. [Churchill] to La Plage, and to the Villa Bicoque, belonging to a very rich old gentleman, M. Godillot, who has done a great deal for Hyères, and is somewhat paralytic. He received us and showed us his Aquarium, which is opened to the public, and contains fishes and sea animals of all kinds, found at and near Hyères. Some were very pretty, but others most hideous, amongst them, a not very large fish of which they make that good soup 'Bouillabaisse', which is so much eaten in the south of France.[30]

The Queen did not record eating bouillabaisse, but one report said she did. Years after her stay in Hyères, a local fisherman told Laurens van der Post that he remembered that as a child he saw Queen Victoria, wearing a purple bonnet, landing on the rocky islet where he lived and sharing his family's bouillabaisse out of a big pot.[31]

She drove in the countryside: 'The fields in the flat parts were quite pink with almond blossoms, and the hedges full of may in flower. The country looks like one big nosegay', she wrote.[32] She also sketched occasionally. The royal Journal shows well the Queen's quest for knowledge and a lively mind:

> The road wound in and out of cork woods and it is very curious to observe the way in which the cork has been cut off the trees. The cork is not removed till the young trees have attained 4 inches in diameter, and every 10 to 15 years it is stripped off again.[33]

The longest journey was a trip to Toulon, which was 20 kilometres away. She was particularly taken by her visit to La Londe, near the older of the salt pans, which constituted one of the chief industries of Hyères.[34] Other places the Queen visited included La Crau, Carqueiranne, the Château de Castille, Sauvebonne, L'Almanarre, La Moutonne, Giens, Pradet, La Garde, les Bormettes, Sylvabelle and San Salvador.

Visitors, including Prince Henry and the Prince and Princess of Saxe-Coburg-Gotha, came over from Cannes and stayed at the Hôtel Albion nearby. The Prince of Wales, who was also staying at the Hôtel Albion in Hyères, had also come over from Cannes, where he had been staying at the Grand Hôtel de Provence. He departed from his usual practice of never staying in the same town as his mother, presumably because he felt their joint sorrow over the death of his son justified an exception. The

Prince of Wales had visited Hyères in 1862 on his first visit to the Riviera. He was there because, oddly enough, his mother had not wanted him to be back home during the first visit to England of his fiancée, Princess Alexandra.

The mournful atmosphere of the Queen's visit continued, and at church on Good Friday the grieving Queen thought the hymn 'O Come and mourn with me a while', which she sang, was pretty and touching.[35] The church in question was All Saints in Costebelle. The *Times* correspondent described it as a pretty little building of iron covered with lattice work, with a thatched roof.[36] It was the last church at which she regularly attended services on the Riviera. Thereafter, with the one exception of her first Sunday in Nice, she always worshipped in her hotel. Curiously, she is not recorded as having visited the grander church of St Paul's in Hyères proper, particularly as she did pay a brief visit to the Catholic church of Notre Dame de Consolation near the hotel. The church was famous for its collection of gifts and pictorial decorations.[37] All Saints is now in private hands and is derelict.[38] St Paul's still exists, but the British Anglicans have not used it since 1953 when they sold it to the town of Hyères for use as a cultural centre. It is now used as a library, cinema and concert room.[39]

The Queen was very pleased to receive a cutting of hair from the head of the deceased Louis, Grand Duke of Hesse and the Rhine, and flowers which had lain on his bed.[40] Her thoughts were much with his family in Darmstadt where she had decided to go after Hyères.

Representative of the vast number of visitors the Queen saw when she was on the Riviera is this list for 1892, which, because of the mourning, was a quiet visit:

The Duke and Duchess of Connaught and their children; the Duke and Duchess of Rutland, Minister in attendance; Lady Harding; Prince Henry of Battenberg; Prince Dietrichstein Mensdorff Nicolsburg; Prince and Princess Philip of Saxe-Coburg; Prince and Princess of Thurn and Taxis; the Marquis of Dufferin and Alva, British Ambassador; Baron von Westerweller-d'Anthoni, Grand Marshall of the Court of Hesse; the Rt. Hon. Hugh and Mrs Childers; Miss Childers; Lady Birch; Major and Mrs Ellis; the Count and Countess de Lieutaud; Commander Tillard of H.M.S. Surprise; the Grand Duke and Duchess of Mecklenburg-Schwerin; the Prince and Princess of Wales, and Prince George and the young Princesses; the Marquis Thezan, the Pope's secretary; Admiral Bossoudie, Maritime Prefect of Toulon; M. Chadenier, Prefect of the Var; Colonel and Lady Constance Barne.

The Queen kept her public engagements to a minimum, but she did receive a deputation of six members of the Horticultural and Agricultural Society of Hyères, bearing a bouquet.[41]

The local people appreciated the fact that the Queen sent Sir Henry Ponsonby and Dr Reid to represent her at the funeral of Louis-André-Manuel Cartigny, the last French survivor of the Battle of Trafalgar. Cartigny, who was 100 when he died, had been born in Hyères on 1 September 1791, and had been taken prisoner on board the *Redoubtable* at Trafalgar and was taken to England, where he was imprisoned for ten years. He had been a great figure in Hyères, doyen of the Chevaliers de la Légion d'Honneur, robust despite his wounds, and usually to be found sunning himself on the Promenade des Palmiers and recounting his battle stories.[42]

Despite the fact that the Hyères visit was one of mourning, in Hyères was the Hon. Alick Yorke, a groom-in-waiting, and known as Master of the Revels – the nearest thing Queen Victoria had to a Court Jester. Yorke has gone down in history as the man to whom the Queen said: 'We are not amused.' Alick was once sitting next to a German to whom he told a slightly risqué story. The German laughed so loudly that the Queen asked Yorke to tell her what had caused the laughter. Alick repeated the story. 'We are not amused', replied the Queen.[43] However, he was forgiven and the Queen continued to send for him after dinner and they would have comic songs.[44] He also organized the Queen's theatricals.

The Queen had enjoyed Hyères so much that she extended her stay by a week and left on 25 April. Her final duty was the distribution of presents. The mayor of Hyères got a portrait of Her Majesty; M. Peyron, the hotel proprietor a photogravure from Agneli's picture of Her Majesty with an autograph; Mme Peyron a gold brooch set with brilliants and pearls; and the postmaster, the two telegraph clerks and the stationmaster a gold pencil case each. The poor of the town got FF1200[45] (£48).[46]

The Queen left Hyères for Darmstadt on 25 April.[47] Numbers of inhabitants and visitors made a pilgrimage to the Hôtel Costebelle to inspect the apartments when the Queen had left. They took away with them as souvenirs any flowers left in the rooms.[48] Reuters reported that she had found her stay so agreeable that she proposed to visit Hyères again the following year.[49] She did not, and instead went to Florence, and again in 1894. The Hôtel Costebelle was shelled in 1945 and no longer exists.

CHAPTER 6

1895: Nice. The young officers and the Battle of the Flowers

On Queen Victoria's first visit to Nice on 15 March 1895 the town greeted her with a welcome unlike anything the Riviera had afforded her before. The square outside the station was lined with a battalion of troops, as were the principal streets, which were decorated and full of people, who gave an enthusiastic welcome. They waved their handkerchiefs and applauded. The band struck up 'God Save the Queen' and General Gebhart, Governor of Nice, made a speech of welcome on behalf of the President of the Republic.[1] He was very nervous when he spoke, the Queen noted in her Journal.[2] She was escorted to the Grand Hôtel at Cimiez, outside Nice, by a party of mounted Gendarmes and Horse Artillery. At the hotel a Company of the 6th Battalion of the Chasseurs Alpins greeted the royal party with a fanfare of clarions. The Press corps covering the visit consisted of 150 journalists.[3]

Cimiez is a former Gallo-Roman town, Cemenelum, on a hill 1½ miles (2.4 kilometres) from the centre of Nice, which was the seat of the proconsul of the imperial province of the Alpes Maritimae. In the third century another royal, Salonina Augusta, wife of the Roman Emperor, Gallienus, had stayed there when the heat of Rome became insufferable. Its attractions include the remains of the Roman amphitheatre and baths and a Franciscan monastery dating from the sixteenth century. Mme Henri Germain, wife of the founder of the bank Crédit Lyonnais, made it fashionable by building a villa, 'Orangini', which became a great social centre from 1879 to 1881. In 1879 her husband, Henri Germain, created an investment company, the Société Foncière Lyonnaise, to build luxury houses and hotels. The builders of the hotels were exploiting the new desire of foreigners for hotels with comforts such as lifts, hot and cold water, private baths and the quiet produced by a large park with sporting facilities like tennis.[4] The Queen was particularly pleased with the lift.[5] In the USA there had been experiments with lifts as early as 1833, but they were not brought into general use for another generation, so the Queen liked the novelty.[6] One of the ladies-in-waiting remarked that the hotel was said to be very damp, but the Queen did not seem to have been bothered because she did not mention it in her diaries.[7] The hotel was set in a great park at a height of 115 metres above sea level, with views over Nice and the Baie des Anges.

Tram operators used the Queen's impending arrival as an argument to apply for a licence to operate a new electric tram service from the centre of Nice to Cimiez, which would be useful not only to the Queen but also to the police. It would replace the tram pulled by horses, who struggled to get up the hill. It started on 27 February, but broke down while it was being shown to the municipal council on 10 March, only five days before the Queen was expected. A new generator had to be rushed across France from the factory at Lyons. The tram started working again on 12 March, only just in time for the royal arrival on 15 March.[8]

The royal staff could also benefit from the mail omnibus with four horses which plied four times a day between the hotel and the centre of Nice.[9] The coach was an exciting part of the life of the visitors to Nice, as the *Eclaireur de Nice* described in its flowery prose of the period:

> Tarara! The footman with his long trumpet ... signals the passage of his four-in-hand on the Place Masséna. It is the hour to return to the hotels. The yellow or green mail-coach is garnished with travellers like a vine covered in grapes in summer. How the sound of the tuba gives so much pleasure on our bustling streets on these splendid December afternoons! This symbolic herald announces the reopening of the season. Nice has found its noisy winter life again. At three in the afternoon go across the Place du Casino: bicycle bells, the galloping of carriages, automobile horns, rattling harnesses, hubbub, tumult. This square has already been named 'The Crossing of the Crushed'.[10]

The first tram, which was battery operated, started in 1895. It was so slow it was called – after the architect – 'M. Biasini's slug'.[11]

There were many hotels. They would cost between FF4 (£0.16) and FF16 (£0.64)[12] a night, depending on the floor and the outlook. Breakfast was FF2 (£0.08), buffet lunch FF3.50 (£0.13), dinner FF6 (£0.24).[13] [14]

Visitors, both foreign and French, mixed well with the locals in the great social whirl for most of the nineteenth century, but tended to go their own ways in the late 1890s as the population grew. Social life consisted of the carnival, balls, concerts, opera, gambling, horseracing, yachting and tennis. At the balls the most beautiful girls were generally

2. The Chalet des Rosiers, Menton, (pictured here with the town in the background) belonged to Charles Henfrey, a wealthy Englishman who lent the house to the Queen in 1882.

Voyage de Madame la Comtesse de BALMORAL

Marche Route
de
CHERBOURG à NICE

Stations	Heures d'arrivée	Temps d'arrêt	Heures de départ	Stations	Heures d'arrivée	Temps d'arrêt	Heures de départ
	h. m.	h. m.	h. m.		h. m. matin	h. m.	h. m. matin
Le Jeudi 11 Mars 1897							
CHERBOURG Dép.	matin —	—	10.25	Macon	2.21	3	2.24
Lison	midi 4	5	midi 9	Lyon	3.33	5	3.38
Caen	1.12	6	1.18	Valence	5.19	3	5.22
Lisieux	2.9	4	2.13	Avignon	7.12	55	8.7
Conches	3.19	4	3.23	Tarascon	8.30	1.15	9.45
Mantes	4.34	15	4.49	Marseille (Bifurcation de Toulon)	11.23	10	11.33
Noisy-le-Sec	5.58	15	6.13	Toulon	midi 45	5	midi 50
Villeneuve-St-Georges (Triage)	6.46	7	6.53	Les Arcs	2.5	5	2.10
Laroche	9.6	43	9.49	Cannes	3.7	5	3.12
Les Laumes	11.18	8	11.26	Nice Arr.	3.45	—	soir
Dijon	min 21	5	min 26	*Le Vendredi 12 Mars 1897*			

G. de Metz

Ed. Blount

3. The Queen's Train Timetable, 1897. the train was scheduled to leave Cherbourg at 10.25 in the morning and arrive in Nice at 3.45 the following day. The Queen liked to travel incognito as 'The Countess of Balmoral', although her luggage was openly labelled 'Queen of England'.

Ne pleures plus Grand-Mère tu peux compter sur moi.

4. ABOVE. Kaiser Wilhelm II telling his grandmother the Queen not to cry any more, but to count on him. He is concealing from her a telegram ordering German warships to Lourenço Marques, maritime gateway to the Transvaal.

5. BELOW. Queen Victoria riding on a bottle of gin. The postcard was published when there was strong anti-British feeling in France at the time of the Fashoda incident in 1898, which almost led to war.

La Reine d'Angleterre à Nice

6. The Queen in an unladylike squabble over China. In the aftermath of the Sino-Japanese War of 1894 the China problem was one of the topics the Queen discussed with Lord Salisbury, the Prime Minster, while they were on the Riviera.

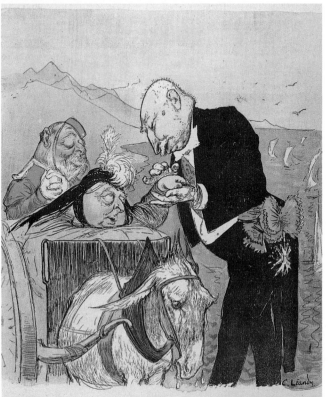

Flirt méridional entre Sa Gracieuse Majesté Victoria et son Élégance Félix Faure.
Dessin de C. Léandre.

7. 'A southern flirtation between Her Gracious Majesty Victoria and his Elegance Félix Faure.' When the French President called on the Queen at her hotel in Nice in 1898 she thought he was very courteous and amiable, and was prepared to overlook the fact that he was the President of a republic.

8. The Winter in Nice. Queen Victoria loved the flower festival with its handsome young army officers in their colourful uniforms.

Le Petit Journal

Le Petit Journal
CHAQUE JOUR 5 CENTIMES

Le Supplément illustré
CHAQUE SEMAINE 5 CENTIMES

SUPPLÉMENT ILLUSTRÉ

Huit pages : CINQ centimes

ABONNEMENTS

SEINE ET SEINE-ET-OISE ... 2 fr. 3 fr. 50
DÉPARTEMENTS ... 2 fr. 4 fr.
ÉTRANGER ... 2 50 5 fr.

Neuvième année

DIMANCHE 24 AVRIL 1898

Numéro 388

Les hôtes de la France
LA REINE D'ANGLETERRE A LA PROCESSION DES PÉNITENTS ROUGES

9. The Queen at the Maundy Thursday procession of the Red Penitents on 7 April 1898. She recorded in her Journal that 'In passing my carriage, the Bishop stopped and bowed, taking his little cap off his head'.

0. The English Sanitary Co. were British manufacturers who benefited from the Queen's visits to the Riviera, which helped to make English goods fashionable.

1. By the end of the Century the Queen's visits had made the Riviera so popular in Britain that the Paris, Lyons and Mediterranean Railway Co. opened offices in London. The Queen led the way in showing the Riviera could be visited not for convalescence but for holidays.

12. ABOVE. 'Old England to the Rescue.' The beginning of the Anglo-Boer War in South Africa, in which the French sided with the Boers. The war lasted from 11 October 1899 to 31 May 1902. Because of the war Queen Victoria cancelled her trip to the Riviera and went to Ireland instead.

13. TOP RIGHT. The Queen distraught as the Boer President, 'uncle' Paul Kruger tells Cecil Rhodes, Chairman of De Beers diamond mining company, to come down from the apple tree, a reference to Kruger's troops besieging Rhodes in Kimberley.

14. ABOVE RIGHT. The Queen as a good farmer in the Anglo-Boer War, sowing lead in order to reap gold. The lead referred to dum-dum bullets which had been banned by international treaty, and which the British were rumoured to have used in the war.

15. RIGHT. The Queen looking very much askance at a fly buzzing by her head. The fly is Paul Kruger, complete with top hat. The Boer War did much to undermine the goodwill towards Britain which the Queen's visits to the Riviera had engendered.

considered to be the Americans and the most elegant the Russians. The most important social centre as the century drew to a close was the Cercle de la Méditerranée. The founders of the company were not only French, but also included a Belgian, a Pole, a Russian, a Swede, a Norwegian and an Englishman with the unlikely name of Edwin Prodgers, who had a beautiful villa on the Promenade des Anglais.[15] No Prodgers appeared in *Who's Who*.

The Grand Hôtel could house 50 of the royal entourage; the overflow stayed in the Hôtel Vitali on the other side of the park. Paoli described some of the entourage:

> A numerous staff of servants used to accompany the Queen on her journeys to the Riviera. It consisted of a first waiting-woman assisted by six dressers; a French chef, M. Ferry, with three or four lieutenants and a whole regiment of scullions under his orders; a coachman, an outrider and a dozen grooms and stablemen, for the Queen always took her horses abroad with her and never drove out except in her own carriage.

> The suite was completed by the small troop of Indian servants, who preferred to form a little set apart from the others. These impenetrable, impassive and supercilious persons were very fine-looking fellows, clad in big turbans and wonderful cashmere garments of dazzling hues. They acted as a sort of attentive and silent body-guard to the Queen and looked as though they had been struck dumb by the almost religious importance of their duties. They enjoyed a few privileges, such as that of practising all the rites of their creed without restrictions, were thoroughly accustomed to discipline and were faithful and devoted to their sovereign in life and death. The Queen also brought with her a Highland gillie, who wore the picturesque costume of his native land.[16]

The staff had plenty to do, Paoli explained, particularly at the beginning and end of the stay because the Queen travelled with almost all the furniture of her bedroom, including the bedding and a high old-fashioned mahogany bedstead. She brought with her a Venetian mirror and a little rosewood table, on which stood many photographs.[17] Taking coals to Newcastle, the accoutrements brought from England included a little orange tree.[18]

Little did Paoli realize in his innocent remarks about the Indian servants how the problem of one of them in particular, Abdul Karim, would soon dominate the royal visits to Cimiez.

Abdul Karim, 24, lately arrived from India, had taken up his duties as one of two table servants to the newly proclaimed Empress of India on 23 June 1887, two days after she had celebrated her Jubilee. The other servant, Mohamed Buxshe, was very dark, and she clearly was most taken by Abdul Karim, who was 'much lighter, tall, and with a fine serious countenance. His father is a native doctor at Agra. They both kissed my feet.'[19] The Queen had never found a replacement in her affections for John Brown, who had died four years before. To the surprise of the Court she soon installed Abdul Karim in John Brown's room at Balmoral. He became even more hated than Brown had been. When Abdul Karim fell ill on one occasion the Queen visited him several times a day and stroked his hand.[20] The Queen Empress was fascinated by India and, with Abdul Karim's help, plunged into a study of its culture and one of its many languages. 'Am learning a few words of Hindustani to speak to my servants. It is a great interest to me, for both the language and the people. I have naturally never come into contact with it before.'[21]

In 1892 Abdul Karim's name appeared for the first time in the Court Circular list of those accompanying the Queen to the Riviera.[22] The accolade clearly went to his head. When he arrived in Italy with the Queen in April 1894 he ordered Dosse, the Queen's courier, to have this announcement published in the *Florence Gazette*:

> The Munshi Mohammed Abdul Karim son of Haji Dr Mohammed Wazirudin an inhabitant of Agra the Cheef City of NWP who left his office in India, and came to England in the service of the Queen Victoria Empress of India in the year 1887.
>
> He was appointed first for some time as Her Majestys Munshi and Indian Clerk. From 1892 he was appointed as her M's Indian Secretary. He is belonging to a good and highly respectful Famiely. All is Famiely has been in Govt. Service with high position. His father is still in the service of the Govn. 36 years ago. One brother of his is a city Collector. All the Indian attendants of the Queen are under him and he also wholes different duties to perfirm in Her Majesty's Service.[23]

This had to be published with a photograph of himself with decorations and sword and his head was to be made 'thinner and less dark'. The announcement was edited before it appeared.

Dr Reid whiled away the time in Florence by noting all the things about the Munshi that had annoyed him:

1. Complaint on arrival to Q of position of his railway carriage from Bologna.

2. Proposal by H.M. to Ponsonby that he should drive with the gentlemen of the Household on occasions.

3. Visit to Rome for one night, £22.

4. Refusal to allow other Indians in any part of the same railway carriage as himself.

5. Deprived H.M.'s maids of bathroom and W.C. and insisted on having it entirely reserved for himself.

6. What the Nurse and Mrs Boyd and Mrs Keith said about his wife and mother-in-law. 'More degraded and dirty than the lowest labourers in England; spitting all over the carpets. Performing functions in sitting room, etc.'

7. In Broge's shop window with large crowds looking at it – A large frame for 10 cabinet photos, of these, 9 various photos of the Queen and the 10th the Munshi in the centre! After a few days Col. Clerk got vice consul Placci to go to Broge and have the M.'s photo removed. The Italians say he is a 'Principe Indiano' with whom the Q. is in love and this accounts for the photo being put where it was.

8. Bigge overheard conversation about him in the English Club, remarking on his low appearance and that he was a man who in India would have no place anywhere but with menials. Much astonished at his being with the Queen and surmises as to the meaning of it and who was responsible.

9. He complained to Dosse that the newspapers took too little notice of him; also to the Q who sent Mrs MacDonald to Dosse to say that he was to see that the newspapers took notice of and mentioned the Munshi more frequently![24]

The sensitivities repeated themselves in 1895. *The Galignani Messenger* on 22 March 1895 carried this corrective:

By telegraphic error it was made to appear that the Munshi assisted the Queen from her carriage on her arrival at Nice, which was of course not the case, as Her Majesty is always assisted by an Indian servant. The Munshi, as a learned man and the Queen's Indian Secretary and preceptor in Hindustani, is one of the most important personages 'auprès de la Reine' having several men under him, and being often privileged to dine with his Royal Mistress and pupil.[25]

But generally the local Press carried more important stories. *Le Petit Niçois* reported that there had been tough negotiations between the hotel and the Queen's representatives but that they finally settled on a special end of season rate of FF40,000 (£1600)[26] for the six weeks.[27]

The attraction of the area of Nice was that it was protected by the maritime alps, which had the dual effect of blocking out cold winter winds from the north and retaining the warmth from the Mediterranean.

The importance attached to the success of the royal visit is shown by the decision of the Nice town council and M. Port, the manager of the hotel, that new sewers, lighting and roads had to be provided. However, a row broke out over who was to pay for them. Finally, the town gave in and met the costs. Two days before the Queen was due to arrive the *Eclaireur de Nice*, in one of its many long articles about the visit, reported that more than 60 workmen were finishing the refurbishment of the hotel and gardens in 'feverish activity'.[28] The usual residents of the hotel had been moved out. Not only did the newspapers carry long detailed articles, but the advertising also exploited the visit. One display advertisement, which appeared regularly, was a drawing of a beautiful girl with long hair, promoting 'Royal Windsor, the Celebrated Hair Regenerator'.

The *Eclaireur de Nice* on 16 March detailed what, dining alone at 9 pm, with the two princesses, Victoria of Schleswig-Holstein and Beatrice, had been laid before the Queen:

POTAGE
Crème de Riz
POISSONS
Filets de soles au gratin
Merlans frits
ENTREES
Croquettes de volaille aux truffes
Noisettes d'agneau aux points d'asperges
RELEVE
Boeuf braisé au macaroni
RÔT
Canetons rôtis
ENTREMETS
Petits pois nouveaux
Pudding soufflé au chocolat
Glace aux fraises
Viandes froides assorties
DESSERT[29]

The Queen's stay was soon clouded by strained relations between Britain and France. On 29 March Lord Rosebery, the Prime Minister, cabled to her that he feared they were rapidly approaching a condition of severe tension with the French government owing to its strange proceedings in

Africa and Siam. A Cabinet meeting had been summoned for the next day, which might prove critical, but he hoped the crisis might be tided over. The same day the Queen replied:

> Your telegram is rather disquieting. While trusting that the Government will preserve a strong attitude against French encroachments, I hope crisis may be averted on national grounds; and also that personally it would be very awkward if complications arose with a country in which I am now residing and receiving marked courtesy and attention.[30]

Sir Edward Grey, Under-Secretary for Foreign Affairs, had given a strong warning to the French in the House of Commons on the previous day:

> The advance of a French expedition under secret instructions right from the other side of Africa into a territory over which our claims have been known for so long would be not merely an inconsistent and unexpected act, but it must be perfectly well known to the French Government that it would be an unfriendly act and would be so viewed by England.[31]

Siam was effectively a buffer state between the French in Indo-China and the British in Burma. The British were therefore very sensitive to any French encroachments in Siam. In 1893 the French had laid claim to the Siamese provinces on the east of the River Mekong and after a brief show of force the Siamese had given way. In January 1896, since the British government concluded that the people would be unwilling to go to war with France over Siam, the British and French concluded an agreement leaving the richest parts of the country intact and guaranteeing her against any third power. Thus did Thailand achieve the distinction of being the only country of south-east Asia never to be colonized. The agreement also covered the delimitation of territory in the lower Niger and relations with Tunis.

But in Cimiez in April 1895 the Queen continued to be bothered. On 1 April she telegraphed the Marquis of Dufferin, the British Ambassador in Paris:

> These questions with France are very annoying and may be serious. Fear our Government are thinking how they can carry on, with trouble in India besides. Trust you can manage to get French Government to do nothing rash and violent, considering that I am here. My having to leave suddenly would create a panic, and be most difficult for me.[32]

Shortly after Grey's warning, the French dispatched the expedition to the Sudan which led to the Fashoda Incident in 1898 and caused the British monarch to worry again about her Riviera holiday.

But the comments in the French Press about the Grey statement were mild and the crisis died down so that the Queen could continue to enjoy her holiday with its usual routines uninterrupted by crises.

Paoli described the routines:

> The Queen usually rose at nine o'clock, proceeded to dress and had her breakfast, the constituents of which varied every morning. She would take coffee, chocolate or tea, with which were served rolls, a dish of eggs, fried fish, grilled bacon and Cambridge sausages, things which she hardly touched.

> Next came the hour for correspondence. Her Majesty regularly received the Foreign Office messengers who brought the official documents for her signature and the ministerial reports. She carefully read through all the administrative papers and exchanged a considerable number of cipher telegrams with her government; and, as she liked answering by return all letters that required replies, her two secretaries were kept very busy. Add to this that she received daily an innumerable quantity of begging letters, which were handed to me in case they needed looking into. Most of these missives eventually found their way into the waste-paper basket.[33]

The most important of the usual routines were the rides in pony and trap to nearby gardens or by carriage to the more distant. The municipality had even built a new road to connect the gardens of the hotel with the Villa Liserb, where Princess Beatrice and her children eventually stayed. In her Journal, the Queen spelt the name Liserbe, which seems to indicate that she had not realized that the owner, Mr Cazalet, an Englishman with South American connections, had named it Liserb, which was Brazil in the French spelling of Brésil, in reverse. In the First World War the property passed into the hands of Lady Michelham, who turned it into a convalescent home for wounded British officers. After the Second World War it was progressively split up into 42 properties.[34]

A special edition of the *Journal de Cimiez* of 7 February 1896, shortly before the Queen's second visit to Cimiez, had an exclusive little story about a meeting of the Nice Poetry Society, which the Queen had attended with some of the Court in 1895. Monsieur Christian Arthaud, the Nice poet, gave a talk on English humour. Victoria smiled at quotations from Edward Lear. In a discussion afterwards on favourite writers, the Queen talked about the writings of Benjamin Disraeli.[35]

The local festivals particularly appealed to the Queen. In the 'festin des reproches', or festival of the reproaches, young couples came together to make admissions to each other of faults committed during the excesses of the carnival. They scolded each other for form's sake, attended a religious service, congregated in the market square, became reconciled, kissed and broke the traditional 'pan bagnat', or blessed bread, together. The 'festin des cougourdons', or festival of the gourds, was the most important fair and the Queen went there with her daughters to buy the prettily decorated fruit.[36]

She was glad to repeat her experience of Grasse and take part in the Battle of the Flowers on the Promenade des Anglais in Nice. The young army officers threw bouquets into her carriage and she threw them back, as the *Eclaireur de Nice* put it, 'with the best grace in the world'.[37] She also had her own supply of bunches of flowers, which the Mayor had supplied.

The Promenade des Anglais was so named in gratitude to the English clergyman, Lewis Way, who had raised the money to build it. In the winter of 1821–22 a bad frost had killed a lot of orange trees in the Nice region. Many men had been thrown out of work and Way persuaded a number of British residents to provide the money to employ them in building a road along the coast.[38]

Other expeditions were to the zoo, where Princess Beatrice photographed Sultan, the lion, and the tigers and to a faience and pottery factory at St-André. She went by train to Grasse to see Alice de Rothschild.

The most important visit was to Empress Eugénie at the Villa Cyrnos on Cap Martin.[39] Empress Eugénie was an old friend. They had first met in 1855 when the Empress had accompanied her husband, Napoleon III, on the visit to England. The Spanish Countess Eugénie de Montijo, who had a Scottish grandfather, William Kirkpatrick, married Napoleon III after he became Emperor in 1853. She lacked royal blood but was startingly beautiful with red hair and blue eyes and transparently white shoulders. The Empress was much more than a figurehead, serving as regent on three occasions during the absence of the Emperor, and at one period attending council meetings. The Empress was a devoted Catholic, believed in a strong Pope and opposed her husband's policies which resulted in a loss of temporal power for the Pontiff. She supported French opposition to a Prussian candidate for the vacant Spanish throne, which led to the Franco-Prussian war of 1870, in which France was defeated. Napoleon III was toppled and he joined her in exile in England, where he lived until his death in 1873.

They had both lived in England before. In exile from France, Napoleon III had even been a Special Constable during the Chartist riots in 1848, when his main contribution had been in the arrest of a very drunk old woman.[40] Eugénie had had the benefits of an English public school education when she was at a school near Bristol where, to her annoyance, she had been known as 'Carrots'.[41]

Queen Victoria welcomed the exiles and saw much of the Empress, whom Victoria called 'my dear sister'. Victoria had written of the Empress: 'Her manner is that most perfect thing I have ever seen – so gentle and graceful, and kind, the courtesy so charming, and so modest and retiring withal.'[42]

It was the tragedy of the death of Eugénie's son, the Prince Imperial, in the British army in the Zulu Wars in 1879 that gave an even more poignant intensity to the relationship, the more so since it was after advice from Queen Victoria that Eugénie had finally produced an heir. In April 1854 the pregnant Eugénie had a fall and took a long hot bath, which Queen Victoria later told her had been inadvisable while she was pregnant. She miscarried this time and on another occasion. Only after intimate chats with Queen Victoria, who had produced eight children, during the April 1855 visit to Windsor, and a session with the Queen's doctor, Lockhart, in London, did all come right. The Queen wrote to her on 29 August 1855: 'My thoughts are often with you. ... Do please remember my plans and don't weaken yourself too much; above all, go out as much as you can in the air without tiring yourself.' Eugénie later recalled: 'Such was my conversation with the Queen, and eleven months afterwards the result was the Prince Imperial.'[43]

Despite the opposition of Disraeli, who had become Lord Beaconsfield and who was then Prime Minister, the two empresses forced through the attachment of the young prince to the British army in South Africa. On 1 June 1879 the prince subaltern rode out into the veldt on reconnaissance with a Captain Carey and some troopers. They were surprised by a party of Zulus. As the prince tried to mount his horse to escape, the holster of his saddle gave way. Carey and the troopers had ridden off and the Zulus killed the prince.[44] Carey was court-martialled, found guilty and cashiered, but with a recommendation to mercy.[45] Oddly enough, the *Times* report of the verdict does not say what he was guilty of. The implication of the report is that it was not cowardice, but 'misbehaviour'.

Sensitive to the fact that the honour of the British army had been impugned, the Queen visited Eugénie no less than three times in the days following the news of the death. 'It showed a gt want of chivalry ... which everyone owes, not only to a Prince, but to any superior, friend or indeed fellow creature', the Queen said.[46]

Edmond Rostand later wrote a play, *Napoleon IV*, charging that Louis had been ambushed with the connivance of Queen Victoria.

'My conscience is clear', declared Disraeli, 'I did all that I could to stop his going. But what can you do when you have to deal with two obstinate women?'[47] The two obstinate women comforted each other when they met on the Riviera.

The Empress bought the estate at Cap Martin in 1894. She had not been allowed by the French Republican government to reside in France for 20 years after her flight at the time of the Franco-Prussian war. Now she was allowed to buy a house, but she was not allowed to have a household of more than eight men, including gardeners and coachmen, and a government inspector visited her once a week. She built a villa in the Italian style, with a loggia decorated with Pompeian frescoes. There were pines and multi-coloured flowers, but the *Eclaireur de Nice* was not complimentary about the property, saying that the house was built with severe lines and was completely isolated in a lost corner. However, the former Empress of the French was not isolated and built an annexe to house the young friends who visited her.[48]

The relationship between Victoria and Eugénie was not without its occasional friction. When the Queen passed through Paris on the way to Switzerland in 1868 the Empress paid her a courtesy call, but the Queen caused great affront by not returning it on her way back. After the Queen visited the Empress at her home in Chislehurst for the first time in November 1870, she sent a message to the head of the household that if she was to come again the windows would have to be opened.[49] So when the Queen was about to visit the Empress in Scotland in 1889, the hostess confided in Sir Henry Ponsonby that, although she enjoyed a visit from the Queen, she sometimes terrified her, and the Empress asked Ponsonby if the room was cool enough.[50]

Eugénie was more at ease with Elizabeth, the Empress of Austria, when she visited the Empress of the French on the Riviera. They shared a passion for horses and would chatter away for hours. Reportedly neither listened to what the other said. They bathed together and hid their jewels behind the same rock.[51]

Paoli described a curious incident in which Dosse, the Queen's courier, arranged for the French soldiers to mount a guard of honour for a visit to the Queen from Empress Eugénie at Cimiez. Just in time, before the Empress arrived, Paoli had the guard stood down. When she arrived he explained what had happened and recorded her reaction:

'Oh, how glad I am that you avoided that incident!' she exclaimed. 'The newspapers would have been sure to hold me responsible; and my position in France, which is already so delicate, would only have suffered in consequence.'

As for me, I am convinced that people would not have failed to see in this simple misunderstanding a political plot, an attempt to restore the imperial family, or goodness knows what.[52]

Queen Victoria did not only mix with royalty and aristocrats when she was at Cimiez. Contacts with the locals started on the first day and continued throughout the stay, as the Queen recorded:

The Fishwives of Nice, to the number of 80, arrived with a huge bouquet. As at Paris, they play a great part, and are called 'les Dames de la Halle.' They were very smartly got up, with gay coloured handkerchiefs on their heads. I received them upstairs and the fat spokeswoman, who carried the bouquet, kissed me on both cheeks! To avoid further kisses, I shook hands with all the others. They were most friendly.[53]

Years later the *Eclaireur de Nice* published an unlikely story. It said the Queen had offered the fishwives a cup of tea. 'In the presence of this hot water they grimaced. They would rather have had a glass of wine.'[54]

The Prior of the Monastery of Cimiez, who, clad in his bronze Franciscan monk's habit, called on her, particularly pleased her by saying he would always pray for her.[55]

The Queen noted for the first time the funny old one-legged beggar, Charles Alberique, on a cart drawn by two dogs, who tried to keep up with the royal carriage and who was to become such a feature of her visits to Nice.[56] She always referred to the beggars as her old friends and gave them money. Octave Galtier, a member of her French guard of honour, recalled her reply when someone said false beggars abused her charity. 'I know I am sometimes exploited, but I prefer to make a mistake in giving than to make a mistake in not giving.'[57] She not only gave coins to the beggars, but at the end of her stay distributed largesse. The *Eclaireur de Nice* reported that she had given the Mayor of Nice FF2500 (£100)[58] to be distributed in numerous charitable works. She also gave the British Consul money for special purposes, such as the Evangelical Shelter and Work of the Crèches.[59]

In the evenings there was often musical entertainment, including a Russian choir of 140 members in national dress, and one lunchtime some strolling musicians and singers rendered Neapolitan songs.[60] For her grandchildren the Queen got some Indian jugglers and a conjuror to perform.

Places the Queen visited, some more than once, included the Gairaut waterfall, Fabron, Villefranche, Bellet, the grottoes of St André, Falicon, St Jean, St Antoine, Aspremont, Roquebrune and Tourette de Levens.

She did not visit Monaco, although Prince Albert and the Princess called on her again in Nice. However, Princess Beatrice was permitted to call on the Prince and Princess.[61]

The statesman, Lord Salisbury, had a house, 'La Bastide', on the Riviera. It was technically in Villefranche, but Salisbury centred his life around the neighbouring Beaulieu. In 1886 he had begun buying up parcels of land in a valley covered in olives, carobs, holm oak and myrtles. In 1890 he started building a villa in Italian style.[62] Furniture was shipped out from England in September 1891 and he let it to Sir Thomas and Lady Lucas for three months from 1 November.[63] He himself moved into it in February 1892. He had a horror of interlopers and the house was surrounded by 'No Entry' signs.

Clearly this huge figure of 6' 4" with his massive beard was regarded locally as a figure of considerable fun. He and his wife went out for walks, she wearing a thick blue veil and he, pipe in his mouth, and with a dirty battered trilby pulled down to his ears. Thus clad he one day entered the casino at Monte Carlo, which had a strict dress code, and after an altercation with the doorman, was refused admission. The management later found out who he was and sent a profuse apology. His next enterprise was to buy a tricycle which he would ride either with his wife or his daughter. A servant brought up the rear and when they came to a hill the English nobility walked and the servant pushed the tricycle. One day he met a Frenchman. 'Is his Excellency francophile or francophobe?' asked the Frenchman. 'Neither one nor the other, I am simply anglophile,' Lord Salisbury replied. He was anglophile enough to contribute generously to the Anglican church of St Michael, which opened in 1894. His donation reflected the fact that one issue on which he felt strongly was defence of the Established Church. Stories of his scientific work at the villa abounded as he conducted experiments in electricity and chemistry. He became good friend of and exchanged many visits with the Mayor of Villefranche, Désiré Pollonnais.[64]

The Queen drove out to call on him on 3 April 1895 and he came to lunch with her on 13 April.[65] Salisbury was not in office when he exchanged these visits, but he had already formed two Cabinets. He was to be Queen Victoria's last Prime Minister and also the last Prime Minister to sit in the House of Lords. When she met Salisbury on the Riviera in April 1895 the Queen was well aware that, although Salisbury was not himself leading the government, the then Prime Minister, Lord Rosebery, was Salisbury's obedient pupil.[66]

Robert Arthur Talbot Gascoyne-Cecil, third Marquess of Salisbury, came from a genuinely Tory family which went back to the two great Cecils, William and Robert, who served Elizabeth I and James I. He had a massive intellect, hated society and social functions and was notoriously absent-minded, even greeting his own son in the grounds of the family home, Hatfield House, as an important, but unrecognized guest.

Salisbury was rather disdainful of what he saw as the upstart German family which reigned in Britain, although he did qualify his opinion: 'If we are doomed for ever to have German royalties', he commented on the marriage of one of the Queen's daughters in the 1860s, 'it is better to have such as have learned the use of the tub by residence in this country.'[67] But he eventually developed a trust in the Queen and paid her the great compliment of saying that talking foreign affairs with her was like talking with a man.[68]

The Queen initially had strong reservations about Salisbury because they differed on foreign policy in his early career, but she soon changed her view and when he visited her in January 1875 she noted in her Journal that he was 'particularly agreeable and gentle, and who one could not believe could be so severe and sarcastic in debate'.[69] In 1885 she had selected him as Prime Minister in preference to his rival Sir Stafford Northcote. Their bonds became closer and in June 1890 she wrote to him: 'She need not say that he knows he possesses her confidence, and how anxious she is to support him in every way.'[70] Most improperly, the Court Circular announced that she had accepted his resignation in August 1892 'with much regret'.[71]

The Queen regarded Salisbury as being in the very front rank of the ten who had conducted the major business of her reign, greater even than Disraeli.[72]

That great maverick historian, A.J.P. Taylor, who, after the Second World War, mesmerized both the undergraduates he tutored at Magdalen College, Oxford, and also radio and television audiences, described the foreign policy of Salisbury thus:

> I would say that Salisbury laid down the lines on which British foreign policy was to develop for many years after his death: he saw that so long as we were

quarelling with France and Russia all over the world – in Egypt, in Persia, in the Far East – we were dependent on German favour and he was determined to escape this favour. Therefore, slowly and persistently, he prepared the way for the Anglo-French entente, which matured in 1904, and the Anglo-Russian entente, which matured in 1907.[73]

... 'Splendid isolation' – not, as is often supposed, a description of his policy, but a reminder that only a Power whose vital interests are not involved can examine a problem in an 'emotional and philanthropic spirit'.[74]

Ten weeks after he saw the Queen at Cimiez, on 25 June 1895, Salisbury went to Windsor to kiss hands as Prime Minister for the third time.

Nice named the main boulevard to Cimiez 'Boulevard Victoria' and down this road she drove on 23 April at the end of her first stay in Nice to take the special train to Darmstadt in Germany.

CHAPTER 7

1896: Nice. Royal visitors, including King Leopold of the Belgians

A pall lay over the second visit to Nice, where the royal party arrived on 11 March 1896. Prince Henry of Battenberg, known in the family as Liko, husband of Princess Beatrice, had died on 20 January.

The Queen's low spirits were not helped by a rough and disagreeable Channel crossing, although the Queen told her Journal that she had not been ill.[1] Very emotional and nervous, she sent for Dr Reid three times during the crossing.[2] Worse was to follow. Driving up to the Grand Hôtel she was shocked to find the building site of 'an enormous new Hotel, which has been most provokingly put up just in front of the Grand Hôtel, taking away all the view and privacy'.[3] There was a good deal of noise from the building in spite of assurances given to the contrary. The Queen does not seem to have been aware that the previous year Colonel John Clerk, an Extra Equerry, had had talks with building promoters about their plans to build a new hotel in time for March 1896 with the Queen's needs specifically in mind.[4] But once the financiers had heard of the encouraging reaction of Colonel Clerk and had become excited about the number of visitors who would surely follow if the Queen of England were to stay in their hotel, they abandoned their relatively modest plans for the Victoria Hôtel and instructed Sébastian Marcel Biasini, the architect, to design a much larger and more ornate project which would be ready a year later.[5]

At the door of the Grand Hôtel the Queen was met by Princess Victoria of Battenberg and Princess Beatrice and her four little fatherless children clutching flowers to give to their grandmother.[6] Their father's death had been particularly painful for his mother-in-law because she so relied on him – in contrast to the Prince of Wales – in her old age and valued his counsel. With Princess Beatrice he had lived under the Queen's roof for all of the marriage and she had become deeply attached to him. In December 1895 he had joined the Ashanti expedition in West Africa.

The British had been trading on the Gold Coast (now Ghana) for two centuries – for much of the time in slaves. The first Ashanti wars of the 1870s had largely subdued the coast, but now King Prempeh in the hinterland had to be dealt with. The hinterland needed to be secured so that newly developed crops like cotton, coffee and indigo could be exploited and also to block French encroachment from neighbouring French colonies. In the second Ashanti war the British seized the capital, Kumasi, without a shot being fired. Conveniently, the British troops found some skulls and other evidence of human sacrifice, which reinforced the case for exiling King Prempeh to Sierra Leone. The Ashanti people had to pay a fine of 50,000 ounces of gold, but were allowed to keep their symbol of power, the Golden Stool.[7]

The Queen had opposed Prince Henry going to Africa because of the danger of catching fever, but Beatrice had told her mother that he had set his heart on the expedition and was smarting under his enforced inactivity in England. Liko also wrote to her to plead his cause. She withdrew her opposition with a heavy heart: 'God grant that dear Liko may be brought back safe to us.'[8]

In tears Beatrice saw her husband off at Aldershot station to the tune of 'Auld Lang Syne'. Prince Henry sailed on 8 December 1895 as an auxiliary, but was later made military secretary to the Commander-in-Chief, Sir Francis Scott. He had marched to within 30 miles of Kumasi in the Gold Coast when he was attacked by a fever.[9] Scott telegraphed Princess Beatrice with news of a slight fever on 10 January and thereafter the Queen's Journal is dominated by reports of her son-in-law's condition. 'Can think of nothing but dear Liko.'[10] By 14 January symptoms were showing a great improvement and by 16 January Liko himself sent Beatrice a telegram from hospital at Cape Coast Castle saying he had been very ill.[11] Prince Henry boarded a ship to return to England but died at sea on 20 January. The Queen was devastated:

> This has been such an awful day that it is almost impossible to describe it. A terrible blow has fallen on us all, especially on my poor darling Beatrice. Our dearly loved Liko has been taken from us! ...

> He was so much better, and we were anxiously awaiting the news of his arrival at Madeira. What will become of my poor child? I said I could not

undertake to tell her, and [Prince] Arthur [Duke of Connaught, the Queen's third son] said he would do so gradually and gently. ...

All she said in a trembling voice, apparently quite stunned, was 'the life has gone out of me'. She went back to her room with Louischen [Louise Margaret, Duchess of Connaught] who as well as dear Arthur have been most tender to her, and I felt as if my heart must break.[12]

Princess Louise, Marchioness of Lorne, deeply wounded Beatrice, according to the Duchess of Teck, 'by calmly announcing that she [Louise] was Liko's confidante & Beatrice, nothing to him, indicated by a shrug of the shoulders'.[13]

Beatrice travelled to Portsmouth to meet HMS *Blenheim*, which was carrying Liko's body preserved in rum in a tank made of biscuit tins. The funeral took place at Whippingham Church on the Isle of Wight on 5 February 1896.[14] On 13 February Princess Beatrice left with the children for Cimiez, where they stayed at the Villa Liserb.

Ten days after the Queen had joined Beatrice in Cimiez she wrote to Lord Salisbury:

We have had beautiful weather; but alas! the contrast to last year is very great, a heavy cloud overhangs our poor house everywhere, and all seems to have lost its charm and interest, though the beautiful scenery and vegetation are soothing and enjoyable. We are well and the beloved Princess quite admirable in her courage and patient resignation.[15]

The many major foreign policy issues which arose early in Salisbury's third administration, or which he had inherited, meant that while she was at Cimiez the Queen was consulted much more than on her previous visits to the Riviera. By 23 September she would have been on the throne longer than any predecessor. She had great experience of foreign affairs and did not fail to remind her ministers of the need to consult her.

She discussed the important subjects with Lord Salisbury in their three meetings at Cimiez and exchanged many telegrams with him and other ministers. The issues included the aftermath of the Jameson Raid, Egypt and the Sudan, Matabeleland, the Ashanti expedition and relations with Germany, France and Russia.

On 29 December 1895 Dr Leander Starr Jameson, the Administrator of the British South Africa Company's territory, had crossed the frontier into the Transvaal Republic with some 500 troopers. The aim was to help the Uitlanders, who were the non-Boer settlers, to obtain by force the civil rights which they considered were unjustifiably denied them by

President Kruger. The Transvaal was technically subject to British suzerainty. The British government immediately repudiated the raid and ordered that it should be stopped. Jameson ignored the order, met a Boer force near Krugersdorp, was defeated and surrendered. The Uitlanders in Johannesburg failed to rise in Jameson's support. President Kruger gave up the prisoners from Jameson's party to be put on trial by the British government. Jameson was sentenced in London in July to 15 months' imprisonment, but was released at the end of the year on grounds of ill health. Kruger arrested and put on trial the leaders of the Uitlander Reformers and four of them were sentenced to death. The British government protested and when the Queen heard the news in Cimiez just before she was due to end her holiday she telegraphed to the Colonial Secretary, Joseph Chamberlain, her strong approval of his firm tone and action with Kruger. 'Cannot think Kruger (whom with his Volksraad I greatly distrust) will commit so monstrous an act as to carry out the sentences', she told him. 'We leave in less than an hour. Pray send news to the principal stations, as I am most anxious to hear.'[16] The sentences were commuted.

The Queen's involvement in the aftermath of the Jameson Raid was very personal. Her grandson, the Kaiser, had sent a telegram to Kruger congratulating him on the preservation of his independence:

I sincerely congratulate you that you and your people have succeeded, by your own energetic action and without appealing for help to friendly Powers, in restoring order against the armed bands that broke into your country as disturbers of the peace, and in safeguarding the independence of the country from attacks without.[17]

The British newspapers were furious. The Prince of Wales conveyed to his mother that he thought the message was:

a most gratuitous act of unfriendliness. ... The Prince of Wales would like to know what business the Emperor had to send any message at all. The South African Republic is not an independent state in any sense of the word, and it is under the Queen's suzerainty. What the Emperor has done therefore is doubly unnecessary and unfriendly. H.R.H. only hopes he will not come to Cowes this year.[18]

The Prince of Wales was still smarting from his nephew's behaviour in England the previous year when he had been heard to refer to the Prince of Wales as 'the old popinjay', quarrelled with Lord Salisbury, kept his grandmother waiting for dinner and angrily went home early.[19]

His nephew did not come again to Cowes with his great white yacht *Hohenzollern* until 1899 and was not invited to the Diamond Jubilee in 1897. The Queen wrote to the Kaiser on 5 January 1896:

My dear William, —

... As your Grandmother to whom you have always shown so much affection and of whose example you have always spoken of with so much respect, I feel I cannot refrain from expressing my deep regret at the telegram you sent President Kruger. It is considered very unfriendly towards this country, which I feel sure it is not intended to be, and has, I grieve to say, made a very painful impression here. The action of Dr. Jameson was of course very wrong and totally unwarranted; but considering the very peculiar position in which the Transvaal stands towards Great Britain, I think it would have been far better to have said nothing. Our great wish has always been to keep on the best of terms with Germany, trying to act together, but I fear your Agents in the Colonies do the very reverse, which deeply grieves us. Let me hope you will try and check this.[20]

The Queen received the Kaiser's reply, which she accepted, declaring that he never intended to offend England, that he looked upon the Jameson raiders as rebels against his grandmother and that he only acted in the interests of peace and of German investments in the Transvaal. The Queen regarded the explanations as lame and illogical.[21]

The Queen reproved the government for not consulting her about sending troops to the Cape, which she learned of from the newspapers.[22] Lord Salisbury apologized but, unknowingly anticipating the problems of the monarchy and government with the Press a century later, said that the newspapers' 'emissaries swarm all over the public offices and it is difficult to keep things from them'. He explained that the plan was to give moral and, if necessary, material support to the Portuguese, who had behaved so well in refusing to allow a passage for German sailors to the Transvaal.[23]

Lord Salisbury was inclined to believe that the Kaiser had been trying to frighten England into joining the Triple Alliance between Germany, Austria-Hungary and Italy. He regarded this as impossible because, as he wrote to the Queen, 'Isolation is a much less danger than the danger of being dragged into wars which do not concern us.'[24] The Queen replied that she could not help feeling that isolation was dangerous.[25]

The Prince of Wales and his current mistress, Lady Daisy Warwick, were on the Riviera at the same time as the Queen. Cecil Rhodes, whom the Prince of Wales greatly admired, had had to resign as Prime Minister of the Cape Colony because of his involvement in the Jameson Raid. It was from the Riviera that Lady Warwick wrote to W.T. Stead, the editor of the *Review of Reviews*, who was also an admirer of Rhodes, offering to get the Prince to write letters for Stead to use on Rhodes's behalf.[26]

In March Salisbury realized an opportunity had arisen to regain the Sudan. In Abyssinia an Italian expeditionary force had been defeated by the Negus at Adowa and its hold on Kassala was threatened by the dervishes, who were in ferment throughout Northern Sudan. Partly as a diversion to help the Italians, Kitchener, the British Sirdar in Egypt, was ordered to advance up the Nile to Dongola, which he captured on 23 September. Lord Salisbury kept the Queen informed and she highly approved of the proposed action 'to help the poor Italians'.[27] An interesting sidelight on how the British constitution has changed is her message to Salisbury congratulating him on the large majorities his government had had in the House of Commons following the debate on the Sudan. Such congratulations would have been unthinkable a few years later.[28] 'Every day I feel the blessing of a strong government in such safe and strong hands as yours', she told Salisbury.[29]

Far to the south of the Sudan there had been an uprising in Matabeleland, in what is now Zimbabwe, in which whites were murdered. The Queen sent telegrams from Cimiez to Chamberlain objecting to Sir Hercules Robinson, Governor and Commander-in-Chief of the Cape Colony, being put in charge of the force sent to restore order because he was not fit for it (he was 62), but her advice was not accepted.[30]

In West Africa the Ashanti expedition, in which Prince Henry had died, deposed King Prempeh and exiled him. The Queen discussed it with Canon Taylor Smith after Sunday church at Cimiez where he had preached a beautiful sermon. He told her what a blessing it was that the 'wicked King Prempeh and his horrible mother' had been removed.[31]

In her meeting with Salisbury on 29 March in Cimiez they agreed that the Russian and French opposition to British policy in Egypt and the Sudan was, 'really too preposterous, as any measures taken have nothing to do with them, but are solely for the safety of Egypt and also to afford some help to the poor Italians.'[32] At the meeting on 8 April in Cimiez they talked about Russia and France again:

> Spoke of the incredible behaviour of Russia, who was urging and encouraging France against us with regard to Egypt. He said there was no sensible statesman in England who was not anxious for a good understanding with Russia; but there is a feeling amongst our people against her, and if she shows herself to be so unfriendly, it will make it very difficult for the Government.[33]

When Marie Feodorovna, Empress-Mother of Russia, had called on her at Cimiez two days earlier, the Queen told her that she was very unhappy that Russia was no longer nearly so friendly to England and begged her to mention it to the Tsar. The Empress-Mother promised to do so and said she could not understand the coolness.[34]

On Germany the Queen and Salisbury noted the Kaiser's wish to put things straight after his congratulatory telegram to Kruger over the outcome of the Jameson Raid, which had caused such offence in Britain.[35] The Queen very much hoped the Kaiser would behave. He was her first grandchild and she never forgot that Prince Albert had doted on him. She had been very attached to him when he was a child, but his arrogance, jealousy of the Prince of Wales and mistreatment of his mother, the Princess Royal, when he became Emperor caused her much pain.

The Queen and Lord Salisbury were much concerned with the African activities of another Riviera resident who was a visitor to the Queen at Cimiez. He was her cousin King Leopold II of the Belgians. The King had acquired part of the Congo region as a personal fief, working with Sir Henry Stanley of 'Dr Livingstone, I presume' fame. At the beginning of the year Salisbury had reported to the Queen on an extraordinary conversation with the King of the Belgians in which he wanted the British to use their influence with the Khedive of Egypt to lease him that part of the valley of the Nile in the hands of the Mahdists. When he had subdued them, the British could use the Mahdists to stop the Armenian massacres.[36] The Queen commented that the proposal was quite preposterous and she felt it really seemed as if King Leopold had taken leave of his senses.[37]

At an earlier meeting with Salisbury, King Leopold had proposed that Britain should throw herself into the arms of France, not caring about Germany, because France carried Russia with her and Russia carried Germany. So if the British had France, she had Germany as well. The British should evacuate Egypt; the French would be so pleased that Britain could then annexe China to the Indian Empire.[38]

Leopold's reputation, particularly in his buying of the sexual favours of little girls, was well known. In 1885 when the London *Pall Mall Gazette* ran its exposures of child prostitution, Mrs Jeffries had named him as a client when she was charged with procuring pre-pubescent virgins. A former servant of the brothel testified that Leopold had paid £800[39] a month for a regular supply of young women, some of whom were 10 to 15 years old and guaranteed to be virgins.[40] People wondered why the Queen entertained him as she did. Marie Mallet described a visit:

We have just been receiving the King of the Belgians in the chilly front Hall [of Balmoral], he can only shake hands with two fingers as his nails are so long that he dares not run the risk of injuring them. He is an unctuous old monster, very wicked, I believe. We imagine he thinks a visit to the Queen gives him a fresh coat of whitewash, otherwise why does he travel five hundred miles in order to partake of lunch.[41]

One diplomat said he had the largest nose he had ever seen. Disraeli wrote of his nose: 'It is such a nose as a young prince has in a fairy tale, who has been banned by a malignant fairy, or as you see in the first scenes of a pantomime, or in the initial letter of a column of Punch.'[42]

When she first met him, Queen Victoria considered him very odd and complained about his fondness for saying disagreeable things to people.[43]

The Queen invited him and his daughter, Princess Clémentine, to Jubilee Day, although many other crowned heads were excluded. The Prince of Wales disliked him. Other European royalty were not so tolerant as Queen Victoria. Empress Augusta of Germany got the Court chaplain to exorcize the apartment in which the King had been staying. The American President Theodore Roosevelt refused to allow him to go to the St Louis Exposition. 'We don't want him. He's a dissolute old rake', he shouted, banging the table.[44]

King Leopold, whose astuteness as a businessman is shown by his success in the establishment of the personal empire in the Congo, bought some land on Cap Ferrat on the Riviera in the mid-1890s. When he saw that Cap Ferrat was about to be developed, through his doctor or his architect, he bought up practically all of the peninsula that came on the market. He had the largest estate on Cap Ferrat. The plants in his greenhouses in Laeken in Belgium were famous, and in his new Riviera properties he concentrated on placing many of them in the open air in the milder climate of the South of France.[45] In 1900 he bought the Villa Polonais, which he renamed Villa Les Cèdres, which became the best known privately owned botanical garden in the world. He used to work in the main cabin of his yacht, *Alberta*, but when he returned to land he would sometimes mount his motor tricycle, which he called 'mon animal', and roar off to the Villa Les Cèdres, where his mistress, Baroness de Vaughan, awaited him. He would take a swim with her in his pool with his long white beard tucked into a rubber envelope. On other occasions he would go by steam launch to a pier leading to the Villa through a subterranean passage. He loved secret and mysterious things. 'Anyone could sell him any house so long as it was built on the side of an abandoned quarry or if it had a secret staircase,' the Baroness wrote.[46]

Leopold had first met Caroline Lacroix, a prostitute, in Paris in 1900 when she was about 16. The Belgian King spirited her away to Bad Gastein in Austria. When she was 18 and he was 67, she became pregnant and Leopold and the French government split the cost of constructing a new road near her villa so that her carriage would have a smooth ride.[47] He installed her in the Villa Les Cèdres, where their son Lucien Delacroix was born. Leopold gave Caroline the title of Baroness de Vaughan and the boy that of Duke of Tervuren.

The Belgian Press relished the Baroness scandal for many years. 'The King no longer stoops to prostitution, like his associates, in wild bursts of sensuality and lasciviousness: prostitution climbs to meet the King,' the Brussels morning newspaper Le Peuple wrote. Leopold married the former prostitute on his deathbed on 13 December 1909. He died four days later.[48]

In 1928 Somerset Maugham bought one of the houses which had been owned by the King, the Villa Mauresque, which had originally been built for the King's confessor, Mgr Charmeton. The writer lived there until his death in 1965.[49]

Sir Frederick Ponsonby described the occasion when King Leopold once came to dinner with the Queen at Cimiez: 'He seemed very nervous and frightened of her and sat twisting his hands like a schoolboy. It was curious that she should like him because his morals were notorious, but the Queen seemed to overlook this.'[50]

The morals did not only concern little girls, but also outrageous cruelty to the Congolese. In the previous spring, Sir Charles Dilke, the republican politician, and H.R. Fox-Bourne, secretary of the Aborigines' Protection Society, had launched a major offensive against Leopold both inside and outside Parliament. As early as 1890, missionaries had presented information to the Aborigines' Protection Society about the atrocities. They mainly concerned the 'rubber system'. If a village was slow to deliver its quota, Leopold's men would carry out punitive raids and bring back to headquarters severed human hands to prove they had done their job.[51] Since this massive slaughter, which, using today's terminology, has been described as the Congo's holocaust, was known at the time, one cannot but help wonder what Queen Victoria thought of it as she entertained Leopold on the Riviera.

When the second son of Caroline was born with a deformed hand, a *Punch* cartoon showed Leopold holding the baby surrounded by Congolese corpses with their hands cut off. The caption read: VENGEANCE FROM ON HIGH.[52]

Stanley said of the King's greed, 'he had the enormous voracity to swallow a million of square miles with a gullet that will not take in a herring.'[53]

Another strange relative the Queen had to contend with was actually in the royal party. She was the Queen's daughter, Princess Helena, married to Prince Christian of Schleswig-Holstein. The Queen spoke frequently to Dr Reid about the Princess's inclination to take drugs, like opium and laudanum. She also indulged in secret smoking sessions. While she was at Cimiez in 1896 she claimed she had facial neuralgia, although Reid did not know if she was faking. Three days later she was still claiming she had neuralgia, so Reid put an end to her malingering by stopping all her narcotics and stimulants.[54] She later worked to improve Britain's nursing facilities and was active in charities.

The most important visitors in 1896 were Francis Joseph, the Emperor of Austria, the doyen of Continental secular sovereigns, and the Empress. Francis Joseph reigned as Emperor of Austria for 67 years (1848–1916), longer even than Queen Victoria, and was also King of Hungary from 1867 to 1916. The Queen witnessed the steady decline of Austria-Hungary during his reign. In 1850 Prussia acknowledged Austria's predominance in Germany but its defeat in the Austro-Prussian war of 1866 sealed Austria's expulsion from greater Germany.

Francis Joseph's wife, the Empress Elizabeth (known as Sisi) was the second daughter of Duke Maximilian in Bavaria and was once considered the most beautiful princess in Europe. She soon tired of the protocol of the Viennese Court and spent more and more time away from Francis Joseph, particularly in Budapest and, as a brilliant horsewoman, hunting in Ireland.

The Queen noted in 1896 that the Empress had lost all her beauty, except her figure, which remained the same.[55] This, no doubt, was because she liked walking. For their visit to the Queen at Cimiez in 1896 the Emperor and Empress arrived incognito at Nice railway station by train, took lunch at Rumpelmayer's patisserie on the boulevard Victor-Hugo, and walked the 1½ miles (2.4 kilometres) uphill to Cimiez. They walked back down again after the meeting.[56]

In conversation with the Queen, the Emperor hoped that their two countries would be on the best of terms, although he understood, said the Journal, that the British could not bind themselves in advance to any particular course of action. He regretted the state of Turkey, which he thought was due to the imprudence of the Kaiser, but trusted England and Germany would always keep well together.[57] It was the only time in her life that the Queen had entertained the Emperor and Empress together. The Austrian newspaper *Pester Lloyd* commented that the meeting could only be attended by beneficial consequences for the whole world.[58]

The 1896 visit lasted nearly three weeks and the Emperor enjoyed the food: 'the prime purpose of life here consists only in eating', he wrote.[59]

The Austrian Emperor had first visited the Riviera in March 1894 when he had joined the Empress at Cap Martin for a fortnight's holiday, but Queen Victoria had not been on the Riviera that year. She would have been eager to entertain him. In 1888, travelling incognito by train from Florence to Potsdam, which involved passing through Austria, she was astounded to find, in full uniform, Francis Joseph on the platform at Innsbruck to greet her. She was even more astonished to learn that he had made an overnight train journey of 17 hours in order to see her. Luncheon had been prepared on the station but unfortunately the Queen had a very bad sick headache and could eat next to nothing.[60] It was, the indisposition apart, a happier occasion than their first meeting, which was in Coburg on 3 September 1863. Francis Joseph told his mother that although the Queen was very gracious she became 'quite grumpy ... inclined to have some bees in her bonnet'.[61]

In February 1895 the Emperor and Empress spent a week on the Riviera, but Queen Victoria did not arrive until March. The Emperor saw Mr and Mrs Gladstone walking in the hotel grounds, but decided to avoid meeting one of the harshest critics of Austria. The Emperor believed Gladstone was hostile because, in the Midlothian election campaign of 1879–80, Gladstone had attacked Austria over its attitude to the Ottoman Empire. The Emperor instructed the Austrian Ambassador, Count A. Karolyi, to complain. Gladstone, by now Prime Minister, replied to Karolyi in a letter of 4 May 1880, in which he denied that he was hostile to Austria. He admitted, however, that he had grave apprehensions in case Austria should play a part in the Balkan peninsula 'hostile to the freedom of the emancipated population and to the reasonable and warranted hopes of the subjects of the Sultan'. He did, however, regret any words of a painful and wounding character.[62]

When the Emperor came to lunch with the Queen in 1897 his visit was noteworthy because she asked him to call her the intimate 'du', which, as she recorded, seemed to please him.[63]

The Empress was assassinated in Geneva in 1898. The assassin, an Italian anarchist, wanted to kill the Comte de Paris but, being deprived of his prey, he stabbed Elizabeth to death instead.

A less important visitor in 1896, judging from the police report, was Prince Albert of Monaco. 'This afternoon at three o'clock the Queen received a visit from Prince Albert of Monaco, who only stayed for a few minutes.'[64]

The *Petit Niçois* published a montage of the 18 royal personages who were on the Riviera in the spring of 1896: the Queen of England at Nice, the Empress-Mother of Russia, the Grand Dukes George and Michael Alexandrovitch, the Grand Duchess Olga at la Turbie, the King of the Belgians and his daughter Clémentine at Nice, the King of Sweden at Cannes, the Emperor and Empress of Austria at Menton, the Prince of Wales at Cannes, the Grand Duke Alexis at Monte Carlo, the Grand Duke Michael at Cannes, the Duke of Leuchtenberg at Nice, the Prince and Princess of Bourbon at Cannes, the Prince Louis of Battenberg at Nice, Prince Boris of Bulgaria at Beaulieu.[65] Not in the montage but also on the Riviera in 1896 while the Queen of England was there were Gustav, the Crown Prince of Sweden, the Crown Prince and Princess of Denmark and Maria-Pia, Queen Mother of Portugal.[66]

Many members of the Russian royal family had come to the Riviera during the French Second Empire which was founded in 1852, but after its fall in 1870 the memories of the Paris Commune and the spectre of 'red municipalities' kept them away. In December 1874 the Empress of Russia decided not to go to France as usual, but instead to San Remo in Italy.[67] But gradually the ruling families drifted back, with a good example having been set by the British monarch in 1882.

The Queen's eyes were troubling her. She had read to her *Fire and Sword in the Sudan* by Slatin Pasha. The Queen thought the account of all he did and suffered was most thrilling. 'What he went through and witnessed before he was in captivity is fearful.'[68] Slatin Pasha (Baron Rudolf Slatin) was an Austrian soldier in the service of Britain in the Sudan, famous for his imprisonment by the Mahdists and his escape after 12 years. Beatrice read to her mother a curious account of the Black Plague in China, but the Queen does not tell us why it was curious.[69]

Rides by carriage and donkey trap were similar to those of 1895, but a highlight of the journeys was that on one of her regular visits to the heights of Gairaut, exceptional atmospheric conditions prevailed and the royal party could see the snow-clad mountains of Corsica.[70] La Turbie was added to the places to be visited because the Empress-Mother of Russia, Marie Feodorovna, was there at her house, the Villa les Terrasses. Marie Feodorovna was close to the Queen because her sister, Alexandra, was married to the Prince of Wales. She had become Empress when her husband succeeded to the throne as Alexander III in 1881 on the assassination of his father, Alexander II. Two years before Queen Victoria visited Marie Feodorovna her husband had died, so she spent more time on the Riviera.

The day before the royal party's departure on 19 April, the Journal brought a sad visit to an end with the plaintive entry:

Our last day here, in this beautiful country, which I so admire and love, and the last time we shall stay in this comfortable Hotel. The new enormous erection, which is nearly finished, will so overshadow it, that it will be impossible to live here.[71]

CHAPTER 8

1897: Nice. The courtiers revolt over the Munshi

A revolution from her own staff faced the monarch before she could leave for her seventh visit to the Riviera. She was determined to include the Munshi in her party, as she had in 1892 and 1895, despite the opposition of her household. The Gentlemen, as the male courtiers were known, charged a brave young lady, the maid of honour, Harriet Phipps, with personally delivering the household's ultimatum to the monarch: she must choose between the Munshi or the household. The Queen's reply was to sweep, with one imperious gesture, all the objects off her desk.

The Munshi affair, which reached its greatest point of crisis while the Queen was on the Riviera, is important, not merely because of the struggle of wills between the monarch and the household, but because the Queen was also fighting for what she saw as her principles on racialism, class and the underdog.

Since December, Reid had been treating the Munshi for a recurrence of gonorrhoea and he told the Queen about it on 20 February. That had not deterred her from wanting to take the Munshi to Cimiez, where he would have to eat with the Gentlemen.[1]

The Court Circular showed who was standing firm, when it announced that the Munshi was in the royal party which left Windsor on 10 March. The household did not resign. On 11 March *The Times* reported that when the Queen arrived at Portsmouth on the first leg of her journey to Nice she leant on the arm of the Munshi when she walked from the train to the royal yacht.[2] On the train the Munshi had his own sleeping saloon, but the Indian attendants were in a corridor carriage.[3] He would have been delighted by being presented to President Faure when he visited the Queen's train, which was reported in the Court Circular, and he got a mention for his dress in the *Times* report of the visit: 'The colours and style of dress worn by the Munshi and Indian Secretary, Hafiz Abdul Karim, added to the effect.'[4]

The Galignani Messenger reported:

> As for the Munshi Abdul Kareem, although every deference is paid to him, and he is generally seen following the Royal carriage in a separate carriage drawn by splendid horses, each Niçois is firmly convinced that he sees in him a captive Native prince, attached, as it were, to the chariot-wheels of the Empress of India.[5]

The Queen had won round one, but the Prince of Wales came to Cimiez and interviewed Reid, as the doctor recorded in his diary, 'about the Munshi and the crisis which the Queen's treatment of, and relations with him is bringing on. I told H.R.H. much that I knew, and how serious I think it. He was much impressed, and promised to support us in any action we may take.'[6]

The trouble came when Raffiuddin Ahmed, a friend of the Munshi's involved with the Muslim Patriotic League and believed by many at Court to be an Afghan spy, arrived. He was suspected of leaking secret dispatches which the Queen had shown the Munshi. Sir John Tyler, Chief of Police of North West India, had earlier told Reid all about the Munshi and Ahmed:

> The Queen had made a vital mistake in giving the Munshi the C.I.E. [Companion of the Order of the Indian Empire]; that he is a man of very low origin and of no education, that he was never anything but a 'Khitmagar' [table servant] in wh. capacity he was sent here; and that the idea of his being considered a gentleman is most ludicrous to those who know him; that the accounts of him published by Raffiudin Ahmed in *Black and White* and other magazines were false in almost every particular, and that Raffiudin Ahmed is a clever but unscrupulous and dangerous man who ought never under any pretext to be admitted into any of the Queen's houses; that he uses the Munshi as a tool for his own purposes; and that when it will serve his purpose, he will be the first man to expose him and turn him into ridicule with the public, wh. he will have no difficulty in doing.[7]

Ahmed had not been invited to Cimiez, where the royal party had arrived on 12 March, so at 48 hours' notice, to the fury of the Munshi, the household banished Ahmed from Cimiez.[8] The Queen later eventually agreed that Ahmed was 'a journalist and a meddler', but still tried to get Lord Salisbury to give him a job. She also wanted Salisbury to apologize to him for his expulsion from Cimiez and to explain that it was entirely because he was a journalist. The Queen seems to have assumed that membership of that profession justified such ill-treatment. Nevertheless she also believed that the 'disgraceful affair' of the expulsion from Cimiez should not prevent him from being invited to at least one Court ball. Lord Salisbury eventually admitted to the Queen that the suspicions about Ahmed were unjust.[9] He also cleared the Munshi.[10]

With Raffiudin on his way back to London from Nice, the Gentlemen turned their attention to the Munshi. On 27 March the Queen brought into the affair Prince Louis of Battenberg, who was married to her granddaughter, Princess Victoria of Hesse and the Rhine, and who was the liaison between her and the household. Prince Louis told Arthur Davidson, the groom-in-waiting, that the Queen wanted the Gentlemen to associate more with the Munshi. The household were up in arms and Reid recorded that 'all agreed to stand together and to resign if H.M. presses the matter'. When Reid told Prince Louis that he had been questioned about Her Majesty's sanity the Prince seemed to agree. There were many conferences and on 30 March, having heard from Reid what he knew about the Munshi, the Queen admitted 'she had been foolish in acceding to his constant requests for advancement but yet trying to shield him.'[11]

Reid also advised the Queen that he had received a letter from the Chief of Police for London, Sir Edward Bradford, warning him of the Munshi's complicity in the affairs of the Muslim Patriotic League:

> H.M. quite caved in. In the evening, before dinner the Queen quite broke down to me, admitted she had played the fool about the Munshi; cried and said she knew what people were saying about her; begged piteously to be "let down easily" and promised to do all we wanted only not abruptly for fear of scandal.[12]

On 4 April Reid had a traumatic meeting with the monarch, in which he boldly told her:

> It seems to me that Your Majesty is only thinking of the Munshi's feelings: but that is of infinitesimal importance compared with the gravity of the situation as regards Your Majesty. As I said to Your Majesty before, there are people in high places, who know Your Majesty well, who say to me that the only charitable explanation that can be given is that Your Majesty is not sane, and that the time will come when to save Your Majesty's memory and reputation it will be necessary for me to come forward and say so: and that is a nice position for me to be in. I have seen the Prince of Wales yesterday and he again spoke to me very seriously on the subject. He says he has quite made up his mind to come forward if necessary, because quite apart from all the consequences to the Queen, it affects himself most vitally. ... Because it af-

fects the throne.[13]

The Queen continued to vacillate. The next day there was a 'very painful interview in the morning with the Queen, who got into a most violent passion and said we had all behaved disgracefully', wrote her doctor. 'I replied to her in such terms that she was obliged to ask me not to repeat what she had said!' The Prince of Wales thanked Reid for all he had done, knowing that there was no one else who would have had the courage to speak to the Queen in such a way.[14]

Reid then met the Munshi and delivered the riot act:

By your presumption and arrogance you have created for yourself a situation that can no longer be permitted to exist. The Queen has believed all the lies you have told her and in her kindness has given you all that you have asked for up to now; but she is beginning to find out what everyone in England and India knows, viz., that you are an impostor. On the subject of your origin we have a certificate from India about your Father, your wife and yourself. You are from a very low class and never can be a gentleman. Your education is nil. To be called 'Secretary' is perfectly ridiculous; you could not write either an English or an Indian letter that would not disgrace the name of Secretary. You have a double face, one which you show to the Queen, and another when you leave her room. The Queen says she finds you humble and 'honest' and kind to everybody! What is the reality? The Queen says the other Indians like and respect you. What do they tell me? And what would they say if they were not afraid of you and the old ones were brought back to give evidence? You have been deceiving the Queen in other ways. ... You have told the Queen that in India no receipts are given for money, and therefore you ought not to give any to Sir F. Edwards [Keeper of the Privy Purse]. This is a lie and means that you wish to cheat the Queen. The Police know this and other things. The Queen's letters in your possession are asked for by H.M. Where are they? Why have you not given them up at once? You had better do so now or it will be the worse for you. If the Queen were to die and any letters of hers were found in your possession no mercy will be shown you. The Queen does not know all I have told you because it would shock her greatly to know how completely you have deceived her and what a scoundrel you are, and she hopes it may be possible for you to stay with her still. But this can only be if your 'position' is altogether taken away. No one of the Queen's Gentlemen can recognise you in any way whatever. But if it be necessary to tell the Queen all about how you have deceived the Queen then it will be impossible for you to remain in England. Prince Louis was to have been sent by the Queen to speak to you but that would be much more serious than my coming. But he will come next if it be necessary. The Queen says you tell her you are in great distress and can't sleep or eat and Her Majesty in her great kindness is sorry to hear it. But if you do this again, and try to humbug the Queen, the Q. will be told everything about you, and then her pity will be turned to anger when she finds out how you have deceived her and you will only hasten your ruin.[15]

Reid said the Munshi was to a certain degree chastened after this diatribe, but some time was to pass before he accepted his true place in the household. Before leaving Cimiez the Queen wrote a memorandum on how the Munshi should be treated, and wished the Gentlemen 'should not go on talking about this painful subject either amongst themselves, or with outsiders and not <u>combine</u> with the Household against the person'.[16]

She wrote to Sir Henry Ponsonby:

to make out that he [the Munshi] is so <u>low</u> is really <u>outrageous</u> & in a country like England quite out of place as anyone can [see] this. She has known 2 Archbishops who were the sons respectively of a Butcher & a Grocer, a Chancellor whose father was a poor sort of Scotch Minister, Sir D. Stewart & Ld Mount Stephen both who ran about barefoot as children & whose parents were very humble & the tradesmen M. & J. P. were made Baronets! Abdul's father saw good and honourable service as a Dr & he [Abdul] feels cut to the heart at being thus spoken of.

It probably comes from some low jealous Indians or Anglo-Indians. ... The Queen is so sorry for the poor Munshi's sensitive feelings.[17]

The Munshi boasted that his father was a Surgeon-General in the Indian Army. Frederick Ponsonby, an equerry, told the Queen that he was not even a doctor, but an apothecary in a hospital, which she hotly denied. Such was the Queen's fury at any aspersions cast on the Munshi that to punish Ponsonby she did not invite him to dinner when they were in Cimiez together one year.[18]

In *Queen Victoria* Elizabeth Longford has made the interesting point that Queen Victoria's love affair with the colonial races should long have been one of the hallmarks of her greatness, but it was scarcely mentioned by historians before the Second World War. She says:

It was only after the disintegration of European colonial empires, Britain's included, that racism became a dirty word. Then, for the first time, it was realised that the Great White Queen held a special brief for her brown and black peoples, and that Queen Victoria could lecture reactionary courtiers on the evils of racial prejudice every bit as eloquently as any member of an international movement today.[19]

Sarah Bernhardt helped the Queen forget about all the trouble over the Munshi for one evening. She had come to Nice from 19 to 27 April to act in plays which included *La Tosca*, *La Dame aux Camélias* and *Lorenzaccio*, and stayed in the Excelsior Régina where she took the whole of the first floor of the east wing for herself and her company.[20] Several members of the household pressed the Queen to invite her to perform, but she at first refused because she thought her code of morality was not quite what it should have been.[21] Her daughter, Victoria, had written to her daughter, Sophie, in 1893 that although Sarah Bernhardt was 'an extraordinary actress from all I have heard, I hope you did <u>not</u> make her acquaintance, as alas no <u>lady</u> can, she is so very bad, and has an awful reputation. It is a pity those immoral pieces are always given, such as you saw.'[22]

Lady Frederick Cavendish had written in her diary on 6 July 1879:

> London has gone mad over the principal actresses in the Comédie Française who are here: Sarah Bernhardt – a woman of notorious shameless character. ... Not content with being run after on the stage, this woman is asked to respectable people's houses to act, and even to luncheon and dinner; and all the world goes. It is an outrageous scandal.[23]

We do not know if the Queen was aware of the goings-on of the Prince of Wales with the actress, or if she was thinking of other reports. On one occasion when Bernhardt came to London, the Prince went to her gala French Fête at the Albert Hall, which was a sort of charity bazaar. The Prince bought a self-portrait in oils from her and Princess Alexandra two blue-eyed white kittens. He stayed at her stall until she had taken £256. Bernhardt did not perform at the theatre that night and also called off a rehearsal. She wrote to her manager, 'I'm just back from the Prince of Wales at twenty past one and can't rehearse now. He has kept me since eleven.'

When, on another occasion in Paris, the Prince confessed to Sarah Bernhardt during an interval of the tragedy *Fédora* that secretly he wished to be an actor, she had him put on a costume and installed him in a bed on the stage. He lay there for much of the last act, pretending to be dead. Finally Sarah entered to find the dead body of her Vladimir and kissed and murmured over the Prince.[24]

The Queen finally gave way and invited Bernhardt to perform. About 30 or 40 people attended. A stage was improvised by placing a dais at one end of the Queen's large reception room, with screens substituting for scenery.[25] The Queen recorded the event in her diary:

1. RIGHT. Sir Henry Ponsonby, the Queen's Private Secretary, had to deal with delicate points of protocol on the Riviera. The Queen detested republics and when in 1898 Félix Faure, President of the French Republic, called on the Queen, who hated republics, Ponsonby had to make arrangements for his reception that showed clearly that he did not quite rank with monarchs.

2. ABOVE. Marie Mallet, the Queen's Maid of Honour, got round the ban on keeping a diary while in the Queen's service by writing letters home, which give a fascinating insight into the Queen's life on the Riviera.

3. RIGHT. Sir James Reid, the Queen's Personal Physician, not only had to deal with the physical health of the Queen but also with the ebb and flow of her emotions.

4. Cannes from the Villa Edelweiss, where the Queen stayed in 1887. She disapproved of Cannes where the Prince of Wales engaged in his womanising, but she went there because her youngest son, Prince Leopold, had died there three years earlier.

5. ABOVE. The Villa Edelweiss and below it the Villa
Nevada, where Prince Leopold had died. He was a
haemophiliac who had slipped on the stairs of the
yacht club.

RIGHT. The memorial fountain to Prince Leopold
near the Villa Nevada was built with money
contributed both by the foreign and local community.

7. Queen Victoria at Grasse in 1891 in the grounds of the Grand Hôtel where she stayed. The principal attraction of Grasse for her was the vast gardens of the fierce Alice de Rothschild, who reproved the Queen for stepping on a flower bed.

8. The royal sitting room, Grand Hôtel, Grasse. The Queen brought many of her photographs and other mementoes to the Riviera to create as familiar a domestic environment as possible. She sent ahead over 70 boxes of luggage together with horses and carriages.

9. OPPOSITE. The Battle of the Flowers in Grasse in 1891 appealed to the old Queen's girlish streak. She would pelt the revellers from the balcony of her hotel, demanding ever more flowers. Her staff had to retrieve the flowers from the street only to have the Queen throw them down again.

10. RIGHT. The Maharajah Duleep Singh in 1877. He visited the Queen in Grasse in 1891 to receive her forgiveness for past sins, which included intriguing in India against the British, who had annexed the Punjab.

11. BELOW. The Queen leaving the Church of All Saints, Costebelle, in 1892. Although she was Head of the Anglican Church, the Queen did not hesitate to visit the nearby Catholic church of Notre Dame de Consolation, which had famous decorations.

12. RIGHT. The Queen driving in her pony trap on a visit in 1892 to the gardens of the Hôtel Hermitage in Hyères, where her courtiers ensured she did not visit the gardens of Sir Charles Dilke, one of the principal critics of the monarchy.

13. BELOW. The Queen's bedroom at the Hôtel Costebelle, where in 1892 she stayed in Hyères, a resort already well used to royalty. It had been a resort for French kings for centuries.

Neuvième année. — N° 424   Huit pages : CINQ centimes   Dimanche 21 Mars 1897

Le Petit Parisien

SUPPLÉMENT LITTÉRAIRE ILLUSTRÉ

TOUS LES JOURS
Le Petit Parisien
5 CENTIMES

DIRECTION: 18, rue d'Enghien, PARIS

TOUS LES JEUDIS
SUPPLÉMENT LITTÉRAIRE
5 CENTIMES.

LA REINE D'ANGLETERRE EN FRANCE
Le Wagon-Salon de la Reine

14. The drawing-room of the Royal Train. The Queen's coaches on her visits to the Riviera consisted of a sitting room and a sleeping car. Xavier Paoli, the French official in charge of royal security, thought it presented '... in its somewhat antiquated splendour, the exact appearance of an old-fashioned apartment in a provincial town.'

15. The Queen's arrival in Nice in March 1897, where she was met by British and French dignitaries.

16. Lord Salisbury, British Prime Minister, who had a house at Beaulieu where he and the Queen exchanged visits. He was regarded locally as a figure of considerable fun. He was refused admission to the Monte Carlo Casino because of his dress, which included a dirty battered trilby pulled down to his ears.

17. Leopold II, King of the Belgians, had a house on Cap Ferrat where he built another one for his mistress, Caroline Lacroix, a former prostitute, who he married on his deathbed.

18. Sarah Bernhardt, the actress, stayed in the same hotel as the Queen, who initially shunned her because she thought her code of morality was not quite what it should have been. But eventually the actress did perform for the Queen.

19. Queen Victoria and Abdul Karim – the Munshi. The courtiers did not like the Indian secretary and threatened to strike when she insisted on bringing him to the Riviera. He came nevertheless. They objected that he dined with them and disliked his airs and graces.

20. The one-legged beggar of Nice, Charles Alberique, would frequently race the Queen on a dog cart, which always amused her. He would be rewarded with money. When he decorated the cart with the inscription 'By special appointment to Her Majesty' the courtiers made him remove it.

21. Tea on a country drive outside Nice. The Queen's Indian servants went ahead to prepare refreshments half an hour before the expected arrival of the royal party. Despite her love of the Riviera, afternoon tea was an English habit she could not forgo.

22. Lunch in the royal dining room at the Hôtel Excelsior Régina, Cimiez, above Nice. The Queen entertained many members of European royalty, who were often her relatives, while she was on the Riviera.

EXCELSIOR
HOTEL RÉGINA
à Nice
CIMIEZ

EXCELSIOR REGINA

CARTE DU RESTAURANT

Menu

Potage Crème d'Orge
Consommé Deslignac
Hors-d'œuvre
Turbans de filets de soles St Nantu
Filet de Bœuf à la Richelieu
Poulardes du Mans truffées
Chaufroix de Cailles à la Chantilli
Salade
Haricots verts
Bombe Nélusko
Desserts

Vins
Médoc en Carafes
Pontet Canet 1869
Corton 1870
Champagne Lyon d'Or frappé

Café et Liqueurs

RESTAURANT
Déjeuners Diners
SOUPERS
à toutes les heures
TABLE D'HÔTE
par petites Tables
SALONS
PARTICULIERS

23. The menu of the Hôtel Excelsior Régina. The Queen usually dined at nine o'clock or later. One of her dinner guests later in her life was the Aga Khan, who commented that 'The Queen, in spite of her age, [she was 79] ate and drank heartily – every kind of wine that was offered, and every course, including both the hot and the iced pudding.'

At ½ p.6 the celebrated & famous actress Sarah Bernhardt, who has been acting at Nice and is staying in this Hotel performed a little piece for me in the Drawingroom, at her own request. The play was called Jean Marie by Adrien Fleuriet [a note in the margin says this should read André Theuriet (1833–1907)], quite short, only lasting ½ an hour. It is extremely touching and Sarah Bernhardt's acting was quite marvellous, so pathetic and full of feeling. She appeared much affected herself, tears rolling down her cheeks. She has a most beautiful voice and is very graceful in all her movements. The story is much the same as that of 'Old Robin Grey'. The 2, who acted with her were also excellent, particularly the one who took the part of Jean Marie. The scene is laid in Brittany. When the play was over, Edith L. presented Sarah Bernhardt to me and I spoke to her for a few moments. Her manner was most pleasing and gentle. She said it had been such a pleasure and honour to act for me. When I expressed the hope she was not tired, she answered 'cela m'a reposé'. She leaves tomorrow for Marseilles.[26]

Sarah Bernhardt had had a great wish to perform before the Queen, and when Lady Lytton called her up to present her to the Queen tears were rolling down the actress's cheeks with emotion. The Queen told Lady Lytton what a pleasure it had been and her lady-in-waiting told her of how good Sarah was to her fellow artists and how she had got a gold medal for attending to the wounded after the Franco-Prussian war.[27]

The Queen put one of her pearl bracelets on Bernhardt's wrist and the actress took off one of hers and gave it to the Queen, who also gave her a photograph.[28] A minor crisis blew up, however, over the Birthday Book. The Birthday Book was where people the Queen had met wrote their names on the appropriate page for their birthday. It accompanied the Queen everywhere, although she could no longer read it. Sometimes it had been mistaken for a bible. When the Queen had left, Sir Frederick Ponsonby asked Bernhardt to sign it on the page for her birthday. To his surprise the actress knelt down on the floor to write and took up nearly a whole page with 'Le plus beau jour de ma vie' and an enormous signature. When the Queen saw it she was much put out and severely reproved Sir Frederick. The actress should have signed in the artists' book, he should not have let her take up a whole page and Sir Frederick was to get Bernhardt to sign again in the correct book. With great difficulty Sir Frederick managed to get access to the actress in an interval of La Tosca in which she was performing before she left for Marseilles. To get her to sign again he had to pretend that the new book was more intimate. But first there was no pen and ink, so one of the companions in the dressing room, whom Ponsonby assumed to be her lover, spent the next act tracking some

down. Then there was no blotting paper and while she was pretending to
wait for the ink to dry, Bernhardt spotted the other names in it and saw
that she had originally signed the wrong book and that this was the second-
class volume. 'She handed back the book to me with a shrug of her shoulders,' poor Sir Frederick recorded.[29]

The Queen needed such distractions because she was worried not only
about the Munshi and the household but about international crises. She
had written in her Journal of her meeting on the train on the way out with
President Faure:

> At a little before 6 stopped at the junction of Noisy-le-Sec on the Ceinture
> railway outside Paris. Here, the President of the Republic Mons: Félix Faure
> came into my saloon and was presented by Sir E. Monson [British Ambassa-
> dor]. I received the President alone and asked him to sit down. We had some
> conversation and he began by compliments about my coming again to France,
> saying the pleasure it gave the people to have me in their country. Then I re-
> marked that the present was a very anxious time, that political affairs seemed
> very difficult, in which he agreed. He was thankful the English and French
> had been able to rescue the unfortunate 3000 Turks. He felt very much for
> Willy of Greece, whom he knew well, but said it would not do to begin to
> dismember Turkey. She might have avoided all, if some time ago, she had
> listened to the advice given her. Mons: Faure is a tall good looking man, eld-
> erly, very gentlemanlike and pleasing, evidently sensible and quiet.[30]

The Queen was particularly concerned about Willy of Greece. William
was his name as a Prince of Denmark, whence he had come to be created
King of Greece at the invitation of the Greeks. He was related to the
Queen by marriage, as his sister Alexandra was the wife of the Prince of
Wales. Crete was part of the Turkish Empire, but Cretan insurgents had
risen against the Turks in May 1896 and demanded union with Greece.
Greece sent troops to help them. The European powers, Austria, Britain,
France, Germany, Italy and Russia decided on intervention. About 600
Turkish soldiers and 2500 Turkish civilians were trapped by the insurgents
in the district of Selinos, including Candanos, and in March 1897 an
international force rescued them.[31] Greece declared war on Turkey in
April 1897. Turkey won, but the European powers intervened and in
1898 Crete was given autonomy. It was united with Greece in 1913. The
idea of the dismemberment of the Turkish Empire was one which had
frequently been mooted. Lord Salisbury, British Prime Minister and
Foreign Secretary, had run the idea past Bismarck in 1887.[32] But, two
months after the French President had expressed his views on its undesir-

ability, a treaty between Austria and Russia, critical players in any break-up, signed on 5 May 1897, saw to it there was no break-up and put the Near East on ice for the next decade.[33]

The British Embassy clearly put up the *Times* correspondent to write a story refuting what French newspapers had written about the political significance of the meeting between the British and French heads of state. He attached great importance to the significance of low-key dress and decorations:

> There has never been any intention or project of giving to this demonstration of natural politeness and sympathy any political signification, and from the first it has been understood and settled that the real purpose of the meeting was the desire of the Queen to give public testimony of her feelings towards the country in which she repeatedly seeks and receives an invigorating and pleasant rest, by meeting the head of the French Republic and expressing to him her sentiments towards France and intrusting him with the agreeable task of acquainting with those sentiments the whole hospitable French nation.

> Noisy le Sec, where the interview took place, from the point of view of landscape charm is, with its monotonous patches of kitchen garden, not much more distinguished in aspect than Clapham, is a railway junction whose outward aspect would seem to suggest that it is the last place in the world that would be chosen as a background for any event even remotely deserving to be classed as historic.[34]

Despite what the correspondent of the Thunderer wrote, the Queen did not consider herself a cypher in international affairs. She met Lord Salisbury in Cimiez on 19 April, just after war had been declared between Greece and Turkey:

> After luncheon saw Lord Salisbury. I expressed to him my great anxiety at the state of affairs, and stated that I thought it would become necessary for us to take action regardless of Germany, (who has been behaving so ill) in order to stop further bloodshed. Lord Salisbury said the time was coming when we should have to break away from Germany and Austria, but not quite yet. He feared Greece would be defeated, which he could not allow. I said it was important we should work well with Russia, which he is also anxious should be the case.[35]

Although Lord Salisbury said they could not allow Greece to be defeated, the Journal reported on 24 April:

> Before dinner received the distressing news of the defeat of the poor Greeks. It makes me very unhappy. Telegraphed to Lord Salisbury to press that something should be done. He answered that he intends proposing a Confer-

ence at Paris, of the Ambassadors, to agree on the terms of an armistice. Feel so distressed for poor Vicky, Sophy and Alix.[36]

Vicky was her daughter and the mother of the Kaiser; Sophie, Vicky's daughter and wife of the Crown Prince of Greece; and Alix, the Princess of Wales and sister of the King of Greece.

Lord Salisbury did not regard the Queen as a cypher: 'received a message from Lord Salisbury saying he thought it very desirable for me to telegraph to Nicky [Nicholas II, Tsar of Russia], urging him to do what he could for the restoration of peace. I accordingly telegraphed in strong terms.'[37] And then two days later: 'Had a very satisfactory answer from Nicky, in which he entirely shares my views of anxiety to put a stop to the war. ... This is very satisfactory.'[38]

On a visit by train to the Hôtel du Parc in Cannes on 26 March to see the Queen of Hanover, Queen Victoria met her old enemy, Gladstone. Princess Louise had invited the Gladstones to tea and then slipped them in to see her mother. The Queen had not seen him since he had resigned as Liberal Prime Minister on 3 March 1894. The meeting was perfunctory, to say the least. Her Journal recorded:

> We went into the drawing room, where we met the dear Queen [of Hanover], whom I had not seen for nineteen years, and she expressed much pleasure at seeing me again. Mr. and Mrs. Gladstone came in for a moment, both looking much aged, and she very shaky and much altered, but she seemed delighted to see me.[39]

Gladstone, now 87, was touched by the meeting, brief though it was. He found her 'decidedly kind, such as I had not seen it for a good while before my final resignation; and she gave me her hand ... which had not happened with me during all my life.'[40] Nevertheless, the brevity of the meeting, which he put at ten minutes, rather than a moment, caused him to comment, 'To speak frankly, it seemed to me that the Queen's peculiar faculty and habit of conversation had disappeared.'[41] He also remarked that the Queen's room was 'populated by a copious supply of Hanoverian royalties'.[42]

Typical of the animosity the Queen had felt for Gladstone was the sentiment contained in her letter to Sir Henry Ponsonby in 1880 that she would 'sooner abdicate than send for or have any communication with that half-mad fire-brand who w[d] soon ruin everything and be a Dictator. Others but herself may submit to his democratic rule, but not the Queen.'[43]

She did not of course abdicate and she did have communication with him. Gladstone resigned for the last time in 1894 because of ill health. When he tendered his resignation at an audience at Windsor they talked about the weather and her plans for an Italian holiday. She did not tell him she regretted his resignation, but only the cause, that is to say, his illness.[44] He was very hurt. He recalled in a memorandum a ride on a mule on a visit to Sicily:

> I well remember having at the time a mental experience which was not wholly unlike a turn of indigestion. I had been on the back of the beast for many scores of hours, it had done me no wrong; it had rendered me much valuable service, but it was in vain to argue; there was the fact staring me in the face. I could not get up the smallest shred of feeling for the brute, I could neither love nor like it.

> A rule of three sum is all that is necessary to conclude with. What that Sicilian mule was to me, I have been to the Queen; and the fortnight or three weeks are represented by 52 or 53 Years.[45]

The issues on which the Queen principally differed with Gladstone concerned foreign policy and the constitution. She regarded as unpatriotic his moralistic attitude to the Ottoman Empire, which she saw as a bulwark against the Russian threat to the route to India, over such matters as the Bulgarian massacres. The constitutional issue was Gladstone's Irish Home Rule policy. The development of her relationship with Gladstone was the reverse of that with Salisbury: in Gladstone's case initial approval had turned to disapproval.

The historian Robert Blake has described Gladstone's relations with the Queen as 'frigid, formal and time-consuming'. To the three monarchical rights of 'the right to be consulted, the right to encourage and the right to warn', as stated by the nineteenth-century writer on the English constitution, Walter Bagehot, she had added a fourth – 'the right to harrass'. Little was known of this relationship outside a very restricted circle while Gladstone was alive. If it had been, Blake considered the monarchy might have been in real danger.

The Queen's book, *More Leaves from the Journal of a Life in the Highlands*, conveyed an image of the Queen as an essentially non-political figure, interested only in country activities. Gladstone took great trouble to shield her and avoid tarnishing this image. This was certainly part of her character, as her Journals on her time on the Riviera showed, and Gladstone described the Highland Journals as 'innocence itself'. But, Blake says, 'He must have known that there was another side which he would not – perhaps could not – reveal.'[46]

While the Queen was on the Riviera in 1897 she was preparing herself for the Diamond Jubilee which was to take place on and around 22 June. But although Gladstone was the senior Privy Councillor, she does not appear to have invited him to play any participatory role.[47]

In contrast to the Queen's relationship with Gladstone, the anniversary of the death of Benjamin Disraeli on 19 April 1881 usually fell in the time of her stay on the Riviera and she dutifully noted it in her Journal.

Over Christmas 1882 Gladstone was suffering from insomnia, which by January had become an obsession. Dr Clark, his physician, recommended six weeks' rest cure on the Riviera. Lord Wolverton, Paymaster-General and a close friend, made his house in Cannes, the Château Scott, available. Members of the party in addition to Lord Wolverton himself, and some of Gladstone's family, included Lord Acton, who went down in history for coining the famous aphorism,'Power tends to corrupt and absolute power corrupts absolutely.' The visit was a great success. 'I am stunned by this wonderful place', Gladstone wrote in his diaries. He liked the routine: 'Here we fall into the foreign hours: the snack early, déjeuner à la fourchette at noon, dinner at 7, break-up at 10.'[48] The 'people's William' even took part in the Battle of the Flowers in Nice and he recorded that he 'was pelted largely'.[49] Gladstone quickly recovered his sleep, although his wife did not.[50] 'I part from Cannes with a heavy heart,' was his last entry about his stay.[51]

In his biography of Gladstone, Roy Jenkins says that Cannes was central to Gladstone's years of decline, a healthful repose, rather than a stimulus, an old man's rest home. He had been there from early January to late March 1895, with a side expedition to Cap Martin, from the end of December 1895 to early March 1896, and from January 1897 for a couple of months.[52]

Nine months after his last meeting with the Queen, Gladstone celebrated his 88th birthday in Cannes, but it was a far from happy occasion, ill as he was with cancer and, as he described, with 'roaring pains'. He was staying with Lord Riddell, whose daughter had married Gladstone's son. He left the house in Cannes in February 1898 and died on 19 May.[53]

Gladstone's comment on the large number of Hanoverians in Cannes was echoed by Salisbury, who joked that on the Riviera one had a choice between royalty in the winter and mosquitoes in the summer.[54]

The Queen did not only entertain the famous. She made friends with a little Dutch girl, Annie, in the grounds of the hotel and gave her and her dog, Johnny, rides in her pony cart. She also invited them to tea.[55]

An indication of the increasing impact on tourism of the Queen's visits over the previous 15 years is given by the report that on 18 March 1897 no less than 100 carriages had assembled near the hotel to see the Queen go out for her daily drive.[56]

The owners of those carriages were able to keep in touch with who else was in town from the English-language newspapers, which published lists of the visitors. Typical was *The Menton and Monte Carlo News – A Society Journal with List of Visitors*. It was published weekly in winter. Hotel keepers provided the lists, with nationality, and visitors in villas registered their names in the Visitors' Book of the newspaper.[57]

The Queen said she felt rather strange in the new Excelsior Hôtel Régina and missed her well-known rooms in the old Grand Hôtel. But she liked the fact that the royal party had a whole wing to itself and a private entrance.[58] She later commented that everything was comfortable and practically arranged and that she liked her rooms.[59] The hotel had been designed to take account of the Queen's difficulty in walking. The English party had 70 rooms in the west wing and the cost was FF80,000 (£3200)[60] for eight weeks.[61] Lady Lytton thought the cooking, done by one of the Queen's cooks and one from the hotel, was excellent.[62]

On her arrival at the hotel she attended a big welcoming dinner.[63] The attentive management had hung copies of famous paintings of the Queen's Hanoverian ancestors in the dining room.[64]

The entrepreneur behind the building of the hotel was Antonin Raynaud, a perfume manufacturer from Grasse, who had had earlier financial connections with Henri Germain.[65] It cost, according to the local paper, FF8 million (£320,000).[66] [67] The hotel was the latest in luxury and the style was the most extravagant Belle Epoque. Aristide Veran, a journalist on *L'Eclaireur de Nice*, was allowed to visit the royal apartments the day before the Queen's arrival. This was his report:

After the awning and gate of the west tower, you cross a sky-blue carpet patterned with fleur de lys, into a hall, the walls rather severely covered with imitation leather, but here and there relieved by plants and delicate flower arrangements.

At the back of the hall a lift with artistic ironwork serves the ground floor and the first floor, the same that houses Her Majesty's room. ...

Do not leave the hall without noting the adjacent charming chapel where the Queen will attend services from a platform draped in red. ...

The Queen's appartments occupy the whole of the first floor. ... The Queen's bedroom has two windows, one giving on to the west and one to the north, the walls being entirely covered in rose silk. There are no pictures. This severity is tempered by a yellow plush rug and green silk blinds.[68]

And so on for column after column for the delectation of the Niçois, so long deprived of a monarch of their own, and eager to read every detail about the Queen's quarters.

The gardens were designed so that the Queen could easily go round them in her wheel chair. There was a cycle path, tennis courts, croquet lawns, boulodrome and a tropical greenhouse. (The tropical greenhouse has now given way to a solarium and a swimming pool.) The Mediterranean gardens were formally laid out with the flower beds mosaic-patterned. The name of the hotel was laid out in plants in the front. Trees and shrubs were date palms, cabbage palm, queen palm, Chusan palm, aloes, algarves and cactuses. There was a liberal provision of terracotta statues and vases.[69]

The hotel was not without its critics. Lord Ronald Gower thought it looked like 'some monstrous stage decoration, with grotesque pinnacles and ugly, bloated, white-domed towers'.[70] Lady Lytton thought it was an insult to dear old Cimiez.[71]

On 12 April 1912 President Raymond Poincaré was present at the unveiling of a statue of Queen Victoria near the hotel. During the Occupation in the Second World War the monarch's head was knocked off. It was replaced in 1945.[72]

The Queen behaved like any proud mother at a school sports day when she visited the Prince of Wales's yacht, which had won many races. With great pride she told her diary:

Shortly before 12 drove down to the Port with Beatrice and Harriet P.[Phipps], Sir A. Bigge having gone on before and where Bertie's yacht was close to the Quay. I stepped easily on board, across a gang way which had been specially prepared. He has been most successful and has won many races here also this time. The yacht is long, but very low in the water and has hardly any bulwarks. I remained sitting for some time on board and Bertie presented to me Mr & Mrs Goellet, who are living on board their yacht, which is lying close to the 'Britannia', also Miss Goellet, and Lady Beatrice Herbert. I gave Bertie's Skipper the Victorian medal.[73]

Although the Queen clearly had reservations about journalists, one evening she received Baron Paul Julius Reuter, the founder of the news agency, who had retired to Nice, where he had a house on the Promenade des Anglais. Lady Lytton reported on the visit: 'The Queen was very shy and did not say much. He has the Jewish face most marked and a tiny figure. He is very civil in supplying the Queen with telegrams but not without payment.'[74] In 1871 Reuter had been enobled by the Duke of Saxe-Coburg-Gotha and in 1891 Queen Victoria allowed him to enjoy the privileges of the foreign nobility in Britain.

An unfortunate incident with a French journalist must have coloured the Queen's view. The journalist wanted to write about the Queen's favourites. 'As if I had any', the Queen commented. It was changed to the Queen's friends, but he got it all wrong and wrote about people she hardly knew or did not like. Nevertheless Lady Lytton said the Queen liked the foreign easy manner.[75]

On 10 April the holiday was marred by the sudden death in Cannes of the Queen's friend the Grand Duke of Mecklenburg-Schwerin. He was found dead in his garden at the foot of an eight-metre-high wall from which he had fallen. Rumours abounded that either his wife Anastasia had shot him or that he had killed himself.[76] 'The papers bring a complete denial of the infamous rumour, that poor Friedrich of Mecklenburg, threw himself out of the window,' the Journal recorded.[77]

Their children did well for themselves: one became Queen of Denmark and one wife of the Crown Prince of Germany.

In 1902 Anastasia became pregnant by her lover, Vladimir Alexandrovitch Paltov, who was a member of her staff, and she let it be known that her largeness was due to a tumour. Her sister-in-law, Countess Torby, commented: 'Of course, we all knew the truth.' The child, Alexis Louis, born in Nice in the same year, was given the surname 'de Wenden', after the villa. Anastasia died in Eze, near Monaco on 11 March 1922.[78]

The Queen left Cimiez for England on 28 April.

CHAPTER 9

1898: Nice. The agonies of King Leopold's daughters

T he Paris Stock Exchange fell on the morning of 8 March 1898 when the market learned that the Queen's departure for her holiday on the Riviera had been delayed. It picked up in the afternoon when the reasons for the delay were received.[1]

Queen Victoria was feeling her 78 years when she prepared for her 1898 journey to the Riviera. Three days before she was due to leave she complained of headaches and tiredness and battled with difficulty through the curious ceremony in the Privy Council of choosing the sheriffs to represent certain of her interests in the counties of England and Wales. With a brass-handled bodkin with a spike some three inches long she pricked the nominations on a long roll of paper tied with green ribbons. According to tradition, Queen Elizabeth I was sewing in the garden when the roll was brought to her for marking. She had no pen handy so she pricked it with her bodkin. It is a good story, given some credence by the fact that earlier rolls were marked with a small black dot and later ones with a small hole. Exhausted by all the pricking, and feeling unwell all day, Queen Victoria could not dress for dinner and could not attend the dinner she was giving for the French Ambassador before she left for France.[2]

She postponed the departure by a day because of her indisposition and forecasts of bad weather in the Channel. The Press Association reported that it had authoritative information that the Queen's indisposition took the form of a slight bilious attack.[3] The royal party left for Portsmouth and Cherbourg on 10 March. Her Journal recorded:

> Arrived here at 4.30 after a rough disagreeable crossing, which tried me a good deal, though I was not sick. We had been told that the sea would be perfectly smooth, but it began rolling soon after I went below, and in the middle of the Channel there was one lurch, just as if the ship had had a blow,

the porthole burst half open, the sea came in, and the chairs were sent spinning. The maids, steward and footmen all rushed in, in a great state, and found part of the cabin full of water. I was taken in the rolling chair across to my bedroom, where I got on to the sofa, feeling much upset. Was very thankful when we got into Cherbourg at last. We had been quite misinformed about the weather.[4]

Doctor Reid wrote to his mother that the Queen's nerves were rather depressed and she was very nervous. He had had to stay nearly the whole of the passage of six hours with her in her cabin and she did not want to be alone.[5]

The fracas about the Munshi had continued throughout 1897 and into 1898 and she had left him behind when she departed for France. On 3 February Reid had heard from Mrs Tuck, the Queen's chief dresser, about a quarrel he had with the Queen: 'the Munshi had had the most violent row with her and had shouted at her. Later she wrote him a long letter.' The cause of the trouble was the Munshi's determination to take Raffiudin Ahmed as a companion to Cimiez in March. The Queen tried to avoid a recurrence of the previous year's rows by refusing the Munshi's demands, but the Munshi's bullying caused her again to vacillate. Reid appealed to Lord Salisbury, and on 18 February the Prime Minister came to Windsor to see the Queen. He strongly advised her not to take Ahmed to Cimiez and reported the conversation to Reid:

> I told the Queen that it would be most unfortunate if the French press got hold of anything and turned her into ridicule, and that was an additional reason for not having Raffiudin there. She quite saw this, and seemed impressed by it, and I am quite sure that this is the argument to use with her.[6]

The Munshi's bullying continued, but Reid reported in his diary that Salisbury said he did not think much of this 'as she could always get rid of him, but that he believes she really likes the emotional excitement, as being the only form of excitement she can have'.[7]

The Queen had arrived at Nice on 13 March and the Munshi turned up at Cimiez on 22 March.[8] To avoid any possible row when the Munshi arrived she had sent Reid a memorandum:

> which is only to be used if there should be any <u>symptom</u> of a <u>return</u> of the very <u>slightest</u> kind of what happened last year. I may mention that the person <u>will have</u> his carriage as he always had, the objection to which Lord Rowton [former Private Secretary to Disraeli] and Lord Salisbury considered most preposterous. His arrival will also be mentioned without title, when he arrives. Burn this now.[9]

Another note told Reid that there was to be no gossip among the Gentlemen.

> Though I deem that all that passed here at Cimiez last year should be buried in oblivion, all be as it was before the lamentable and unnecessary occurrence, still I think it right that I cannot allow any remarks about my people being made by my Gentlemen, or any gossip and reports or stories being listened to by them; but [they] are at once to be stopped.[10]

The Aga Khan visited Europe for the first time at the age of 20 in 1898, three years after he had succeeded as head of the Ismaili sect of the Shia Muslim community. He landed at Marseilles and immediately went to Nice. 'A considerable proportion of the Royalty, nobility and gentry of Europe was concentrated along this strip of coastline,' he recalled in his memoirs.[11] Despite his elevated position, a room had not been booked for him and he had difficulty finding one. Finally he found accommodation in the Excelsior Hôtel Régina. His wealth did not stop him from commenting that it was very expensive. His daily bill, without any extravagences, including the accommodation of his two valets, was FF200 (£4).[12] He liked the show of wealth on the Riviera. 'I stared at the shop windows, and what shop windows, the jewellers especially,' he recounted. He did not meet the Queen, but he saw her and her Indian servants. He commented in his diary:

> They were distinctly second-class servants of the kind you found around hotels and restaurants, the kind that the newly-arrived or transient European is apt to acquire in the first hotel in which he stays – very different from and very inferior to the admirable, trustworthy and very high-grade men whom, throughout the years of British rule in India, you would encounter at Viceregal Lodge or at Government house in any of the provinces. It seemed highly odd, and frankly it still does. Was the explanation possibly that the pay offered was not good enough to attract the first-rate men overseas?[13]

The Queen invited the Aga Khan to Windsor when he was in England and he again commented – to himself – on the poor quality of the servants of the Empress of India who served them dinner. He noted that 'The Queen, in spite of her age [she was 79], ate and drank heartily – every kind of wine that was offered, and every course, including both the hot and the iced pudding.'[14]

The Court Circular of 1 May announced the Munshi's return to Windsor, but, despite the Queen's orders, the announcement included his title.[15]

The Queen narrowly averted being involved in another drama, this time with her Coburg relatives. As she travelled on the train to Portsmouth, unbeknown to her she passed a train carrying her cousin Princess Louise, daughter of Leopold II and wife of Prince Philip of Coburg. She had entertained the Prince and Princess at Grasse in 1891 and at Hyères in 1892. By now it was apparent why Princess Louise had not accompanied her husband when the Queen received him in Nice in 1896.

Philip and Louise had married on 18 February 1875. Her mother did nothing to prepare Louise for her sexual initiation. Louise was 17 and Philip was 14 years her senior. Despite the fact that he was fat, bald and myopic, Louise described in her memoirs how she weaved dreams of married love and happiness:

> I gave myself up to delightful hopes, and described the magnificence of my trousseau, which was enriched with fairy-like gifts of Belgian lace and intricate embroideries.

> Loaded with jewels, I soared higher and higher, flattered by homage, congratulations and good wishes, without perceiving that, although my fiancé was so much older than myself, I had now become a certain personality in his dreams and in his thoughts.[16]

The wedding night shattered these dreams of the young girl:

> I am not, I am sure, the first woman who after having lived in the clouds during her engagement, has been as suddenly hurled to the ground on her marriage night, and who, bruised and mangled in her soul, has fled from humanity in tears. ... On the evening of my marriage at the Château of Laeken, whilst all Brussels was dancing amid a blaze of lights and illuminations, I fell from my heaven of love to what was for me a bed of rock and a mattress of thorns.

> The day was scarcely breaking when, taking advantage of a moment when I was alone in the nuptial chamber, I fled across the park with my bare feet thrust into slippers, and, wrapped in a cloak thrown over my nightgown, I went to hide my shame in the Orangery.[17]

A guard found the distressed Princess. Her mother rushed to her from Brussels, scolded her, coaxed her and told her of her marital duties, which she finally understood and reluctantly accepted.

When the trains carrying Queen Victoria and Louise passed each other, Louise was on her way from the Riviera accompanied by her lover, Count Mattacic from Croatia, to 'implore the help and protection of Queen Victoria who had given me so many evidences of her affection'.[18] They missed her, despite the fact that the Queen had left Windsor late because of her indisposition.[19]

In 1896 Princess Louise had fallen in love with Count Mattacic and wanted to divorce Philip. King Leopold refused, but raised no objection to her continuing the liaison with discretion. Indiscreetly she travelled to Nice with her daughter, Dora, and joined Mattacic in the Villa Paradis. Soon two seconds of Philip arrived and challenged Mattacic to a duel. Philip met the fit young Mattatic on the sanded floor of the Spanish Riding School in Vienna. They were handed pistols. Philip's shots went wild; Mattacic fired his into the air. They were handed swords. Mattacic touched Philip lightly on the right hand.[20] It was the end of the duel but not of the hounding of Mattacic. He was accused of forging the signature of Louise's sister, Stephanie, on Louise's enormous bills. The bills had to be paid and the couple travelled to England to get the help of the Queen. Having missed her they followed her back to Nice, but wise friends dissuaded them from approaching her at Cimiez. When King Leopold arrived on the Riviera, he would neither see Louise nor give her any money. (Oddly enough she dedicated her memoirs to, 'the Great Man, to the Great King, who was MY FATHER'.[21]) The Nice newspapers carried announcements that Philip was not responsible for his wife's debts. This caused tradesmen and moneylenders to storm the lovers' hotel room and seize anything of value they could lay their hands on.

Desperate for money they secretly fled to Croatia, which was Austrian territory. They were discovered. Mattacic was arrested for forgery, flung into prison and sentenced to six years' imprisonment.

Louise was offered the alternative of returning to Philip or being sent to a lunatic asylum. She chose the latter and was certified insane. King Leopold told the superintendent of the asylum to 'keep a strict watch upon the madwoman'. When Mattacic got out of prison he rescued Louise from the asylum. They settled in Germany and, after Mattacic had died, she divorced Philip in 1907. She published her memoirs, which are very one-sided, in 1921 and died in 1924.

The third daughter of Leopold II, Clémentine, who sometimes accompanied the King on his visits to Queen Victoria on the Riviera, had the happiest marriage of the three sisters, although her father stopped her marrying in his lifetime. She married Prince Victor Napoleon Bonaparte, head of the house following the death in exile of Napoleon III.[22]

Another Coburg preoccupied the Queen at Cimiez in 1898. This time it was her second son, Prince Alfred, Duke of Edinburgh and Saxe-

Coburg-Gotha, who was known as 'Affie'. Alfred had often been a problem to the Queen. In November 1862, only a year after the Prince of
Wales's adventure in Dublin, Alfred, a naval officer, had an affair with a
young woman in Malta, where he was stationed.[23] 'Affie makes me very
unhappy,' his mother wrote of a visit he paid her shortly after he had been
made Duke of Edinburgh in 1866. 'He hardly ever comes near me, is
reserved, touchy, vague and wilful and I distrust him completely.'[24] He
was married to Grand Duchess Marie of Russia and inherited the Duchy of
Coburg.

He had a serious drink problem. He came to dinner with the Queen at
Cimiez on 24 March and brought with him his daughter, Crown Princess
Marie of Romania, and her husband Ferdinand, Crown Prince of Romania.[25] 'Missy', as she was known in the family, was very different from her
father. She was one of the Queen's most talented grandchildren. She was a
great beauty, rode and danced well, wrote novels, painted and sculpted
and was an accomplished botanist. But what was to develop into a tragedy
two years later started the day after the family dinner party, when the
Queen's doctor, Reid, was summoned to Alfred's yacht the *Surprise* at
Villefranche and found the Prince in agony with developed rectal inflammation. Reid decided he needed urgent surgery. This was successfully
carried out on 26 March.[26] The Queen visited him in his cabin on the yacht
a week later: 'Went into Affie's cabin, which is small and dark and sat by
his bed for half an hour. Thankful to have found him really much better.'[27]

Reid complained in a letter to his mother that the place was swarming
with Royalties and other big people whom he had to keep dealing with.
(The Queen even sent Reid to check up on Empress Eugénie.)[28] Alfred's
mother most improperly asked Reid for her son's medical notes. We do
not know whether he committed a breach of medical etiquette by showing
them to her. By July 1900 Alfred was suffering from inoperable cancer of
the tongue and throat and he died in Coburg on 31 July at the age of 56.
The Queen had not been shown his medical notes and had not known how
seriously ill he was. His death came as a great shock to her.[29]

The casual nature of much of the contact between the royals on the
Riviera is shown by this passing comment in the Journal for 4 April: 'On
our way down to Villefranche we met Leopold of Belgium walking. He
had arrived in Villefranche harbour on his yacht this morning.' He came to
dinner that evening.[30]

Nevertheless the farce of protocol sometimes became ridiculous.
Wilhelmina, the Queen of the Netherlands, then 18, came to visit the

Queen of England, 60 years older. Sir Frederick Ponsonby complained about it in his memoirs:

> It appeared to be the custom for the suite of the visited to write their names and leave cards on the suite of the visitor. I had therefore to go to Cannes and write the names of all the Queen's suite in the Queen of Holland's book. The farce of leaving cards struck me as being so absurd; as there were six of Queen Victoria's suite and twelve of the Dutch suite I had to leave seventy-two cards.[31]

Carrying out his protocol duties got Ponsonby into difficulties on another occasion:

> I went to Cannes to bid farewell from the Queen to the Prince of Wales and I found that a train back to Nice started five minutes after the Prince of Wales' train left. I determined to catch this, but unfortunately so many people came to the station to see him off that I had only one minute in which to get to another platform and catch my train. I remained bowing on the platform till the Prince's train started and then ran like a hare. But a tall hat and frock-coat were never intended as suitable attire for running, and there was something ridiculous in my bounding over the line to catch my train.

> I reached the train just as it was starting, rushed to the first carriage I saw and swung myself in. Now the train on leaving Cannes goes immediately into a tunnel and it so happened that in the carriage which I had selected were two maiden ladies who had been nervous about travelling for fear of thieves and who had therefore tipped the guard to give them a compartment to themselves. When they saw me jump in as the train rushed into the tunnel they never waited a moment but pulled the emergency cord, with the result that the train stopped and glided back into Cannes station. There the stationmaster appeared supported by gendarmes, and the two French ladies monopolized the conversation, but they were so excited and incoherent that the stationmaster found it difficult to understand what exactly had happened. I sat quiet to start with, but as I wanted to get back I quietly pushed them aside and emerged from the carriage. The gendarmes eyed me suspiciously, but I explained in a few words what had happened, and I offered to go to another carriage. The stationmaster took me to another carriage and on the train went.[32]

Protocol reared its ugly head when the Queen met M. Faure, the French President, again. The arrangements for his reception, which she so innocently described in her Journal hid a snake's nest of nuances:

> At half-past three M. Faure, the President of the Republic, who has been spending some days at the Riviera Palace, came to see me. Bertie received

him below, and brought him up, and the three Princesses with the ladies were at the top of the stairs. I stood at the door of the drawing-room and asked him to sit down. He was very courteous and amiable, with a charming manner, so grand seigneur and not at all parvenu. He avoided all politics, but said most kindly how I was aimée par la population, that he hoped I was comfortably lodged, etc. Bertie and the others came in, and after a little while the President's two gentlemen were presented and then he left.[33]

These seemingly innocent arrangements had been discussed at length by the Queen, the Prince of Wales and the household. The Queen intensely disliked all republics. Although she had to admit that M. Faure was head of a sovereign state, she refused to treat him as a sovereign. The Prince of Wales had come over from Cannes for the occasion and he supported the idea of a little difference being made. Instead of going down to the door to meet the President on his mother's behalf, he met him on the stairs, which was all the Queen would allow. But Félix Faure was no walk-over, as Ponsonby explained:

> In the Hall Lady Southampton, Miss Phipps, and Miss Evelyn Moore, Sir Arthur Bigge, Sir William Carington, and myself awaited the President. When he arrived, he looked round to see who was there to meet him, and seeing neither the Queen nor the Prince of Wales, kept his hat on to imply that the visit had not properly begun. He shook hands with the three ladies still with his hat on, and of course did the same with the men. Such a proceeding was hardly dictated by the Protocol, and it surprised us all. When Paris heard of this afterwards I was told that everyone said it was outrageous and very bad manners. The President was then conducted upstairs, and the Prince of Wales came hurrying down as if he were late. It was then and only then that the President took his hat off. He remained a quarter of an hour.[34]

The Nice Press either did not know or did not want to know the nuances of the visit: 'The Queen of England awaited him at the entrance to the salon ... she made a few steps towards him', L'Eclaireur reported and it saw in this movement a symbolic gesture of rapprochement. 'The conversation was conducted in French and was of an exquisite cordiality', important persons present at the meeting told L'Eclaireur.[35]

The next day the Queen sent a present of wine to the French guard of honour with orders to drink President Faure's health.[36]

The Queen's main political preoccupations, which she discussed with Salisbury (who, the Queen noted with an exclamation mark, was wearing a black skull cap) at his villa at Beaulieu, were China and the threat of a

Spanish-American war.[37] She thought America had behaved monstrously over Spain.[38]

Cuba had revolted against Spanish rule. When on 15 February the USS *Maine* was blown up in Havana harbour with heavy loss of life there was soon a clamour in the USA for war against Spain with the cry 'Remember the *Maine*'. On 29 March President McKinley sent an ultimatum to Spain which included the demand of an immediate armistice for the Cuban rebels and American mediation between Spain and Cuba. Although McKinley later admitted a peaceful solution might have been had, the USA considered the Spanish reply unsatisfactory and on 25 April declared war.[39] The war ended in August and Spain lost Cuba, Puerto Rico and the Philippines.

Maria Christina, the Queen Regent of Spain, had appealed to the Queen, who was, of course, able to do nothing.[40] Victoria had met Maria Christina in San Sebastian in 1889 and thought her charming and delightful. She was an Austrian Archduchess and it pleased the English Queen that she spoke German to her, with a pleasant Austrian accent. 'The Queen has a very charming face and manner, brown eyes, a good nose, and a slight graceful figure.' A little Queen-to-Queen intimacy appealed to Victoria: 'The Queen kindly took us upstairs to her room, where I tidied myself up and put on my cap.'[41]

Queen Victoria may have thought America was behaving monstrously toward Spain, but her government, concerned at Britain's international isolation and the possible need one day to have an ally against Germany, supported the Americans, and so blocked any collective European intervention. Indeed, on one occasion at Manila the British naval commander interposed his ships between the American and German squadrons to prevent any action by the Germans.[42] Although he considered the position of the Queen Regent of Spain most lamentable and grievous, Salisbury warned the Queen on 1 April not to give any undertaking to assist her.[43] So Victoria's letter to her friend Maria Christina ('poor thing') the next day had to be a bromide.

The China problem which the Queen discussed with Lord Salisbury was the aftermath of the Japanese defeat of China in the first Sino-Japanese war of 1894. China was taking the place of Turkey, which the Queen had discussed the previous year with President Faure, as the sick man. Russia had led the triple intervention with Germany and France at the end of the war to save Liaodong for China – and eventually Russia – but Britain and the USA had held back. The Western powers had supported the unity and integrity of China in their different ways. But, now that it seemed possible that China would break up, they hastened to set up contingency plans by staking out spheres of influence. These plans demanded acquisition of naval bases on the Chinese coast. Russia was in the van, getting control of Dairen and Port Arthur. Germany exacted a 99-year lease of Jiaozhou and France later leased Guangzhou Bay. Britain leased Weihaiwei and the Hong Kong New Territories.[44] The latter were handed back to China in the presence of the great-great-great-grandson of Queen Victoria, Prince Charles, on 30 June 1997.

China was discussed again at a dinner at Cimiez on 21 March attended by Sir Edmund Monson, British Ambassador to France. 'He thought people ought not to be unreasonable about some of the demands made by China', the Queen wrote in her Journal. 'I observed I could not quite understand why nobody was to have anything, anywhere, but ourselves, in which he quite concurred.'[45]

But the holiday was not all work. One morning some people sang under the window after breakfast.[46] Mrs Austen Lee, wife of one of the Paris Embassy staff, a powerful mezzo-soprano, sang beautifully one evening with an expression and pathos which the Queen considered was not to be surpassed by a professional singer.[47] The next night the ladies dined alone and an extraordinarily good Hungarian gypsy band played in the drawing room.[48] One afternoon the Queen went to the dark and empty church of Notre Dame and listened to the organ, which had some remarkable stops.[49]

The Queen drove with the princesses to Villefranche and saw all their old friends the beggars.[50] The old man in the dog cart always got FF10 (£0.40) when the Queen saw him and she sent him FF50 (£2)[51] when she left. The cart eventually carried the inscription 'By special appointment to Her Majesty'. Orders were given for it to be erased, but the presents continued.[52] The highlight of the expeditions was the Maundy Thursday procession, which the Queen wrote up in her Journal:

> In the afternoon drove with my 2 daughters, Marie E. and the children to the old part of the town to witness the annual Maunday Thursday procession of the 'Pénitents Rouges,' which starting from the Cathedral, visits 7 churches in Nice. First came women, followed by men, then more women with white veils on their heads, carrying wax lighted tapers, and a number of girls in blue with white veils from seminaries. Later came clergy and acolytes, carrying lanterns and a large cross. One man carried a very large crucifix in front of the Bishop of Nice, who wore purple robes. In passing my carriage, the

Bishop stopped and bowed, taking his little cap off his head. He then made the tour of the Place, blessing the people as he passed and laying his hands on the heads of the children. A few more members of the Confraternities followed, and kept up a sort of chant as they walked.[53]

The Queen paid one of her rare visits to Cannes one afternoon when she went by special train to attend the confirmation of Princess Alice of Albany at St George's Church, the memorial to her father, Leopold.[54] A break from the usual routine of carriage rides was a trip across the River Var to Villeneuve and Loubet.[55]

Awards were much sought after at the end of each visit and ranks carefully compared. Sir Frederick said the French regarded them as like a collector's rare stamp or an unknown egg.[56] For the 1898 visit the awards were: M. Paoli, Head of the Railway Police and Detectives: Royal Victorian Order, Third Class[57] (he had received the Fourth Class in 1896, just after the Order had been created);[58] M. Le Roux, Prefect of the Alpes-Maritimes: Royal Victorian Order, Second Class; M. Sauvan, Mayor of Nice: Royal Victorian Order, Third Class; Mr Gambart, no description: Royal Victorian Order, Fourth Class; General Gebhart, Governor of Nice: Royal Victorian Order, Second Class.[59]

The Queen derived great pleasure from distributing presents. She brought with her a large trunk with watches and chains, pins, statuettes, photographs, pens and inkstands and cigarette holders. She gave them to all ranks and did not forget the humblest hotel staff with whom she came in contact. She kept a gift book and carefully recorded the individual recipients and the presents so that she never gave the same present twice.[60]

The Queen left Nice on 28 April but the weather in the English Channel delayed the journey and the Queen did not arrive back at Windsor Castle until 2 May.

CHAPTER 10

1899: Nice. The Fashoda Incident threatens the visit

On 10 July 1898 five bearded and haggard Frenchmen sat by the banks of the Upper Nile in the cool of the evening and drank champagne to toast their arrival at Fashoda in the Sudan, which that day they had claimed for France. Under the leadership of the explorer Jean-Baptiste Marchand they had brought the champagne from the Atlantic to the Upper Nile in a journey that had taken them two years. They also brought claret, fresh uniforms, a mechanical piano and haricots verts seeds. Two months later, on 18 September, the British general, Herbert Kitchener, Sirdar of the Egyptian army, arrived from Egypt by steamer and claimed Fashoda for Egypt. Thus was created the Fashoda Incident, which much preoccupied Queen Victoria and the hoteliers and shopkeepers of Nice for the next three months. Would she, or would she not, cancel her annual visit to the Riviera?

Presumably Marchand still had some champagne left after two months, because he and Kitchener entertained each other with whisky and champagne.[1] Kitchener was particularly impressed with the haricots verts.

The Fashoda Incident represented the apogee of Anglo-French rivalry in the scramble for Africa, which had repercussions in the struggle for power in Europe and in the rest of the world. In March 1877 Lord Salisbury, Secretary of State for India and soon to become British Prime Minister and Foreign Secretary, had written, 'English policy is to float lazily down-stream, occasionally putting out a diplomatic boat-hook to avoid collisions.'[2] We can imagine that on one bank of the river was the Triple Alliance of Germany, Austria and Russia. On the other was France, which sometimes got Russia to put a foot over to its bank.

But over-hanging the drift downstream was always India and the need to protect access to it. For that reason Britain had occupied Egypt in 1882 to safeguard the Suez Canal. It knew that eventually it would have to reconquer the Sudan from the Mahdists and, in order to strengthen its hold on the Upper Nile, it annexed Uganda in 1894. This had the additional attraction of bringing the day nearer when a railway could stretch from Cairo in Egypt to Capetown in South Africa.

The French also wanted a railway to span Africa, not north–south, but east–west. They wanted it to run Congo–Upper Nile–Djibouti and as part of this audacious plan decided to seize the valley of the Upper Nile. This they planned to do from West Africa.[3] In 1894 they hired the French explorer Pierre Monteil to travel across Africa and place the French flag on the Upper Nile. The project was cancelled at the last minute.[4]

The unfriendly act, to which Sir Edward Grey had previously referred in his House of Commons speech of 28 March 1895, took much longer to achieve than the French had expected. The French government learned in early 1896 that Kitchener had been authorized to head for Dongola in the Sudan, as the first move in the campaign to wrest the country from the hands of the Mahdists, who had seized it from Egypt in 1855. The French government therefore lent a ready ear to the proposal of the 31-year-old veteran of colonial wars in West Africa to mount an expedition to move by water and land up the Congo river and its tributaries and plant the tricolor on the fort at Fashoda. That would avenge the insult of the exclusively British occupation of Egypt in 1882.

By mid-1896 Marchand had left Marseilles for the four-week journey to the French Central African headquarters in Libreville. The expedition rendezvoused at Loango in the French Congo. The first aim was to get to the 13-mile-wide 'Pool' of the Congo at Brazzaville, above the 200-mile cataract region, which effectively blocked river communications between the Atlantic and the swelling of the river. By December the expedition, comprising a handful of Frenchmen, porters and Senegalese soldiers, against appalling odds of disease and attacks by local tribes, had moved 5000 loads, or 45,000 kilograms of supplies to the Pool. That part of the journey had taken twice as long as Marchand had expected. But, in early January 1897, Marchand wrote that he expected to be in Fashoda by November of that year. He again underestimated the difficulties, which included dismantling the expedition's steamer, the *Faidherbe*, and moving it across land in parts. The two-ton boiler was rolled along a three-metre-wide path hacked through the jungle. Lack of communications and news was a major disadvantage. In May 1898 Marchand received eight-month-old newspapers from Paris reporting that the expedition had been massacred.

The contrast with Kitchener's resources could not have been more marked. He defeated the Mahdists at Omdurman on 2 September. For that victory the Queen bestowed a barony on him, although she complained to Salisbury that her telegram telling him of the honour never reached him. 'It is most annoying, as the good effect of the early recognition of his services has thus been marred', she telegraphed. In fact the cable was not lost; it had arrived in Omdurman after the Sirdar had gone south.[5] The Queen had also been upset by hearing that the Mahdi's tomb had been destroyed and the bones improperly disposed of. Kitchener wrote to explain and she replied from Nice on 24 March:

> She never believed that the Sirdar had given the order for the remains of the Mahdi to be destroyed. That the tomb was destroyed she quite understands was absolutely necessary. But she felt – [as to] the destruction of the poor body of a man who, whether he was very bad and cruel, after all was a man of a certain importance – that it savours in the Queen's opinion, too much of the Middle Ages not to allow his remains to be buried in some private spot where it would not be considered as of any importance politically or an object of superstition. The graves of our people have been respected, and those of our foes should, in her opinion, also be.
>
> However, now she is quite satisfied, as the skull has been buried.[6]

In fact the skull had not been buried but was turned into an inkpot. The Queen was not told.[7]

Kitchener had gone south to deal with Marchand. He steamed up river in the *Dal* with five gunboats, 2500 local troops and 100 Highlanders, bagpipes skirling. Kitchener had had instructions from London not to be too hard on Marchand and he allowed him to stay at Fashoda until he received instructions from Paris. Those instructions had to come via the only available communications, which were Kitchener's. The French government were preoccupied with the Dreyfus affair, where a Jewish French officer had been wrongly convicted of treason, and it took a month before Marchand received a message. And that was merely a brief telegram of congratulation.[8]

Relations between France and Britain were very strained through October and November with much vituperation in the Press of the two countries. But neither side wanted war. On 4 December Marchand started to carry out the orders to withdraw that he had finally received. On 21 March 1899 Britain and France signed an agreement, which left the British with Egypt and the Sudan.[9] It marked the end of confrontation between the two powers and it cleared the decks for the eventual Entente.

The Queen had favoured a placatory line over Fashoda. She tele-graphed to Lord Salisbury from Balmoral on 30 October:

> I feel very anxious about the state of affairs, and think a war for so miserable
> and small an object is what I could hardly bring myself to consent to. We
> have had so many losses on the Indian frontier, and to think of sacrificing any
> more is too horrible and too wrong. We must try and save France from <u>hu-miliation</u>.[10]

Again a few days later she said, 'It will be important I think to help the
French as much as is proper and dignified out of the foolish and horrible
<u>impasse</u> they had got into.'[11]

Rumours were rife that Kitchener was a homosexual. 'They say he dis-likes women, but I can only say he was very nice to me', the Queen
commented.[12]

The Queen's love of France was qualified by her dislike of its republi-can government, based partly on her affection for Napoleon III and
Empress Eugénie and her distress at their overthrow, and partly on her
natural dislike, as a monarch, of republicanism. In 1884 the constitutional
changes that had been made caused her to believe that her government
was following 'the dreadful example of France'.[13] During the Franco-Prussian war she described the French as 'that nation w^h, with but few
exceptions, seems to be entirely devoid of <u>truth</u>, & to live upon vanity,
deception, amusement, and self-glorification'.[14] Ten years later she drew
Gladstone's attention 'to the frightful tyranny & <u>want</u> of religious liberty
now existing in the French Republic. ... Is monarchical constitutional
Great Britain to look on & be on the most intimate terms with a Republic,
which in fact approaches the Commune? There is no oppression & tyranny
so great as that of a Republic.'[15] The year she first visited the Riviera, in
1882, she wrote, 'Do not approve single action with France, especially
<u>Republican</u> France.'[16]

The Queen expected to have her say in foreign affairs. She wrote to
Palmerston in 1863, 'She wishes to state once more her desire that <u>no step</u>
is taken in foreign affairs <u>without</u> her <u>previous sanction</u> being obtained.'[17]
In the case of Fashoda she was more conciliatory than her government.
'Would it be safe to promise commercial access to the Nile and delimita-tion of that region suggested in Sirdar's letter of 8th October to Lord
Cromer on condition of French withdrawal from Fashoda?', she asked
Salisbury.[18]

A further reason for a possible cancellation of the visit to the Riviera
was the risk of civil disturbance arising from the Dreyfus affair. There was

a possibility of a right-wing coup by the officers who had cashiered Dreyfus. When the Queen had heard of the verdict on 9 September 1899 from
Michael Herbert, Secretary of the Embassy in Paris, she sent a telegram to
him: 'Thanks for your telegram with the news of this monstrous verdict
against this poor martyr.' Unfortunately, the telegram was not coded and
it leaked out in Paris. The result was abuse of England and the Queen in
the French Press.[19]

The *Petit Niçois* of 14 November reported rumours from the British
and French Press that the Queen had cancelled her visit to the Riviera and
instead would rent a villa near Florence.[20]

Nevertheless, Sir Edmund Monson, the British Ambassador, wrote
from Paris on 30 November:

> Your Majesty is doubtless aware that great interest is taken in France in the
> decision which your Majesty may eventually take in regard to visiting Cimiez;
> and that there is much anxiety lest circumstances should cause your Majesty
> to alter the intention to which it is understood you have arrived. Whatever
> may be the condition of the international relations between England and
> France, the respect entertained for your Majesty throughout this country and
> the appreciation of your Majesty's yearly visits to the French coast of the
> Mediterranean, remain unchanged.[21]

Paoli expressed his worry:

> The mere thought that political events might interfere with her annual holi-
> day were enough to cause her acute distress. I remember, for instance, the
> time of the unfortunate Fashoda incident, which happened just at the moment
> when she was about to start for Nice. An ill-disposed section of the press had
> written to cry out against the journey; and the Queen caused her hesitation
> and anxiety to be brought to my knowledge. Realizing the great harm which
> her absence — necessarily involving the absence of a large number of her sub-
> jects — was likely to do to our Mediterranean coast, I instituted a summary
> enquiry into the feeling of the population, as a result of which I strongly ad-
> vised Her Majesty to make no alteration in her plans. Fortunately I was not
> alone in this opinion: I found a valuable ally in the person of the late Lord
> Salisbury, who was prime minister at the time. He never wearied of repeat-
> ing:

> 'It is more than ever essential that the Queen should go to France this year.'[22]

Salisbury's wife was already on the Riviera at their house at Beaulieu. She
took the crisis all very phlegmatically, staying on at Beaulieu and writing
to relatives about her plans to disguise herself and get back to Britain if
there were hostilities.[23]

The Queen's Journal records that Salisbury told the Queen that she could perfectly well go to Cimiez and that her putting it off might create a panic.[24]

Salisbury told the Queen's Private Secretary, Sir Arthur Bigge:

> There are revolutions and revolutions. If President Faure were flying for his life, it might be difficult for the Queen to remain at Cimiez. But if they went no farther than locking out the Court of Cassation, or lodging a certain number of Jews in Mazas, I do not know why H.M. should take any notice of the transaction. But if she were nervous, she could always, with her horses, find herself on the other side of the frontier in two hours. Such a change of plans might not be entirely dignified, but it would be better than countermanding the preparations now. I can suggest no precautions except perhaps taking a suite of rooms at Bordighera in the name of one of the Ladies in Waiting. But as far as I can venture to forecast the situation, a bad revolution is improbable; and if it occurs, it is likely to be accompanied by an immediate peril of war, which will entirely alter the position of the Royal party.[25]

In early January Monson met President Faure, who expressed his pleasure that the Queen had positively decided to return to Nice in the spring. 'Sir Edmund replied that he believed your Majesty had in fact never varied from this intention,' Sir Edmund told the Queen.[26]

Her Majesty may not herself have wavered from the intention to go to Nice, but shortly before her departure Windsor Castle telegraphed Nice – presumably to the British Consul – to ask if it would be safe for her to go. The reason was a report in the London newspaper, *The Globe*, of an impersonation of the Queen by an actress called Mrs Norris, which the newspaper said was insulting. So serious was the possibility of cancellation, with its consequent damage to the economy of the area, that the Prefect ordered a police enquiry. The police reported on 25 February. Mrs Norris's speciality, the report said, was to imitate sovereigns and other celebrities. Her imitation of Queen Victoria had the monarch saying, 'At the head of a great nation, I am loved by my people and I am proud of it.' The whole of the hall of the Palais de la Jetée Promenade, frequented only by the foreign colony, applauded. If the police report was true, it is odd that they reported that the manager of the Jetée Promenade had told Mrs Norris to stop imitating Queen Victoria. The conclusion of the police was that the story had been whipped up by the Nice correspondent of *The Globe*, Monsieur Lequeux. In a bit of muddled thinking, the police also thought the English people did not want the Queen to come, for reasons the police did not try to explain.[27]

Reuters reported that the Mayor of Nice, M. Honoré Sauvan, travelled to Paris to apologize to the British Embassy for the incident. The Mayor hotly denied the Reuters report and said he had gone to Paris merely to find out when the Queen would be coming to Nice and to say how welcome she would be.[28]

Two days after Mrs Norris's final imitation of the Queen, a telegram from America reported, according to the police, an 'outrage' perpetrated against some Americans and English riding on a float in the Battle of the Flowers. This time the railway police carried out an investigation. Inspector Renucci interviewed Mr Arthur Horncastle and Mr Byron Harker, staying at the Grand Hôtel, Nice. With friends they were on a float, draped with British and American flags, and they wore white suits and straw hats. As they came on to the Promenade des Anglais some urchins shouted out 'Down with the Americans; long live Spain'. Seeing the joke, Mr Horncastle replied with 'Vive la France', the report said. Mr Horncastle and Mr Harker said it was no incident and contrasted with the great welcome they got from the people on the stands and from the army officers, who covered them with flowers. The police again attributed the storm in the Anglo-American teacup to M. Lequeux, correspondent of *The Globe*, who resided at the Pension Anglaise, Promenade des Anglais.[29] Curiously enough the police did not report that they had interviewed M. Lequeux. The police did not comment on how well informed the urchins were on world affairs. The USA had won the war with Spain the previous year.

The police were nevertheless getting nervous about the arrival of the Queen. With their reports they sent the Prefect a copy of an article from the *Libre Parole* of February 1899, which said, 'this year, the Empress of India, protectress of the faith, would do better to stay at home than go anywhere else.' 'Is it impossible that demonstrations might occur?', the police commented.

What became known as 'The Campaign for the Denigration of Nice' centred on rumours of a typhoid epidemic and on the possibility that the Queen might cancel her visit because of the bad relations between Britain and France and go to Florence instead. The French Press said the English had started the rumours. The implication was that in the atmosphere of war following the Fashoda Incident they wanted to ruin local business. The weekly *The Anglo-American Society on the Continent*, which was, after all, a local business, did not want to see its advertising, which frequently mentioned the Queen, dry up. Typical was the display advertisement:

> The Riviera Supply Stores
> English Grocers
> Purveyors to Her Majesty the Queen
> Afternoon Tea Room at the Head Office, 39 rue d'Antibes, Cannes, where
> Refreshments of all kinds may be had, including Tea, Cocoa, and Coffee as
> supplied to the Queen

Or the classified:

> As Concierge or Caretaker of Villa. A highly respectable man employed at
> the Excelsior Regina Hotel during the Queen's visit desires situation. Write
> Baptiste Autié, 30 rue de l'Escarène, Nice.30

The Anglo-American strongly scotched the rumours. Its issue of 21 November 1898 carried a column headed 'Busy Bodies and News Mongers'. It said it had investigated the terrible, blood curdling reports, which owed their origins to a certain sect of newsmongers. Some two months earlier there had indeed been typhoid fever at the nearby village of Riquier and a few cases in Nice itself, but there was no panic by the authorities or doctors. It concluded:

> To all those who have studied and appreciated the wonderful tact of our
> Queen, the reasons given for her change of Winter quarters is absurd. Even if
> her Majesty had thought of deserting Nice, the very fact of relations being, or
> having been, strained between the two countries would have been quite suffi-
> cient to turn the scale in favour of another visit to Cimiez. As a matter of fact
> the Queen <u>will</u> come to Cimiez as usual provided nothing unforeseen happens
> in the meantime.[31]

The British Consul, Sir James Harris, had earlier written to *The Anglo-American* (in French, presumably so that it would be read by the local community) explaining that the attacks on Nice by the British Press were due to the attacks on England and the English in the French Press. He cited the correspondent of the *Phare du Littoral*, whom he considered inaptly byelined as 'Diplomat', for describing the English as 'robbers, crooks and brigands'.[32]

The local English-language Press bemoaned the lack of English visitors to Nice in the 'Winter of Discontent' and blamed it on 'that fickle Jade Fashion'.[33] Alongside a drawing of the Queen captioned 'The Queen God Bless Her', *The Anglo-American* consoled itself a little by the influx of

Germans and Austrians, 'although they are not so lavish in their expenditure as the English and Americans'.

The Librairie Rontani on the rue Alexandre Mari, near the flower market in Nice, was the sort of local business which would have been particularly distressed if the visit had been cancelled. Above the door was a stained glass window: 'By appointment Stationer to H.M. The Queen Victoria.' The window is still there and the Rontani family still own the shop the Queen patronized.

The British businesses in Nice fought back and the British Chamber of Commerce launched an advertising campaign in the British Press to entice visitors for the next season.[34]

We do not know if the Queen saw the French postcard of this period of her riding on a bottle of gin.

For the first time the royal caravanserai planned to travel from Folkestone, where the Queen had never been, to Boulogne instead of from Portsmouth to Cherbourg. Bad weather delayed the departure for a couple of days until 11 March. They could have gone earlier, but the Queen as always would not travel on a Friday. Marie Mallet reported that the household was very upset by the delay: 'all this uncertainty is very tiresome as our books are packed away in boxes, also our work, so we have no employment and the men have no clean shirts and are growling like grizzly bears at the delay', she wrote to her husband from Windsor.[35] The Court Circular felt it was appropriate in describing the arrangements for the channel crossing to note that the Queen had forwarded her annual subscription of £50[36] to the Royal National Lifeboat Institution.[37] Although there was some cheering on the arrival at Boulogne, it was less than in previous years, no doubt a reflection of the aftermath of Fashoda. A week before the Queen passed through Toulon there had been an explosion in a gunpowder factory which killed 60 and injured 150.[38] When she arrived in Toulon, with her usual considerateness, she did not fail to convey her deep regrets to the sub-Prefect, who was at the station to welcome her.[39]

Marie Mallet had cheered up by the time they arrived in Cannes on 12 March:

> The Prince of Wales and Princess Louise were on the platform at Cannes looking very well; he has taken to golf determined not to be behind the times. ... The weather is glorious, perfect summer, everyone in white dresses and flowery hats, I feel like a little black mole and a dowdy one too, for this place is smarter than Paris.[40]

Over-hanging this visit was the illness of the Queen's daughter, Victoria (Vicky), the Empress Frederick of Prussia. She was suffering from inoperable cancer of the spine. She visited her mother at Cimiez in April. The two empresses, Victoria and Vicky, met up with Empress Eugénie. An impressive sight was the empresses, Vicky and Eugénie, walking either side of the Empress Victoria's little carriage drawn by the white donkey.[41]

The holiday took its usual form of daily rides in the pony and trap, particularly to the nearby Liserb Gardens. The Queen was very energetic and Mary Mallet had to dissuade her from going out to see a funeral at a quarter to ten one morning, which the maid of honour thought much too early.[42] There were visits to such as Lady Salisbury, who, in a huge hat covered with lilly of the valley, complained about the delay in Lord Salisbury's arrival because he had attended a funeral. The Queen was very amused when she told her, 'I entirely agree with Sir William Jenner who said: "I never mean to attend any funeral but my own".'[43]

One day the Queen went to visit a private zoo owned by the Comtesse de la Grange (whom Marie Mallet described as a former cocotte and a doubtful Countess) and was given a newly laid ostrich egg, which her chef made into an omelette, and which Her Majesty pronounced delicious. On the egg the Comtesse had scrawled her name, 'Just as if she had laid it herself', the Queen remarked naively. 'Why cannot we have ostrich eggs at Windsor? We <u>have</u> an ostrich.' 'Yes, mama, a male one', was Princess Beatrice's reply.[44]

There was much musical entertainment. Ruggiero Leoncavallo played selections from his operas La Bohème and I Pagliacci. ('He plays quite beautifully and the pieces out of his new opera are charming.'[45]) Monsieur Redman, a Polish pianist, also played quite beautifully and included some pieces of Chopin the Queen had not heard before.[46] The Nice Choral Society and six municipal bands turned out for the birthday of Princess Henry of Battenberg and the Queen appeared on the balcony.[47] Other performers included Senor Costada's orchestra, which played a selection of Spanish music after dinner; Neapolitan musicians played at breakfast.

Marie Mallet read to the Queen.[48] One book the Queen very much liked was Taquisara by Marion Crawford,[49] a romance set in Italy, many elements of which would have appealed to the Queen, including probity and loyalty, and a lot about death.

The fishwives paid their usual visit. 'The "Dames de la Halle" appeared today with vast bouquets for the Queen and Duchess of York', Marie Mallet told her husband. 'The latter had to submit to a smacking kiss on either cheek from the fattest and most "garlicky" of the worthy fish-wives, and they also insisted on embracing Colonel Carington and Sir James Reid.'[50]

There were many royals on the Riviera. Marie Mallet, in one of her usual uninhibited letters to her husband, wrote:

> I cannot imagine why the whole of our Royal family should have decided to descend 'en masse' upon their august relative today, about 2 p.m. the hotel was literally crawling with Royalties and one could not take a step without falling foul of one or other. The Princess of Wales and her daughters look very seedy and Princess Maud has dyed her hair a canary colour which makes her look quite improper and more like a milliner than ever.[51]

On Sundays there was a service in the chapel in the hotel. Marie Mallet led the singing and Princess Beatrice played the organ.[52] Although there were two Anglican churches in Nice, the Queen did not normally go to them, preferring one of the clergymen, or a visitor, sometimes a bishop, to come to conduct a service at the hotel. She went to Holy Trinity once on her first visit to Nice because the chapel in the hotel was not ready. When the Excelsior Hôtel Régina closed in 1937 the royal coat of arms, which had hung above the door in the chapel, was moved to hang above the inside of the door of Holy Trinity.[53]

Religious services played an important role in the Queen's visit to the Riviera, where the Church of England had established a strong presence. The Society for the Propagation of the Gospel (SPG), which had been founded by the Church of England in 1699 to provide missions to the plantations in North America, had had its first mission to France in 1702 to ameliorate the condition of the galley slaves. In 1842 the Church of England created the Diocese of Gibraltar to look after 'English merchants, traders, artisans, miners, jockeys and horse trainers' resident on the Mediterranean coast and in 1863 the SPG started to establish churches. They opened them in Menton, Beaulieu and La Turbie (for Monaco) and local residents opened them in other centres. The Americans had their own church in Nice, but elsewhere they joined the English church services, in which a prayer for the President of the United States was said after the prayer for the British monarch. The churches did not proselytize the local people.[54]

A frequent visitor to the Queen on the Riviera was William Boyd Carpenter, Bishop of Ripon, known as 'the silver-tongued Bishop of Ripon', who not only preached, but also joined the monarch for dinner. He was no doubt an excellent dinner guest at Cimiez because he was versatile in his writings, producing not only *An Introduction to the Study of the Scriptures*, but also a 'shilling shocker', *The Last Man in London*.[55]

The Queen was so pleased with Canon J.N.B. Woodroffe, who preached to her in Nice, that she gave him a gold pen. He had told the congregation that 'I have a sting of the flesh' meaning simply eye-strain caused by malaria.[56]

The Queen had a number of meetings to discuss affairs of state, including relations with the French, with Lord Salisbury, the Prime Minister. The treaty which brought to an end the Fashoda Incident, which had brought in doubt the Queen's visit to the Riviera, had been signed five days before her first meeting on 26 March. 'We talked of many things and rejoiced at the success of the arrangement with the French, which gives us entire possession of the valley of the Nile.'[57] However, French historians have also seen the Fashoda Incident positively because it forced the British to negotiate on French interests in Egypt and led eventually to the Entente Cordiale of 1904.[58]

Prince Albert of Monaco called. She did not deign to give him luncheon, but saw him afterwards. He 'talked very interestingly of his discoveries and soundings taken in his yacht, in the North Sea &c.'[59] Albert was a leading authority on oceanography, having studied under the expert Professor Henri Milne-Edwards in Paris, who had written a book on crustaceans, molluscs and corals. The Prince had undertaken no less than 26 research voyages.[60] He was the founder of the Paris Institute of Oceanography and the Oceanography Museum of Monaco.

The highlight of the public engagements was the opening of a bridge in Nice. She described the event in her Journal of 27 April:

> At a quarter to four started with Lenchen [Princess Helena], Beatrice, Thora [Princess Helena Victoria, daughter of Princess Helena], [Prince] Leopold, [son of Princess Beatrice] and the two ladies following, the gentlemen and Sir E. Monson [British Ambassador] having preceded us, for the new bridge at the end of the Boulevard Carabacel, which I was asked to open. The bridge was beautifully decorated with flags and garlands. The Maire and his Adjunct met us on arrival, the band playing <u>God Save the Queen</u>, and he addressed a few words to me, thanking me for the honour I had conferred on the town, also presenting a most enormous and lovely bouquet. I answered in faltering words, 'Je suis bien touchée que vous m'ayez demandé d'inaugurer votre nouveau pont, et je fais des voeux bien sincères pour la prospérité de la ville de Nice et de ses environs.' Flowers were given to the Princesses. We then drove over the bridge, the band playing the <u>Marseillaise</u>. There were great crowds, who were all most enthusiastic.[61]

A strange event was the painting of Angele Gastaud. She was a peasant child of a characteristic Cimiez type and the Queen caused her to sit as a model to Monsieur Perrot, the pastel artist, for a portrait for her Majesty. The Queen later received Angele and gave her a gold chain and cross.[62] The Queen gave to charity and also distributed presents on each of her visits. Her generosity on this her last visit included 'pecuniary aid' for the widow of the railway guard who was accidentally killed while working on the line traversed by the special royal train.[63] She gave £120[64] for the poor of Nice, FF3700 (£148)[65] for various charities and FF500 (£20)[66] for the endowment fund of Holy Trinity Church in Nice. The incumbent of the church, the Rev. J.F. Langford was given a handsome travelling clock.[67]

Sensitivity about the Munshi continued. He was not mentioned in the Court Circular announcement of the outward party, but on 1 April it said he had arrived in Cimiez the previous day. The Duchess of York, later Queen Mary, wrote to her husband that he arrived on 1 April.[68] The Court Circular of 2 May, the day before the Queen's departure from Nice, announced that the Munshi Abdul Karim had left Cimiez.[69] But he became less prominent on his return to England, and later in 1899 went to India for a year. When the Queen died he had a place in her funeral procession, as she had earlier decreed. The Prince of Wales had his papers burnt and sent him back to India, where he lived in comfortable retirement, as arranged by the Queen in 1898. He died in 1909.[70]

The Queen was liking Cimiez so much that she extended her stay into May. At 51 nights it was the longest of her visits, which, as she got to like the area more and more, had progressively built up from the 27 nights of Menton in 1882. Leaving aside nights on boat and train, the Queen passed no less than 332 nights on the Riviera out of the total time spent on the continent of Europe during her reign of 886 nights. Other parts of France accounted for 113 nights, making a total for France of 445. If the short stay of four nights in Cannes in 1887 is excluded, she averaged 41 nights, or almost six weeks, for each holiday on the Riviera.[71]

The entry in the Journal for 1 May was:

Drove to Beaulieu. ... Had our tea at St. Jean, where Lenchen [Princess Helena] and Beatrice joined us. Alas! My last charming drive in this paradise of nature, which I grieve to leave, as I get more attached to it every year. I shall mind returning to the sunless north, but I am so grateful for all I have enjoyed here.[72]

This poignant entry in the Queen's Journal on 2 May was the last she was to write on the Riviera:

The morning was again beautiful and added to one's sadness at leaving. Every year I grow fonder of dear Cimiez.[73]

Queen Victoria left Nice on 2 May 1899. She was never to return.

CHAPTER 11

Epilogue: The cancelled visit

The Anglo-Boer War broke out on 11 October 1899. The anti-British stance of the French, exacerbated by the humiliation of Fashoda, caused the Queen to cancel her annual visit to the French Riviera in 1900. She originally planned to go instead in March for several weeks to the Hôtel Angst at Bordighera on the Italian Riviera, where rooms had been booked the previous year in case she had had to flee France because of the ill-feeling generated by the Fashoda Incident.[1] Special furniture was sent from Windsor Castle to Buckingham Palace on the first stage of its journey to Italy. The hotel went to the expense of printing postcards of the hotel and the Queen's portrait.[2] But on 6 March the Palace announced that she had cancelled her visit, 'as her Majesty feels unwilling to be abroad at this time'. The Rome correspondent of *The Times* reported that the cancellation had caused keen disappointment in Italy.[3]

The Menton and Monte Carlo News rather lamely explained that the real reason for the cancellation of the visit to the French Riviera was the combined effect of the noise caused during the last visit by the laying of tramways and the horrible smell of petroleum which hung about the roads following the passage of automobiles.[4]

The British Ambassador to France, Sir Edmund Monson, told the Queen on 1 October that 'The only redeeming point in the systematic abuse of England is the never-failing respect which characterises every allusion to your Majesty.'[5] But when the war started the respect failed and by 11 December, the Queen was complaining of the atrocious personal attacks on her in the French Press.[6]

Perhaps not surprisingly, an exception was the *Petit Nice*, which claimed to have 'energetically protested against the exhibition of caricatures ridiculing Queen Victoria'.[7] It had been pleased to reproduce an article from the *Figaro*, which reported that the Queen's staff had said that the Queen planned to come back to Nice again for two months in 1901.

Proof of this was that she had left a number of things at the hotel and had asked if she could rent the bedroom and sitting room for the 1900 season so that no one else could use them. 'Very courteously the management of the hotel has refused to take the money for this rental and has informed Her Majesty that the appartment would stay closed until it pleased her to come back again,' *Figaro* reported.[8]

Paris became the collection centre for the volunteers from France, Italy, Spain, Portugal, Germany, the Low Countries, Russia and the USA who came to fight the British in the Anglo-Boer War. The French volunteers were particularly prominent. They included Prince Louis d'Orléans et de Braganze, cousin of the French pretender, whom Lord Salisbury expelled from Britain for writing to congratulate the cartoonist Adolphe Willette on his vicious caricatures of Queen Victoria in the French Press[9], and René de Charette, a descendant of the Vendéan guerrilla, François-Athanase Charette de la Contrie. He was a particularly appropriate volunteer given the parallels often drawn between the guerrilla tactics of the Boers and the counter-revolutionaries from the Vendée, in the west of France, who fought against the central government at various times from 1793 to 1832. Most important of the volunteers was the 20th Count Villebois-Mareuil, formerly a French Army colonel and novelist and founder of Action Française, who was a military adviser to the Transvaal. He was killed in a reckless attack on 5 April 1900 near Boshof. The British buried him with full military honours and his death was greeted with widespread mourning in France. Streets were named after him in Paris and Lyons. When President Kruger arrived in France in November 1900 he was greeted by the French President Loubet and presented with many addresses and commemorative medals.

Queen Wilhelmina, whom Queen Victoria had entertained on the Riviera two years earlier, sent a Dutch warship to bring Kruger to Europe and she herself received him when he came to the Hague.[10]

The continental European Press carried many stories of atrocities by the British, which were, of course, denied. On 9 October 1999 the great-great-great-grandson of Queen Victoria, the Duke of Kent, launched centenary commemorations of the war in South Africa and admitted the 'dreadful abuses' of the British concentration camps. A total of 27,927 Boers died in the camps from disease, about 10 per cent of the Boer population.[11] In a speech in the Orange Free State he said, 'Let us all agree on one thing – never again war in South Africa, never again the rightly criticised policies of Kitchener and never again the dreadful abuses caused by the camps.'[12]

On 7 March Queen Victoria wrote to her daughter, Victoria, the Empress Frederick:

> I cannot tell you how grieved I am not to go and see you at Bordighera, or how I pine for the sunny, flowery south, but with the abuse against England and even me, and the war still going on and much to be settled, I feel I could not, with safety almost, go abroad. ... You will be startled when I tell you that I am going early next month to visit Ireland. It is entirely my own idea as was also my giving up going abroad. It will give great pleasure and do good.[13]

Gratitude for the gallantry of Irish soldiers in South Africa largely influenced the Queen's decision to spend her spring holiday of 1900 in Ireland, which she had not visited for 39 years. The Queen was very satisfied with the visit and said she would always retain a most grateful remembrance of the warm-hearted sympathetic people.

So it was the cancellation of a visit to the Riviera which, nine months before she died, led to the reconciliation with Ireland of the Queen of the United Kingdom of Great Britain and Ireland and Empress of India.

The question arises of why, despite Queen Victoria having spent nearly a year of her life on the Riviera, with many of her visits involving important events, her biographers have given it only a passing mention, despite what it reveals about her. The answer may be because it took so long for significant British memoirs and collections of letters to appear. The first of an important quintet was Henry Ponsonby's letters published in 1942; then Frederick Ponsonby's recollections in 1957; Lady Lytton's diary in 1961; Marie Mallet's letters in 1968; and finally, and best, Dr Reid's life, which was not published until 1987.

The Victorians and Victorianism became unpopular even before the First World War, typified by the publication in 1918 of Lytton Strachey's *Eminent Victorians*, which tumbled from their plinths such seeming heroes and heroines as Cardinal Manning, Florence Nightingale, Dr Arnold of Rugby School and General Gordon. When Strachey published his biography of Queen Victoria in 1921, readers expected a similar hatchet job. They were astonished by the largely favourable portrait, one which Michael Holroyd, Lytton Strachey's biographer, has described as 'a whimsical, teasing, half-admiring, half-mocking view'.[14] Virginia Woolf said that 'In time to come Lytton Strachey's queen Victoria will be Queen Victoria, just as Boswell's Johnson is now Dr Johnson.'[15]

If one looks back over a century of biographies it is, perhaps, surprising that the assessment of the Queen has little changed. Not surprisingly, the anonymous hagiography which appeared in the *Quarterly Review* in April 1901, which has been attributed to Lady Ponsonby, carried no breath of criticism – even her obstinacy was a virtue.[16] But a few months later, writing in *The Dictionary of National Biography*, Sir Sidney Lee ventured: 'The queen was not altogether free from that morbid tendency of mind that comes of excessive study of incidents of sorrow and suffering' and 'The queen's artistic sense was not strong.'[17] The consistent theme of later biographies over a century was, put simply, that she was a good woman and a good queen.

Queen Victoria died on 22 January 1901.

Note on the Queen's Journal

The Journal played an important part in the monarch's life, not least on the Riviera, where she wrote an average of some 2000 words on each of her visits. The Journals had started on 31 July 1832 with the entry 'This book, Mama gave me, that I might write the journal of my journey to Wales in it. Victoria, Kensington Palace, July 31st.'[1] The Queen was very methodical with her private papers and after her accession her letters were bound into volumes. In many cases the Queen had extracts from her Journal copied with the letters.

On her death Edward VII entrusted Arthur Christopher Benson and Viscount Esher to select letters and Journal entries from the volumes. The three volumes of the first series, called *The Letters of Queen Victoria: A Selection of her Majesty's Correspondence between the years 1837 and 1861*, which drew on 500–600 volumes of letters and Journal extracts, were published in 1907. In fact the correspondence started in May 1821, when Princess Victoria was two. The first letter was from the Duchess of Clarence, afterwards Queen Adelaide: 'My dear little heart, – I hope you are well and don't forget Aunt Adelaide, who loves you so fondly.'[2]

Esher was a friend of Queen Victoria and of Edward VII, and Benson was master of Magdalene College, Cambridge. King George V chose George Earle Buckle, a historian and former editor of *The Times*, to edit the second and third series. They were each of three volumes and appeared between 1926 and 1932. In his preface to the second series Buckle explained that:

> the present Editor has been privileged to have access to the written volumes of Queen Victoria's private Journal, which have been compiled, under the authority of King Edward and of his present Majesty, by Princess Beatrice, to whom the Queen left the manuscript, with instructions to modify or destroy any portions which appeared, in her Royal Highness's judgment to be unsuitable for preservation.[3]

The Dictionary of National Biography commented on Buckle's work: 'Buckle's editing was a triumph of self-suppression.'

Princess Beatrice copied out the Journals from 1 January 1837. We do not know what she suppressed, for many of the originals were burnt. The text from 1832 to 10 February 1840 survives in typescript. It was made for Lord Esher for use in his book *The Girlhood of Queen Victoria*, which was published in 1912 in two volumes.[4] The Queen herself published three volumes of Journals: *Leaves from the Journal of Our Life in the Highlands from 1848 to 1861* in 1868,[5] *More Leaves from the Journal of a Life in the Highlands from 1862 to 1882* in 1884[6] and *Leaves from a Journal: A record of the visit of the Emperor and Empress of the French to the Queen and of the visit of the Queen and HRH the Prince Consort to the Emperor of the French, 1855*, which was published privately in 1880 and publicly in 1961.[7]

The copyright is, of course, owned by the monarch of the day. The Journals have never been published in their entirety. Writers can apply to consult the Journals in the Royal Archives at Windsor Castle.

Notes

Introduction (pages 1–15)

[1] Xavier Paoli, *My Royal Clients* (trans Alexander Teixeira de Mattos) (London: Hodder and Stoughton, 1911), pp 331–2.

[2] Robert Latouche, *Histoire de Nice* (Nice: Ville de Nice, 1951–65), vol ii, p 198.

[3] Dominique Escribe, *La Côte d'Azur: Genèse d'un Mythe* (The Côte d'Azur: Genesis of a Myth) (Nice: Gilbert Vitaloni et le Conseil Générale des Alpes-Maritimes (A.C.A.M.), 1988), p 7.

[4] James Haug, *Leisure and Urbanism in Nineteenth Century Nice* (Lawrence, Kansas: The Regent Press of Kansas, 1982), p 5.

[5] James Boswell, *The Life of Samuel Johnson, LL.D.* (London: Charles Dilly, Third Edition, 1799. Reprint, London: Oxford University Press, 1938), vol ii, pp 24–5.

[6] Keith Thomas, *Man and the Natural World: Changing Attitudes in England 1500–1800* (London: Allen Lane, 1983), pp 15–22.

[7] Robert Southey, *Letters from England*, quoted in Thomas, *Man and the Natural World*, p 267.

[8] Quoted in James Buzard, *The Beaten Track: European Tourism, Literature and the Ways to Culture, 1800–1918* (Oxford: Oxford University Press, 1993), p 1.

[9] Daniel Boorstin, 'From Traveller to Tourist: The Lost Art of Travel' in *The Image: A Guide to Pseudo-Events in America*, revised edition (New York, 1987), pp 77–117, quoted in Lynne Withey, *Grand Tours and Cook's Tours: A History of Leisure Travel, 1750–1915* (London: Aurum Press, 1998), pp viii–ix.

[10] William Wordsworth, *The Poems* (ed John O. Hayden) (New Haven, Connecticut: Yale University Press, 1981), vol i, p 402, quoted in Buzard, *The Beaten Track*, p 19.

[11] Louis Burnet, *Villégiature et tourisme sur les côtes de France* (Holidays and Tourism on the French Seaboard) (Paris: Bibliothèque des guides bleus, Librairie Hachette, 1963), p 10, quoted in Haug, *Leisure and Urbanism in Nineteenth Century Nice*, pp 129, xiv.

[12] Escribe, *La Côte d'Azur*, p 8.

[13] Arthur Young, *Travels in France and Italy* (London, 1792; Dent reprint, 1976), p 220.

[14] Letter of 11 April 1787, quoted in Roy Moore and Alma Moore, *Thomas Jefferson's Journey to the South of France* (New York: Stewart, Tabori & Chang, 1999), p 99.

[15] Letter of 12 April 1787, quoted in Moore and Moore, *ibid.*, p 100.

[16] Tobias Smollett, *Travels through France and Italy, Containing Observations on Character, Customs, Religion, Government, Police, Commerce, Arts and Antiquities. With a particular Description of the Town, Territory and Climate of Nice, to which is added a Register of the Weather, kept during a residence of Eighteen Months in that city* (London: R. Baldwin, 1766. Reprint Fontwell, Sussex: Centaur Press, 1969).

[17] Charles Graves, *Royal Riviera* (London: William Heinemann, 1957), p 36.

[18] Paulette Leques, *Aspects de Nice du XVIIIe au XXe siècles* (Aspects of Nice from the 18th to 20th Century), Annales No 19 (Nice: Faculté des Lettres et Sciences Humaines de Nice and Les Belles Lettres, 1973), p 93.

[19] Charles Delormeau and Robin Avillach, 'Les Cimetières Anglais à Nice' (The English Cemeteries in Nice), *Nice Historique*, No 4, 1991, p 167.

[20] Escribe, *La Côte d'Azur*, p 9.

[21] Leques, *Aspects de Nice*, p 93.

[22] Anthony Trollope, *Travelling Sketches* (1866), p 101, quoted in John Pemble, *The Mediterranean Passion: Victorians and Edwardians in the South* (Oxford: Clarendon Press, 1987), p 1.

[23] Patrick Howarth, *When the Riviera Was Ours* (London: Routledge & Kegan Paul, 1977. Reprint, London: Century, 1988), pp 17–20.

[24] Robert Stewart, *Henry Brougham 1778–1868: His Public Career* (London: The Bodley Head, 1986), pp 354–60.

[25] Alexandre Dumas, *Une Année à Florence* (Paris: Editions Bourin, 1991), p 88, quoted in Colin Dyer, 'Hivernants et habitants sur la Riviéra Française: Nice et Cannes jusqu'à l'arrivée du chemin de fer' (Winter visitors and inhabitants on the French Riviera. Nice and Cannes up to the arrival of the railway), in *Recherches régionales Alpes-Maritimes et contrées limitrophes* (Archives Départementales, Conseil Général des Alpes-Maritimes), No 143, 1988, p 24.

[26] Escribe, *La Côte d'Azur*, p 11.

[27] Michel Saudan, Yolande Blanc and Sylvia Saudan-Skira, *De l'Hôtel-Palais en Riviera* (The Hotel Palace on the Riviera) (Geneva: Atelier d'edition 'Le Septième Fou', 1985), p 55.

[28] Escribe, *La Côte d'Azur*, p 12.

[29] Saudan, Blanc and Saudan-Skira, *De l'Hôtel-Palais en Riviera*, p 55.

[30] *Ibid.*

[31] Escribe, *La Côte d'Azur*, p 9.

[32] *Ibid.*, p 11.

[33] A.J.P. Taylor, *The Struggle for Mastery in Europe 1848–1918* (Oxford: Clarendon Press, 1954, Reprint, 1971), pp 103–19.

[34] Graves, *Royal Riviera*, p 24.

[35] Smollett, *Travels through France and Italy*, pp 78, 116, 132.

[36] Graves, *Royal Riviera*, p 39.

[37] Saudan, Blanc and Saudan-Skira, *De l'Hôtel-Palais en Riviera*, p 32.

[38] Dyer, 'Hivernants et habitants', p 19.

[39] James Henry Bennet, *Winter and Spring on the Shores of the Mediterranean*, fifth edition (London: J & A Churchill, 1875), p 642.

[40] Withey, *Grand Tours and Cook's Tours*, p 170.

[41] Henry Alford, *The Riviera (1870)*, pp 2–3, quoted in Pemble, *The Mediterranean Passion*, p 27.

[42] Withey, *Grand Tours and Cook's Tours*, p 173.

[43] Karl Baedeker, *South-Eastern France, including Corsica: Handbook for Travellers*, third edition (London: Dulau & Co., 1898), p xv.

[44] Withey, *Grand Tours and Cook's Tours*, p 179.

[45] Leques, *Aspects de Nice*, p 96. Leques quotes *Le Messager de Nice* of 17 and 18 March 1861 and *Les Echos de Nice* of 15 March 1861, giving total visitors of 4560. But, despite the fact that Nice was now part of France, the French were included with the foreigners. There were about the same number of French and English, making up together 61 per cent. Therefore if 30.5 per cent of French visitors, making 1390, is deducted from the total, foreigners totalled 3170. Statistics were often published in terms of families. Most commentators have taken the family to be five persons.

[46] Population Censuses, 1886, 1891, 1896, ADAM 06M0011 to 06M0026.

[47] Maurice Bordes, *Histoire de Nice et du pays niçois* (Toulouse: Edouard Privat, 1976), pp 307–8.

[48] Département des Alpes-Maritimes, *Annuaire Administratif, statistique et historique* (Nice: Librarie Ch. Cauvin, 1861–1901).

[49] Haug, *Leisure and Urbanism in Nineteenth Century Nice*, p 32.

[50] Latouche, *Histoire de Nice*, vol i, p 116.

[51] Haug, *Leisure and Urbanism in Nineteenth Century Nice*, pp 1–3.

[52] Fernand Braudel, *The Mediterranean and the Mediterranean World in the Age of Philip II* (trans Siân Reynolds) (London: Fontana/Collins, 1975), vol i, p 43.

[53] Haug, *Leisure and Urbanism in Nineteenth Century Nice*, pp 3–5.

[54] *Ibid.*, p xiv.

[55] Dyer, 'Hivernants et habitants', pp 24–5.

[56] *Ibid.*

[57] Bennet, *Winter and Spring on the Shores of the Mediterranean*, pp vii–viii.

[58] Howarth, *When the Riviera Was Ours*, p 34.

[59] Bennet, *Winter and Spring on the Shores of the Mediterranean*, p 7.

[60] *Ibid.*, p 8.

[61] Howarth, *When the Riviera Was Ours*, p 50.

[62] Henry James, *Hawthorne* (New York: Collier Books, 1966, originally published 1879), pp 47–8.

[63] Robert Tomes, 'The Americans on Their Travels', *Harper's New Monthly Magazine*, 31, p 57, quoted in William W. Stowe, *Going Abroad: European Travel in Nineteenth-Century American Culture* (Princeton: Princeton University Press, 1994), p 8.

[64] Edith Wharton, *A Backward Glance* (London: J.M. Dent, 1993, originally published 1934), p 31.

[65] *Ibid.*, p 58.

[66] J.A. Lindsay, *The Climatic Treatment of Consumption* (1887), pp 40–1, quoted in Pemble, *The Mediterranean Passion*, p 247.

[67] Lindsay, *The Climatic Treatment of Consumption* (1887), pp 29–30, quoted in Pemble, *The Mediterranean Passion*, p 250.

[68] James Johnson, *Change of Air*, quoted in Pemble, *The Mediterranean Passion*, p 251.

[69] Lindsay, *The Climatic Treatment of Consumption* (1887), p 182, quoted in Pemble, *The Mediterranean Passion*, pp 251–2.

[70] Pemble, *The Mediterranean Passion*, p 252.

[71] *Ibid.*, p 246; Thomas Linn, *The Health Resorts of Europe: A medical guide to the mineral springs, climatic mountain and seaside health resorts, milk, whey, grape, earth, mud, sand and air cures of Europe* (London: Henry Kimpton, 1899), p 190.

[72] Lindsay, *The Climatic Treatment of Consumption* (1887), pp 40–1, quoted in Pemble, *The Mediterranean Passion*, p 247.

Chapter 1. Prologue (pages 16–19)

[1] David Duff, *Victoria Travels: Journeys of Queen Victoria between 1830 and 1900, with Extracts from her Journal* (New York: Taplinger Publishing Company, 1971), pp 59–67.

[2] Stanley Weintraub, *Victoria: An Intimate Biography* (New York: Truman Talley Books/Dutton, 1987. Reprint, New York: Truman Talley/Plume, 1992), pp 71–2.

[3] Letter from St Cloud to the King of the Belgians, 23 August 1855 in A.C. Benson and Viscount Esher (eds), *The Letters of Queen Victoria: A Selection of Her Majesty's Correspondence between the year 1837 and 1861* (London: John Murray, 1907), vol iii, p 172.

[4] Letter from St Cloud to the King of the Belgians, 23 August 1855 in Benson and Esher (eds), *The Letters of Queen Victoria*, vol iii, p 173.

[5] Monica Charlot, *Victoria: The Young Queen* (Oxford: Blackwell, 1991), p 364.

[6] Weintraub, *Victoria: An Intimate Biography*, p 251.

[7] Letter from St Cloud to the King of the Belgians, 29 August 1855 in Benson and Esher (eds), *The Letters of Queen Victoria*, vol iii, p 175.

[8] Duff, *Victoria Travels*, p 152.

[9] Charles Greville, *The Greville Memoirs: A Journal of the Reigns of King George IV, King William IV and Queen Victoria* (ed H. Reeve) (London: Longmans, Green, 1888), vol vii, p 291.

[10] Delia Millar, 'Queen Victoria Goes South', *Country Life*, 26 September 1985, pp 860–1.

[11] Arthur Ponsonby, *Henry Ponsonby, Queen Victoria's Private Secretary: His Life from his Letters* (London: Macmillan, 1942), p 284.

[12] Millar, 'Queen Victoria Goes South', pp 860–1.

Chapter 2. 1882: Menton (pages 20–36)

[1] *The Times*, 15 March 1882.

[2] Duff, *Victoria Travels*, p 11.

[3] *The Times*, 15 March 1882.

[4] *The Times*, 14 March 1882; Weintraub, *Victoria: An Intimate Biography*, p 404.

[5] Letter of 28 February 1882, PRO, FO 27/2561.

[6] Reuters reports in *The Times*, 11 and 12 April 1899.

[7] Frederick Ponsonby, *Recollections of Three Reigns* (London: Eyre & Spottiswoode, 1957), pp 52–3.

[8] Michaela Reid, *Ask Sir James: The Life of Sir James Reid, Personal Physician to Queen Victoria* (London: Viking, 1987), pp 47–8.

[9] Frederick Ponsonby, *Recollections*, p 53.

[10] *The Times*, 16 March 1882.

[11] Paoli, *My Royal Clients*, p 333.

[12] Duff, *Victoria Travels*, pp 333–4.

[13] Paoli, *My Royal Clients*, pp 333–4.

[14] Patrick Kingston, *Royal Trains* (London: Spring Books, 1989), pp 129, 136.

[15] Reid, *Ask Sir James*, p 48.

[16] Howarth, *When the Riviera Was Ours*, p 70.

[17] *The Times*, 15 March 1882.

[18] Mary Lutyens (ed), *Lady Lytton's Court Diary, 1895–1899* (London: Hart-Davis, 1961), p 95.

[19] Reuters report in *The Times*, 17 March 1882.

[20] Court Circular, 17 March 1882.

[21] Royal Archives, Queen Victoria's Journal, 16 March 1882.

[22] *The Times*, 17 March 1882.

[23] RA QVJ, 16 March 1882.

[24] RA QVJ, 30 March 1882.

[25] Quoted in Alan Sillitoe, *Leading the Blind: A Century of Guide Book Travel 1815–1914* (London: Macmillan, 1995), p 120.

[26] Millar, 'Queen Victoria Goes South', p 862.

[27] Reid, *Ask Sir James*, p 48.

[28] *Ibid.*, pp 49–50.

[29] Reuters report in *The Times*, 18 March 1882.

[30] Reuters report in *The Times*, 4 April 1882.

[31] Letter of 17 March 1882, PRO, FO 27/2561.

[32] *British Medical Journal* reports in *The Times*, 17 March and 14 April 1882.

[33] Bennet, *Winter and Spring on the Shores of the Mediterranean*, pp vii–viii.

[34] RA QVJ, 27 April 1882 in Christopher Hibbert (ed), *Queen Victoria in her Letters and Journals* (London: John Murray, 1984. Reprint, Harmondsworth, Middlesex: Penguin, 1985), p 273.

[35] Reuters report in *The Times*, 1 April 1882.

[36] *The Lancet* report in *The Times*, 14 April 1882.

[37] RA QVJ, 7 April 1882.

[38] Elizabeth Longford, *Victoria R.I.* (London: Weidenfeld & Nicolson Ltd, 1964), p 447.

[39] RA QVJ, 28 March 1882.

[40] RA QVJ, 20 March 1882.

[41] *The Times*, 27 March 1882.

[42] *The Times*, 10 April 1882.

[43] *The Times*, 25 March 1882.

[44] *The Times*, 6 April 1882.

[45] Bennet, *Winter and Spring on the Shores of the Mediterranean*, pp 96–8.

[46] Howarth, *When the Riviera Was Ours*, p 59.

[47] Letter of 26 January 2000 to the author from Lady de Bellaigue, Registrar, the Royal Archives.

[48] Reuters telegram, *The Times*, 25 March 1882.

[49] Charles Quest-Ritson, *The English Garden Abroad* (London: Viking, 1992), pp 63–4.

[50] HRH The Duchess of York and Benita Stoney, *Travels with Queen Victoria* (London: Weidenfeld and Nicolson, 1993), p 192.

[51] Quest-Ritson, p 63.

[52] *Ibid.*, pp 63–75.

[53] Vivian Russell, *Gardens of the Riviera* (London: Little Brown, 1993), p 46.

[54] The Hanbury Gardens are four kilometres from Menton on the right-hand side of the coast road into Italy.

[55] Vivien Noakes, *Edward Lear: The Life of a Wanderer* (London: Collins, 1968), pp 295–6.

[56] Angus Davidson, *Edward Lear: Landscape Painter and Nonsense Poet (1812–1888)* (London: John Murray, 1968), p 263.

[57] Quest-Ritson, *The English Garden Abroad*, pp 23–4.

[58] Edward Lear's diary, 2 August 1882, quoted in Noakes, *Edward Lear: The Life of a Wanderer*, p 296.

[59] Peter Levi, *Edward Lear: A Biography* (London: Macmillan, 1995), p 236.

[60] Davidson, *Edward Lear: Landscape Painter and Nonsense Poet*, p 263.

[61] Letter of 25 March 1882 and the Queen's reply of 29 March, quoted in Roger Fulford (ed), *Beloved Mama: Private Correspondence of Queen Victoria and the German Crown Princess 1878–1885* (London: Evans Bros, 1981), pp 116–17.

[62] RA QVJ, 30 March 1882.

[63] Anne Edwards, *The Grimaldis of Monaco* (New York: William Morrow, 1992), p 132.

[64] Louis Turner and John Ash, *The Golden Hordes: International Tourism and the Pleasure Periphery* (London: Constable, 1975), p 61.

[65] Graves, *Royal Riviera*, pp 60–75.

[66] *British Medical Journal* report in *The Times*, 14 April 1982.

[67] Graves, *Royal Riviera*, p 61.

[68] Burney Yeo, *Health Resorts*, p 295, quoted in Pemble, *The Mediterranean Passion*, p 252.

[69] Bennet, *Winter and Spring on the Shores of the Mediterranean*, pp 179–80.

[70] Edward Isaac Sparks, *The Riviera: Sketches of the Health Resorts of the Northern Mediterranean Coasts of France and Italy* (1879), p 299, quoted in Pemble, *The Medi-*

terranean Passion, p 252.

[71] Graves, *Royal Riviera*, p 74.

[72] Quoted in Mary Blume, *Côte d'Azur: Inventing the French Riviera* (London: Thames and Hudson, 1992), p 61.

[73] J.R. Green, *Stray Studies from England and Italy* (London: Macmillan, 1876), p 65.

[74] Mary Blume, *Côte d'Azur*, pp 61–2.

[75] Reid, *Ask Sir James*, p 49.

[76] Blume, *Côte d'Azur*, p 62.

[77] Howarth, *When the Riviera Was Ours*, p 51.

[78] RA QVJ, 7 April 1882.

[79] *The Times*, 12 April 1882.

[80] Reuters report in *The Times*, 23 March 1882.

[81] Reuters report in *The Times*, 11 April 1882.

[82] Reuters report in *The Times*, 17 March 1882.

[83] Howarth, *When the Riviera Was Ours*, p 70.

[84] Reid, *Ask Sir James*, p 48.

[85] Letter of 20 March 1882 in Arthur Ponsonby, *Henry Ponsonby, Queen Victoria's Private Secretary*, p 285.

[86] RA QVJ, 19 March 1882.

[87] W.E. Gladstone, *The Gladstone Diaries* (eds M.R.D. Foot and H.C.G. Matthew) (Oxford: Clarendon Press, 1986), vol x, p 151.

[88] RA QVJ, 5 April 1882.

[89] Court Circular, 8 April 1882.

[90] Court Circular, 13 April 1882.

[91] RA QVJ, 12 April 1882.

[92] Court Circular, 14 April 1882.

[93] RA QVJ, 14 April 1882.

[94] *The Lancet* report in *The Times*, 14 April 1882.

[95] £40,479 at 1999 values.

[96] PRO, LC 11/249.

[97] The Chalet des Rosiers is best seen from the gardens of the Val Rahmeh. Exit Menton on the coast road, Porte de France, towards Italy; turn left after the second church on the left, up the Avenue St Jacques. The gardens are at the top of the hill on the left.

Chapter 3. 1887: Cannes (pages 37–50)

[1] Charlotte Zeepvat, *Prince Leopold: The Untold Story of Queen Victoria's Youngest Son* (Stroud: Sutton Publishing, 1998), pp 184–5.

[2] The Cercle Nautique is now the Hôtel Noga-Hilton on the Croisette.

[3] Letter of 27 March 1884, Royal Archives Add A30/418, quoted in Zeepvat, *Prince Leopold*, p 187.

[4] *Central News* interview with Perceval, 30 March 1884, quoted in Zeepvat, *Prince Leopold*, p 186.

[5] Zeepvat, *Prince Leopold*, pp 187–8.

[6] D.M. Potts and W.T.W Potts, *Queen Victoria's Gene* (Stroud: Alan Sutton Publishing, 1995), p 149.

[7] Minutes of the Annual General Meeting of the Société Foncière de Cannes et du Littoral of 2 April 1884, ADAM 8 J 312.

[8] RA QVJ, 28 March 1884, quoted in Hibbert (ed) *Queen Victoria in Her Letters and Journals*, p 285.

[9] Register of St George's Church, Cannes, 2 April 1887.

[10] Interview by author with Mme Emy Cabot, caretaker of St George's Church, Cannes, 11 November 1999. St George's Church is at 29 Avenue Roi Albert, Californie, Cannes.

[11] Charlotte Zeepvat, 'In Royal Footsteps', *Royalty Digest*, June 1998, p 363.

[12] In January 2000 the Villa Nevada came on to the market at a price of FF12,000,000 (£1,200,000).

[13] The Villas Edelweiss and Nevada and the Memorial Fountain are on the Boulevard des Pins, Californie, Cannes.

[14] The Villa Victoria is at 5 Avenue Docteur Picaud, west Cannes.

[15] Zeepvat, *Prince Leopold*, pp 25–34.

[16] *Ibid.*, pp 178–9.

[17] Letter to Princess Frederica, 18 January 1884, Royal Archives LI/129, quoted in Zeepvat, *Prince Leopold*, p 184.

[18] Zeepvat, *Prince Leopold*, p 184.

[19] Letter of 15 March 1884, Hessisches Staatsarchiv Darmstadt, Grossherzogliches Familienarchiv Abt D24 Nr.15/6, original in German, quoted in Zeepvat, *Prince Leopold*, p 186.

[20] Letter from the Prince of Wales to the Queen, 22 January 1887, Royal Archives Z.162/10, quoted in Philip Magnus, *King Edward the Seventh* (London: John Murray, 1964), p 197.

[21] Margaret Maria Brewster, *Letters from Cannes and Nice* (Edinburgh: Thomas Constable, 1857), pp 48, 151.

[22] *The Times*, 29 March 1887.

[23] *The Times*, 2 April 1887.

[24] Duff, *Victoria Travels*, p 263.

[25] *The Times*, 7 April 1887.

[26] *The Times*, 1 April 1887.

[27] £5,281 at 1999 values.

[28] Brewster, *Letters from Cannes and Nice*, p 33.

[29] £42.24 to £62.84 at 1999 values.

[30] Brewster, *Letters from Cannes and Nice*, pp 37–8.

[31] J. Mossop, *Thomas Robinson Woolfield's Life at Cannes and Lord Brougham's First Arrival* (London: Kegan Paul, Trench, Truebner, 1890), pp 6–13.

[32] *Ibid.*, pp 29–45.

[33] Quoted in Henri Sappia, 'Les Anglais sur la Côte d'Azur' (The English on the Côte d'Azur), *Nice Historique*, No 6, March 1899, p 84.

[34] Walburga Paget, *In my Tower* (London: Hutchinson, 1924), vol i, p 165.

[35] Letters of 17 and 18 December 1856, quoted in Quest-Ritson, *The English Garden Abroad*, p 16.

[36] Quest-Ritson, *The English Garden Abroad*, p 16.

[37] Lear's diary, 2 February 1870, quoted in Noakes, *Edward Lear: The Life of a Wanderer*, p 241.

[38] Horatio F. Brown, *John Addington Symonds: a biography*, no page, quoted in Davidson, *Edward Lear: Landscape Painter and Nonsense Poet*, p 171.

[39] 'Ecologue', *The Complete Nonsense of Edward Lear* (ed Holbrook Jackson) (London: Faber and Faber, 1947), pp 277–8, quoted in Noakes, *Edward Lear: The Life of a Wanderer*, pp 221–2.

[40] *The Times*, 4 April 1887.

[41] RA QVJ, 3 April 1887.

[42] Interview by author with Rev. Ian Barclay, Priest-in-Charge, Holy Trinity Church, Cannes, 9 November 1999. The church is at 2–4 rue Général Ferrié, off the rue du Canada, behind the Carlton Hotel.

[43] RA QVJ, 3 April 1887.

[44] Court Circular, 6 April 1887.

[45] Letter to Crown Princess Victoria, 26 December 1861, quoted in Fulford (ed), *Dearest Mama*, p 30.

[46] Letter to Crown Princess Victoria, 18 June 1862, quoted in Fulford (ed), *Dearest Mama*, p 78.

[47] Paoli, *My Royal Clients*, p 208.

[48] *The Times*, 30 January 1883.

[49] *The Times*, 30 January 1883.

[50] *The Times*, 1 and 5 February 1883.

[51] Virgina Cowles, *Edward VII and His Circle* (London: Hamish Hamilton, 1956), p 144.

[52] Theo Aronson, *The King in Love: Edward VII's Mistresses* (London: John Murray, 1988), p 116.

[53] Agnes De Stoeckl, George Kinnaird (eds), *Not all Vanity* (London: John Murray, 1950), p 67.

[54] Aronson, *The King in Love*, p 224.

[55] Magnus, *King Edward the Seventh*, p 175.

[56] Latouche, *Histoire de Nice*, vol ii, p 168.

[57] Aronson, *The King in Love*, p 227.

[58] J.P.C. Sewell, *Personal Letters of King Edward VII: Together with Extracts from the Correspondence of Queen Alexandra, the Duke of Albany and General Sir Arthur and Lady Paget* (London: Hutchinson, 1931), p 221.

[59] Yvette Guilbert, *Chanson de ma vie* (Song of my Life), pp 218–24, quoted in Magnus, *King Edward the Seventh*, p 246.

[60] Frank Harris, *My Life and Loves* (ed John F. Gallagher) (London: W.H. Allen, 1964), p 466.

[61] Magnus, *King Edward the Seventh*, p 262.

[62] *Ibid.*, pp 176–7.

[63] Alfred E.T. Watson, *King Edward VII as a Sportsman* (London: Longmans Green, 1911), pp 295–6, 372–81.

[64] Paoli, *My Royal Clients*, pp 201–2.

[65] *Ibid.*, p 225.

[66] Musée Masséna, Nice, *Les Anglais dans le Comté de Nice et en Provence depuis le XVIIIme siècle: L'Art Anglais au Musée Masséna* (The English in the County of Nice and in Provence since the XVIIIth Century: English Art at the Musée Masséna) (Nice: Editions des Amis du Musée Masséna, 1934), p 89.

[67] Blume, *Côte d'Azur*, p 60.

[68] Letter from the Prince of Wales to the Queen, 22 January 1887, Royal Archives Z.162/10, quoted in Magnus, *King Edward the Seventh*, p 197.

[69] Court Circular, 6 April 1887.

[70] Arthur Ponsonby, *Henry Ponsonby, Queen Victoria's Private Secretary*, p 285.

[71] RA QVJ, 23 April 1887, quoted in Duff, *Victoria Travels*, pp 265–7.

[72] Ponsonby Letters, 22 December 1888, quoted in Longford, *Victoria R.I.*, p 498.

[73] £422.40 at 1999 values.

[74] Duff, *Victoria Travels*, p 304.

[75] Lutyens (ed), *Lady Lytton's Court Diary*, p 102.

[76] £37,917 at 1999 values.

[77] PRO, LC 11/269.

Chapter 4. 1891: Grasse (pages 51–69)

[1] Duff, *Victoria Travels*, pp 282–5.

[2] Lutyens (ed), *Lady Lytton's Court Diary*, p 98.

[3] PRO, FO 27/3059.

[4] Saudan, Blanc and Saudan-Skira, *De l'Hôtel-Palais en Riviera*, p 29.

[5] Stephen Liégeard, *La Côte d'Azur* (Paris: Académie Française, 1887 & 1894. Reprint of 1894 edition, Nice: Serre, 1988), p 208.

[6] *Le Commerce*, 22 February 1891.

[7] *Le Commerce*, 22 March 1891.

[8] *Le Commerce*, 22 March 1891.

[9] The former Grand Hôtel is at 26 Avenue Victoria.

[10] Roger Grihangne, *La Reine Victoria à Grasse* (*Queen Victoria in Grasse*) (trans and ed David Lockie) (Grasse: Ville de Grasse, 1991).

[11] *Ibid.*, pp 33–5; Miriam Rothschild and others *The Rothschild Gardens* (London: Gaia Books, 1996), p 20.

[12] Russell, *Gardens of the Riviera*, pp 30–2.

[13] Marcel Gaucher, *Les jardins de la fortune* (The gardens of fortune) (Paris: Hermé, 1985), p 27.

[14] *Ibid.*, pp 15–16.

[15] Constance Battersea, *Reminiscences* (London: Macmillan, 1922), pp 114–15.

[16] Gaucher, *Les jardins de la fortune*, p 25.

[17] *Ibid.*, p 32.

[18] *Ibid.*, p 18.

[19] *Ibid.*, p 13.

[20] *Ibid.*, p 16.

[21] RA QVJ, 22 April 1891.

[22] The former Villa Victoria is at 46 Avenue Victoria, Grasse.

[23] The teahouse is now at 198 Boulevard Président Kennedy in Super Grasse.

[24] *Le Commerce*, 8 April 1891, quoted in Grihangne, *Queen Victoria in Grasse*, pp 25–6.

[25] Letter of 25 April 1891 to Bernard Mallet, quoted in Victor Mallet (ed), *Life with Queen Victoria: Marie Mallet's letters from Court 1887–1901* (London: John Murray, 1968), pp 53–4.

[26] Letter of 26 April 1891 to Bernard Mallet, quoted in *ibid.*, p 54.

[27] £5116 at 1999 values.

[28] Letter of 24 April 1891 to Bernard Mallet, quoted in Mallet (ed), *Life with Queen Victoria*, pp 52–3.

[29] *The Times*, 17 April 1891.

[30] The Villa Wenden is now called Villa le Rouve and is at 15/19 Avenue de la Favorite, Californie, Cannes.

[31] Ricardo Mateos Sainz de Medrano, 'A Child of the Caucasus' in *Royalty Digest*, July 1993, pp 12–14.

[32] *The Times*, 20 April 1891.

[33] *The Times*, 28 April 1891.

[34] PRO, FO 27/3059.

[35] *The Times*, 11 April 1891.

[36] Gaucher, *Les Jardins de la fortune*, p 26.

[37] Letter to the Empress Frederick of 27 April 1891, quoted in Agatha Ramm (ed), *Beloved and Darling Child: Last Letters between Queen Victoria and her Eldest Daughter 1886–1901* (Stroud: Alan Sutton Publishing, 1990), pp 125–6.

[38] RA QVJ, 30 March 1891.

[39] Battersea, *Reminiscences*, pp 115–16.

[40] *The Times*, 28 April 1891.

[41] £256 at 1999 values.

[42] *The Times*, 28 April 1891.

[43] Reid, *Ask Sir James*, p 159.

[44] *The Times*, 21 April 1891.

[45] Roland Allison and Sarah Riddell (eds), *The Royal Encyclopedia* (London: Macmillan, 1991), p 627.

[46] Edwards, *The Grimaldis of Monaco*, pp 141–2.

[47] *Ibid.*, p 154.

[48] *Ibid.*, p 161.

[49] Letter to Lady Elizabeth Biddulph of 2 April 1891, quoted in Mallet (ed), *Life with*

Queen Victoria, p 43.

[50] Dulcie M. Ashdown, *Victoria and the Coburgs* (London: Robert Hale, 1981), pp 14, 112–13.

[51] Roger Fulford, *Your Dear Letter: Private Correspondence of Queen Victoria and the German Crown Princess 1865–1871* (London: Evans Bros, 1971) p 201.

[52] HRH Princess Stephanie of Belgium, *I Was To Be Empress* (London: Ivor Nicholson & Watson, 1937), pp 113–14.

[53] Ashdown, *Victoria and the Coburgs*, p 138.

[54] Princess Stephanie, *I Was To Be Empress*, p 248.

[55] Alan Palmer, *Twilight of the Hapsburgs: The Life and Times of Emperor Francis Joseph* (London: Weidenfeld and Nicolson, 1994), p 215.

[56] Princess Stephanie, *I Was To Be Empress*, p 210.

[57] *Ibid.*, p 72.

[58] *Ibid.*, p 254.

[59] Palmer, *Twilight of the Hapsburgs*, p 265.

[60] Theo Aronson, *The Coburgs of Belgium* (London: Cassell, 1968), p 135.

[61] Letter of 15 April 1891, quoted in Mallet (ed), *Life with Queen Victoria*, pp 51–2.

[62] Letter of 24 April 1891, quoted in *ibid.*, pp 52–3.

[63] F. Eyck, *The Prince Consort* (London: Chatto & Windus, 1959), p 19, quoted in Ashdown, *Victoria and the Coburgs*, p 95.

[64] Ashdown, *Victoria and the Coburgs*, p 95.

[65] RA QVJ, 31 March 1891.

[66] Letter to Bernard Mallet of 31 April 1891, quoted in Mallet (ed), *Life with Queen Victoria*, p 48.

[67] £390,000 at 1999 values.

[68] Michael Alexander and Sushila Anand, *Queen Victoria's Maharajah: Duleep Singh, 1838–1893* (New York: Taplinger Publishing, 1980), pp 2–20.

[69] RA QVJ, 6 July 1854, quoted in Alexander and Anand, *Queen Victoria's Maharajah*, p 43.

[70] *Ibid.*, pp 43–53.

[71] E. Dalhousie Login (ed), *Lady Login's Recollections* (London, 1916), no page, quoted in Alexander and Anand, *Queen Victoria's Maharajah*, p 58.

[72] Alexander and Anand, *Queen Victoria's Maharajah*, pp 100–16.

[73] Letter (undated) to Lord Cross, Secretary of State for India, RA 010/97, quoted in Alexander and Anand, *Queen Victoria's Maharajah*, p 290.

[74] Letter of 1 August 1890 from Lord Cross to Duleep Singh, RA 010/102, quoted in Alexander and Anand, *Queen Victoria's Maharajah*, p 290.

[75] Alexander and Anand, *Queen Victoria's Maharajah*, p 292.

[76] Lena Login, *Sir John Login and Duleep Singh* (London: W.H. Allen, 1890), pp 374–5.

[77] Annotation on a draft of a letter from Sir Henry Ponsonby to the Prince of Wales, quoted in Alexander and Anand, *Queen Victoria's Maharajah*, p 294.

[78] Letter of 28 October 1893, RA 010/119, quoted in Alexander and Anand, *Queen Victoria's Maharajah*, p 299.

[79] *The Times*, 30 July 1999.

[80] Alexander and Anand, *Queen Victoria's Maharajah*, p 301.

[81] *Daily Mail*, 30 July 1999.

[82] RA QVJ, 8 April 1891.

[83] Reid, *Ask Sir James*, p 160.

[84] RA QVJ, 9 April 1891; Reid, *Ask Sir James*, pp 159–60.

[85] RA QVJ, 9 April 1891.

[86] Letter to Lady Elizabeth Biddulph of 10 April 1891, quoted in Mallet (ed), *Life with Queen Victoria*, p 44.

[87] Letter to Bernard Mallet of 13 April 1891, quoted in *ibid.*, p 50.

[88] Letter to Bernard Mallet of 21 April 1891, quoted in *ibid.*, p 52.

[89] RA QVJ, 21 April 1891.

[90] RA QVJ, 27 March 1891.

[91] £10,399 at 1999 values.

[92] £39,688 at 1999 values.

[93] Brochure and pamphlet of the Association des Amis de la Chapelle de Victoria de Grasse.

[94] St John's Church is at 65 Avenue Victoria, Grasse.

[95] Reuters report in *The Times*, 28 March 1891.

[96] St George's Church Register, 22 April 1891.

[97] Mallet (ed), *Life with Queen Victoria*, p xvii.

[98] Letter to Lady Elizabeth Biddulph of 26 March 1891, quoted in *ibid.*, pp 41–2.

[99] Letter to Bernard Mallet of 28 March 1891, quoted in *ibid.*, p 47.

[100] Letter to Bernard Mallet of 28 March 1891, quoted in *ibid.*, p 47.

[101] Letter to Bernard Mallet of 14 April 1891, quoted in *ibid.*, p 51.

[102] Letter to Bernard Mallet of 25 March 1891, quoted in *ibid.*, p 47.

[103] Letter to Bernard Mallet of 1 April 1891, quoted in *ibid.*, p 49.

[104] RA VIC/Z 258 110.

[105] RA QVJ, 27 April 1891.

[106] £119,203 at 1999 values.

[107] PRO, LC 11/284.

[108] *Le Commerce*, 30 April 1891, quoted in Grihangne, *Queen Victoria in Grasse*, p 29.

Chapter 5. 1892: Hyères (pages 70–78)

[1] Court Circular, 22 March 1892.

[2] RA QVJ, 2 April 1892.

[3] *The Times*, 16 April 1892.

[4] Alphonse Denis, *Hyères ancien et moderne: Promenades pittoresques, scientifiques et littéraires sur son territoire, ses environs et ses îles* (Hyères Ancient and Modern: Picturesque, Scientific and Literary Walks on its Territory, Surroundings and Islands) (Hyères: c.1835. Reprint of 1910 edition, Marseilles: Laffite Reprints, 1995), p 658.

[5] Leaflet 'Eglise Anglicane' of the Service des Affaires Culturelles d'Hyères.

[6] Aubin-Louis Millin, *Voyages dans les départements du Midi de la France* (Journeys in the Departments of the South of France) (Paris: Imprimérie Impériale, 1807), pp 450, 568, quoted in Dyer, 'Hivernants et habitants sur la Riviéra Française', p 21.

[7] Denis, *Hyères ancien et moderne*, pp 660–2.

[8] £1228 to £8186 at 1999 values.

[9] John Murray, *A Handbook for Travellers in France*, 15th Edition (London: John Murray, 1881), vol ii, pp 170–1.

[10] Claire Caronia, 'La Communauté Protestante à Hyères de 1800 à 1945' (The Protestant Community in Hyères from 1800 to 1945), summary of a Master's thesis at the University of Nice, *Recherches régionales Alpes-Maritimes et contrées limitrophes*, Archives Départementales, Conseil Géneral des Alpes-Maritimes, 1998, No 143, pp 35–61.

[11] Leaflet 'Eglise Anglicane' of the Service des Affaires Culturelles d'Hyères.

[12] Howarth, *When the Riviera Was Ours*, pp 121–3.

[13] *Ibid.*; James Pope-Hennessy, *Robert Louis Stevenson* (London: Jonathan Cape, 1974), pp 161–7.

[14] Letter to John Addington Symonds, January 1883, in Sidney Colvin (ed), *The Letters of Robert Louis Stevenson* (London: Methuen, 1899, new edition, 1911), vol ii, p 95.

[15] Letter to Mr Simoneau, summer 1883, in *ibid.*, p 128.

[16] Howarth, *When the Riviera Was Ours*, p 122.

[17] Quoted in Giles St Aubyn, *Queen Victoria: A Portrait* (London: Sinclair Stevenson, 1991), p 566.

[18] E. Benson, *Queen Victoria* (London: Longmans, 1935), p 335.

[19] St Aubyn, *Queen Victoria: A Portrait*, pp 566–7.

[20] Ponsonby letters, 13 April 1892, quoted in Longford, *Victoria R.I.*, p 516.

[21] Longford, *Victoria R.I.*, pp 517–22.

[22] *Ibid.*, p 516.

[23] *Ibid.*

[24] Weintraub, *Victoria: An Intimate Biography*, pp 369–70.

[25] Stephen Gwynn and Gertrude Tuckwell, *The Life of the Rt. Hon. Sir Charles W. Dilke Bart., M.P.* (London: John Murray, 1917) vol ii, pp 523–4.

[26] Longford, *Victoria R.I.*, p 516.

[27] Arthur Ponsonby, *Henry Ponsonby, Queen Victoria's Private Secretary*, p 285.

[28] *The Times*, 24 March 1892.

[29] RA QVJ, 18 April 1892.

[30] RA QVJ, 2 April 1892.

[31] Longford, *Victoria R.I.*, p 516.

[32] RA QVJ, 6 April 1892.

[33] RA QVJ, 11 April 1892.

[34] *The Times*, 28 March 1892.

[35] RA QVJ, 15 April 1892.

[36] *The Times*, 28 March 1892.

[37] *The Times*, 29 March 1892.

[38] All Saints Church is on the Boulevard Félix Descroix, near the Catholic Church of Notre Dame de Consolation.

[39] St Paul's Church is on the corner of Avenue Alexis Godillot and Avenue de Beauregard.

[40] RA QVJ, 29 March 1892.

[41] *The Times*, 16 April 1892.

[42] *The Times*, 23 and 24 March 1892; Henri Letuaire, *Combat de Trafalgar*, pamphlet (Hyères: G. Bloch, 1891).

[43] Mallet (ed), *Life with Queen Victoria*, p xiii.

[44] *Ibid.*, p 25.

[45] *The Times*, 23 April 1892.

[46] £2456 at 1999 values.

[47] *The Times*, 26 April 1892.

[48] Reuters report in *The Times*, 26 April 1892.

[49] Reuters report in *The Times*, 18 April 1892.

Chapter 6. 1895: Nice (pages 79–93)

[1] Court Circular, 15 March 1895.

[2] RA QVJ, 15 March 1895.

[3] *Eclaireur de Nice*, 16 March 1895.

[4] Saudan, Blanc and Saudan-Skira, *De l'Hôtel-Palais en Riviera*, p 56.

[5] RA QVJ, 15 March 1895.

[6] Daniel J. Boorstin, *The Americans: The Democratic Experience* (New York: Vintage Books, 1974), p 103.

[7] Lutyens (ed), *Lady Lytton's Court Diary*, p 94.

[8] Jean Robert, *Les Tramways de Nice et de la Côte d'Azur* (The Tramways of Nice and the Côte d'Azur) (Neuilly-sur-Seine: J. Robert, 1988), p 27.

[9] Latouche, *Histoire de Nice*, vol ii, p 150.

[10] *Ibid.*

[11] *Ibid.*, p 140.

[12] £9.03 to £36.12 at 1999 values.

[13] Latouche, *Histoire de Nice*, vol ii, p 149.

[14] £4.52, £7.34 and £13.55 at 1999 values.

[15] Latouche, *Histoire de Nice*, vol ii, pp 158–60.

[16] Paoli, *My Royal Clients*, p 338.

[17] *Ibid.*, pp 337–40.

[18] *The Times*, 14 March 1895.

[19] RA QVJ, 23 June 1887, in George Earle Buckle, *The Letters of Queen Victoria. Third Series 1886–1901* (London: John Murray, 1930–32), vol iii, p 344.

[20] Reid, *Ask Sir James*, pp 128–33.

[21] RA QVJ, 3 August 1887, in Buckle, *Third Series*, vol iii, p 344.

[22] Court Circular, 19 March 1892.

[23] Reid, *Ask Sir James*, p 138.

[24] *Ibid.*, pp 138–9.

[25] *Ibid.*, p 141.

[26] £90,320 at 1999 values.

[27] Guy-Junien Moreau and Catherine Moreau, *Le Régina: de la Reine Victoria à nos jours, splendeurs et métamorphoses d'un Palace, Nice 1897–1997* (The Regina: Queen Victoria in Our Times, Splendours and Metamorphoses of a Palace, Nice 1897–1997) (Nice: Serre, 1996), p 9.

[28] *Eclaireur de Nice*, 13 March 1895.

[29] *Eclaireur de Nice*, 16 March 1895.

[30] Cypher telegrams of 29 March 1895, in Buckle, *Third Series*, vol ii, p 490.

[31] Buckle, *Third Series*, vol ii, p 491.

[32] Cypher telegram of 1 April 1895, in Buckle, *Third Series*, vol ii, p 492, n 1.

[33] Paoli, *My Royal Clients*, p 340.

[34] Moreau and Moreau, *Le Régina*, pp 88–9.

[35] *Journal de Cimiez*, 7 February 1896.

[36] Paoli, *My Royal Clients*, pp 351–3.

[37] *Eclaireur de Nice*, 22 March 1895.

[38] Howarth, *When the Riviera Was Ours*, p 17.

[39] *Eclaireur de Nice*, 5, 9, 13, 17 April 1895.

[40] David Duff, *Eugénie and Napoleon III* (London: Collins, 1978), p 53–4.

[41] *Ibid.*, p 65.

[42] Weintraub, *Victoria: An Intimate Biography*, p 246.

[43] Robert Sencourt, *The Life of Empress Eugénie* (London: Ernest Benn, 1931), p 125.

[44] *Ibid.*, p 330.

[45] *The Times*, 29 August 1879.

[46] Letter of 26 July 1879, quoted in Longford, *Victoria R.I.*, pp 427–8.

[47] Weintraub, *Victoria: An Intimate Biography*, p 435.

[48] Duff, *Eugénie and Napoleon III*, pp 264 and 272; *Eclaireur de Nice*, 1 April 1895 et seq.

[49] Duff, *Eugénie and Napoleon III*, pp 186 and 224.

[50] Arthur Ponsonby, *Henry Ponsonby, Queen Victoria's Private Secretary*, p 382.

[51] Duff, *Eugénie and Napoleon III*, p 273.

[52] Paoli, *My Royal Clients*, p 335–6.

[53] RA QVJ, 15 March 1895.

[54] *Eclaireur de Nice*, 3 November 1922.

[55] RA QVJ, 17 April 1895.

[56] RA QVJ, 19 April 1895.

[57] *Le Miroir des modes*, January 1914.

[58] £5645 at 1999 values.

[59] *Eclaireur de Nice*, 21 April 1895.

[60] RA QVJ, 1 and 18 April 1895.

[61] Reuters report in *The Times*, 29 March, 1895; Court Circular, 3 April 1895.

[62] André Cane, 'Dans le Sillage de la Reine Victoria Lord Salisbury à Villefranche-sur-Mer.' (In the wake of Queen Victoria and Lord Salisbury at Villefranche-sur-Mer) in *Nice Historique*, No 2, April–June 1984, p 48.

[63] Letter of 1 February 2000 to the author from Robin Harcourt Williams, Librarian and Archivist to the Marquess of Salisbury.

[64] Cane, 'Dans le Sillage de la Reine Victoria', pp 48–51.

[65] Reuters report in *The Times*, 4 April 1895; *The Times*, 15 April 1895.

[66] A.J.P. Taylor, *British Prime Ministers and Other Essays* (ed Chris Wrigley) (London: Allen Lane, The Penguin Press, 1999), p 79.

[67] David Steele, *Lord Salisbury: A Political Biography* (London: UCL Press, 1999), p 2.

[68] Andrew Roberts, *Salisbury: Victorian Titan* (London: Weidenfeld and Nicolson, 1999), p 317.

[69] RA QVJ, 14 January 1875, in Buckle, *Second Series*, vol ii, p 369.

[70] Letter of 27 June 1890, in Buckle, *Third Series*, vol i, p 617.

[71] Roberts, *Salisbury*, p 581.

[72] Algernon Cecil, *Queen Victoria and Her Prime Ministers* (London: Eyre & Spottiswode, 1953), p 333.

[73] Taylor, *British Prime Ministers*, pp 79–80.

[74] *Ibid.*, p 78.

Chapter 7. 1896: Nice (pages 94–106)

[1] RA QVJ, 9 March 1896.

[2] Reid, *Ask Sir James*, p 82.

[3] RA QVJ, 11 March 1896.

[4] Moreau and Moreau, *Le Régina*, p 11.

[5] *Ibid.*, p 13.

[6] RA QVJ, 11 March 1896.

[7] Thomas Pakenham, *The Scramble for Africa, 1876–1912* (London: George Weidenfeld and Nicolson, 1991), pp 507, 513.

[8] RA QVJ, 17 November to 6 December 1895, in Buckle, *Third Series,* vol ii, pp 575–7.

[9] Oxford University Press, *Dictionary of National Biography on CD-ROM*, entry on Prince Henry Maurice of Battenberg.

[10] RA QVJ, 11 January 1896, in Buckle, *Third Series*, vol iii, p 19.

[11] RA QVJ, 14 and 16 January 1896, in Buckle, *Third Series*, vol iii, pp 21, 23.

[12] RA QVJ, 22 January 1896.

[13] James Pope-Hennessy, *Queen Mary, 1867–1953* (London: George Allen and Unwin, 1959), p 317.

[14] Weintraub, *Victoria: An Intimate Biography*, pp 565–6.

[15] Letter of 21 March 1896, in Buckle, *Third Series*, vol iii, p 36.

[16] Cypher telegram of 29 April 1896, in Buckle, *Third Series*, vol iii, pp 41–2.

[17] RA QVJ, 3 January 1896, in Buckle, *Third Series*, vol iii, p 7.

[18] Letter of 4 January 1896 from Sir Francis Knollys, Private Secretary to the Prince of Wales, to Sir Arthur Bigge, Private Secretary to the Queen, in Buckle, *Third Series*, vol iii, pp 7–8.

[19] Longford, *Victoria R.I.*, p 543.

[20] Letter of 5 January 1896, in Buckle, *Third Series*, vol iii, pp 8–9.

[21] RA QVJ, 10 January 1896, in Buckle, *Third Series*, vol iii, pp 17–18.

[22] Letter of the Queen to Lord Salisbury, 8 January 1896, in Buckle, *Third Series*, vol iii, pp 19–20.

[23] Letter of Lord Salisbury to the Queen, 8 January 1896, in Buckle, *Third Series*, vol iii, pp 12–13.

[24] Letter of the Queen to Lord Salisbury, 12 January 1896, in Buckle, *Third Series*, vol iii, p 12.

[25] Letter of the Queen to Lord Salisbury, 14 January 1896, in Buckle, *Third Series*, vol iii, pp 19–20.

[26] Aronson, *The King in Love*, p 171.

[27] Cypher telegram to Lord Salisbury, 13 March 1896, in Buckle, *Third Series*, vol iii, p 33.

[28] Message of 21 March 1896 to Lord Salisbury, in Buckle, *Third Series*, vol iii, p 35.

[29] Cypher telegram to Lord Salisbury, 22 March 1896, in Buckle, *Third Series*, vol iii, p 37.

[30] Cypher telegrams of 3 and 15 April to Joseph Chamberlain, in Buckle, *Third Series*, vol iii, pp 38–40.

[31] RA QVJ, 22 March 1896.

[32] RA QVJ, 29 March 1896, in Buckle, *Third Series*, vol iii, pp 37–8.

[33] RA QVJ, 8 April 1896.

[34] RA QVJ, 6 April 1896, in Buckle, *Third Series*, vol iii, p 39.

[35] RA QVJ, 29 March 1896, in Buckle, *Third Series*, vol iii, pp 37–8.

[36] Letter of Lord Salisbury to Sir Arthur Bigge, 17 January 1896, in Buckle, *Third Series*, vol iii, pp 24–5.

[37] Letter of Queen Victoria to Sir Arthur Bigge, 21 January 1896, in Buckle, *Third Series*, vol iii, p 25.

[38] Letter of Lord Salisbury to Sir Arthur Bigge, 5 December 1895, in Buckle, *Third Series*, vol ii, pp 557–9.

[39] £39,688 at 1999 values.

[40] Adam Hochschild, *King Leopold's Ghost: A Story of Greed, Terror and Heroism in Colonial Africa* (London: Macmillan, 1999), p 88.

[41] Letter to Bernard Mallet, 25 May 1897, quoted in Mallet (ed), *Life with Queen Victoria*, p 106.

[42] Aronson, *The Coburgs of Belgium*, pp 34–5.

[43] *Ibid.*, p 35.

[44] *Ibid.*, p 134.

[45] Quest-Ritson, *The English Garden Abroad*, p 21.

[46] Hochschild, *King Leopold's Ghost*, p 255.

[47] *Ibid.*, p 224.

[48] Neal Ascherson, *The King Incorporated: Leopold II in the Age of Trusts* (London: George Allen & Unwin, 1963), pp 292–7.

[49] Quest-Ritson, *The English Garden Abroad*, p 21–2.

[50] Frederick Ponsonby, *Recollections*, p 55.

[51] Ascherson, *The King Incorporated*, pp 244–5.

[52] Hochschild, *King Leopold's Ghost*, p 224.

[53] *Ibid.*, p 74.

[54] Reid, *Ask Sir James*, p 106.

[55] RA QVJ, 13 March 1896.

[56] Latouche, *Histoire de Nice*, vol ii, p 196.

[57] RA QVJ, 13 March 1896.

[58] *The Times*, 14 March 1896.

[59] Palmer, *Twilight of the Hapsburgs*, p 280.

[60] RA QVJ, 23 April 1888, in Buckle, *Third Series*, vol i, pp 400–1.

[61] Palmer, *Twilight of the Hapsburgs*, pp 133, 280.

[62] W.E. Gladstone, *The Gladstone Diaries* (ed M.R.D. Foot and H.C.G. Matthew) (Oxford: Clarendon Press, 1986), vol ix, p 514.

[63] RA QVJ, 17 March 1897, in Buckle, *Third Series*, vol iii, p 145.

[64] ADAM IM 496.

[65] Latouche, *Histoire de Nice*, vol ii, p 195.

[66] *Ibid.*, p 196.

[67] *Ibid.*, p 195.

[68] RA QVJ, 24 March and 24 April 1896.

[69] RA QVJ, 8 April 1896.

[70] *The Times*, 15 April 1896.

[71] RA QVJ, 28 April 1896.

Chapter 8. 1897: Nice (pages 107–121)

[1] Reid, *Ask Sir James*, pp 142–3.

[2] *The Times*, 11 March 1897.

[3] Reuters report in *The Times*, 11 March 1897.

[4] *The Times*, 12 March 1897.

[5] Sushila Anand, *Indian Sahib: Queen Victoria's Dear Abdul* (London: Duckworth, 1996), pp 79–80.

[6] Reid, *Ask Sir James*, p 143.

[7] *Ibid.*, p 141.

[8] Longford, *Victoria R.I.*, p 539.

[9] *Ibid.*, pp 540–1.

[10] Roberts, *Salisbury*, p 680.

[11] Reid, *Ask Sir James*, pp 143–4.

[12] *Ibid.*, p 144.

[13] *Ibid.*

[14] *Ibid.*

[15] *Ibid.*, pp 145–6.

[16] *Ibid.*, p 146.

[17] Letter of 10 April 1894, Arthur Ponsonby, *Henry Ponsonby, Queen Victoria's Private Secretary*, pp 131–2.

[18] Frederick Ponsonby, *Recollections*, pp 13–15.

[19] Elizabeth Longford, *Queen Victoria* (Stroud: Sutton Publishing, 1999), p 99.

[20] Moreau and Moreau, *Le Régina*, p 62.

[21] Frederick Ponsonby, *Recollections*, p 37.

[22] Lutyens (ed), *Lady Lytton's Diary*, pp 102–4.

[23] Virginia Cowles, *Edward VII and His Circle*, pp 143–4.

[24] Allen Andrews, *The Follies of King Edward VII* (London: Lexington Press, 1975), pp 145–6.

[25] Moreau and Moreau, *Le Régina*, p 62.

[26] RA QVJ, 22 April 1897.

[27] Lutyens (ed), *Lady Lytton's Diary*, pp 102–3.

[28] Moreau and Moreau, *Le Régina*, pp 62–3.

[29] Frederick Ponsonby, *Recollections*, pp 38–9.

[30] RA QVJ, 11 March 1897.

[31] Telegram from Sir Alfred Biliotti, British Consul, who had accompanied the rescue party, to Lord Salisbury, British Prime Minister and Foreign Secretary, 11 March 1897, PRO, FO 421/158.

[32] Taylor, *The Struggle for Mastery in Europe*, p 319.

[33] *Ibid.*, p 370.

[34] *The Times*, 12 March 1897.

[35] RA QVJ, 19 April 1897.

[36] RA QVJ, 24 April 1897.

[37] RA QVJ, 25 April 1897.

[38] RA QVJ, 27 April 1897.

[39] RA QVJ, 26 March 1897, in Buckle, *Third Series*, vol iii, p 146.

[40] Philip Guedella, *The Queen and Mr. Gladstone* (London: Hodder & Stoughton, 1933), vol ii, pp 76–7.

[41] Brooke and Sorenson (eds), *The Prime Ministers' Papers: W.E. Gladstone*, vol i, pp 173–4, quoted in Roy Jenkins, *Gladstone* (London: Macmillan, 1995, corrected edition, 1996), p 623.

[42] Howarth, *When the Riviera Was Ours*, p 93.

[43] Letter of 4 April 1880, quoted in Arthur Ponsonby, *Henry Ponsonby, Queen Victoria's Private Secretary*, p 184.

[44] RA QVJ, 28 February 1894, in Buckle, *Third Series*, vol ii, pp 367–8.

[45] Gladstone Memorandum, 19 March 1894, taken from the Gladstone Papers, quoted in Guedella, *The Queen and Mr Gladstone*, vol ii, pp 75–6.

[46] Robert Blake, *Gladstone, Disraeli and Queen Victoria* (Oxford: Clarendon Press,

1993) pp 23–4.

[47] Jenkins, *Gladstone*, p 623.

[48] Gladstone, *Diaries*, vol x, p 397.

[49] *Ibid.*, p 403.

[50] Jenkins, *Gladstone*, p 466.

[51] Gladstone, *Diaries*, vol x, p 409.

[52] Jenkins, *Gladstone*, p 622.

[53] Howarth, *When the Riviera Was Ours*, p 93–4.

[54] Weintraub, *Victoria: An Intimate Biography*, p 574.

[55] Typescript by Annie Quarles Van Upford, entitled 'Mémoires d'Enfant, 1957' in a dossier labelled 'La Reine Victoria', Bibliothèque du Chevalier Victor Spitalieri de Cessole, Nice.

[56] Reuters report in *The Times*, 19 March 1897.

[57] Jean Watelet, *Bibliographie de la presse française et politique et de l'information générale. 1865–1944: 6 Alpes-Maritimes et Principauté de Monaco* (Bibliography of the French Press, both Political and General Information. 1865–1944: 6 Alpes-Maritimes and the Principality of Monaco) (Paris: Bibliothèque Nationale, 1972), p 92.

[58] RA QVJ, 12 March 1897.

[59] RA QVJ, 24 April 1897.

[60] £180,640 at 1999 values.

[61] Moreau and Moreau, *Le Régina*, pp 24–6.

[62] Lutyens (ed), *Lady Lytton's Court Diary*, p 99.

[63] Moreau and Moreau, *Le Régina*, p 16.

[64] Karl Heinz Wocker, *Koenigin Victoria: Eine Biographie* (Queen Victoria: A Biography) (Duesseldorf: Claassen, 1978), p 443.

[65] Moreau and Moreau, *Le Régina*, pp 8–9.

[66] *Ibid.*, p 15.

[67] £18,064,000 at 1999 values.

[68] Moreau and Moreau, *Le Régina*, pp 24–6.

[69] *Ibid.*, pp 20–1.

[70] Pemble, *The Mediterranean Passion*, p 171.

[71] Lutyens (ed), *Lady Lytton's Court Diary*, p 98.

[72] *Liberté*, 5 December 1945.

[73] RA QVJ, 7 April 1897.

[74] Lutyens (ed), *Lady Lytton's Court Diary*, p 102.

[75] *Ibid.*, pp 100–1.

[76] Ricardo Mateos Sainz de Medrano, 'A Child of the Caucasus', *Royalty Digest*, July 1993, p 14.

[77] RA QVJ, 13 April 1897.

[78] Sainz de Medrano, 'A Child of the Caucasus', pp 14–15.

Chapter 9. 1898: Nice (pages 122–132)

[1] *The Times*, 9 March 1898.

[2] RA QVJ, 7 March 1898.

[3] *The Times*, 9 March 1898.

[4] RA QVJ, 11 March 1898, in Buckle, *Third Series*, vol iii, p 236.

[5] Reid, *Ask Sir James*, pp 82–3.

[6] *Ibid.*, p 154.

[7] *Ibid.*, pp 154–5.

[8] Court Circular, 22 March 1898.

[9] Reid, *Ask Sir James*, p 155.

[10] *Ibid.*, p 155.

[11] Aga Khan, *The Memoirs of the Aga Khan: World Enough and Time* (London: Cassell, 1954), pp 40–3.

[12] £218 at 1999 values.

[13] Aga Khan, *Memoirs*, pp 42–3.

[14] *Ibid.*, p 47.

[15] Court Circular, 1 May 1898.

[16] Princess Louise of Belgium, *My Own Affairs* (trans Maude M.C. ffoulkes) (London: Cassell, 1921), p 58–9.

[17] *Ibid.*, p 60–2.

[18] *Ibid.*, p 179.

[19] *The Times*, 9 March 1898.

[20] Louise, *My Own Affairs*, p 177.

[21] *Ibid.*, frontispiece.

[22] Ashdown, *Victoria and the Coburgs*, p 145.

[23] Dulcie M. Ashdown, *Queen Victoria's Family* (London: Robert Hale, 1975), p 123.

[24] *Ibid.*, p 124.

[25] Reuters report in *The Times*, 26 March 1888.

[26] Reid, *Ask Sir James*, pp 108–9.

[27] RA QVJ, 1 April 1898, in Buckle, *Third Series*, vol iii, p 239.

[28] Court Circular, 2 April 1898.

[29] Reid, *Ask Sir James*, pp 108–9.

[30] RA QVJ, 4 April 1898, in Buckle, *Third Series*, vol iii, p 240.

[31] Frederick Ponsonby, *Recollections*, p 55.

[32] *Ibid.*, pp 55–6.

[33] RA QVJ, 13 April 1898, in Buckle, *Third Series*, vol iii, pp 243–4.

[34] Frederick Ponsonby, *Recollections*, p 54.

[35] Moreau and Moreau, *Le Régina*, p 40.

[36] Reuters report in *The Times*, 15 April 1898.

[37] RA QVJ, 2 April 1898.

[38] RA QVJ, 21 April 1898, in Buckle, *Third Series*, vol iii, p 244.

[39] Samuel Eliot Morison, *The Oxford History of the American People* (New York: Oxford University Press, 1965), pp 800–1.

[40] RA QVJ, 4 April 1898, in Buckle, *Third Series*, vol iii, p 240.

[41] RA QVJ, 27 March 1889, in Buckle, *Third Series*, vol i, pp 481–2.

[42] R.C.K. Ensor, *England 1870–1914* (Oxford: Clarendon Press, 1936), pp 256–7.

[43] Letter of 1 April, in Buckle, *Third Series*, vol iii, p 238.

[44] Jack Gray, *Rebellions and Revolutions: China from the 1800s to the 1980s* (Oxford: Oxford University Press, 1990), pp 120–1.

[45] RA QVJ, 21 March 1898.

[46] RA QVJ, 23 March 1898.

[47] RA QVJ, 31 March 1898.

[48] RA QVJ, 1 April 1898.

[49] RA QVJ, 26 April 1898.

[50] RA QVJ, 14 March 1898.

[51] £21.83 and £109.15 at 1999 values.

[52] Duff, *Victoria Travels*, p 339.

[53] RA QVJ, 7 April 1898.

[54] Court Circular, 9 April 1998.

[55] Reuters report in *The Times*, 17 April 1898.

[56] Duff, *Victoria Travels*, p 345.

[57] Court Circular, 27 April 1898.

[58] RA QVJ, 28 April 1896.

[59] Court Circular, 27 April 1898.

[60] Duff, *Victoria Travels*, pp 345–6.

Chapter 10. 1899: Nice (pages 133–146)

[1] Sarah Searight, 'Steaming through Africa', *History Today*, July 1998, pp 17–18.

[2] Lady Gwendolen Cecil, *Life of Robert, Marquis of Salisbury* (London: Hodder and Stoughton, 1921–32), vol ii, p 130.

[3] René Girault, *Diplomatie européenne et imperialismes* (European Diplomacy and Imperialism), Histoire des relations internationales contemporaines, vol i, 1871–1914 (Paris: Masson, 1979), p 183.

[4] Searight, 'Steaming through Africa', p 14.

[5] Cypher telegram of 30 October 1898, in Buckle, *Third Series*, vol iii, pp 283–4.

[6] Letter of 24 March 1899, in Buckle, *Third Series*, vol iii, pp 353–4.

[7] Weintraub, *Victoria: An Intimate Biography*, p 600.

[8] Searight, 'Steaming through Africa', pp 12–18.

[9] Kenneth Bourne, *The Foreign Policy of Victorian England 1830–1902* (Oxford: Oxford University Press, 1970), pp 160–1.

[10] Cypher telegram of 30 October 1898, in Buckle, *Third Series*, vol iii, pp 305–6.

[11] Cypher telegram of 5 November 1898, in Buckle, *Third Series*, vol iii, p 309.

[12] Jad Adams, 'Was "K" Gay?', *History Today*, November 1999, p 27.

[13] Frank Hardie, *The Political Influence of Queen Victoria, 1861–1901* (Oxford: Oxford University Press, 1935), p 121.

[14] Guedella, *The Queen and Mr. Gladstone*, vol i, p 258; letter from the Queen to Gladstone, 10 October 1870, quoted in Hardie, *The Political Influence of Queen Victoria*, p 168.

[15] Guedella, *The Queen and Mr. Gladstone*, vol ii, p 120; letter from the Queen to Gladstone, 11 November 1880, quoted in Hardie, *The Political Influence of Queen Victoria*, p 168.

[16] Letter to Sir Henry Ponsonby, 30 May 1882, in Buckle, *Second Series*, vol iii, p 301.

[17] Letter of 11 August 1863, in Buckle, *Second Series*, vol i, p 102.

[18] Cypher telegram of 30 October 1898, in Buckle, *Third Series*, vol iii, pp 305–6.

[19] Telegram of 30 October 1898, in Buckle, *Third Series*, vol iii, p 396.

[20] *Petit Niçois*, 14 November 1898.

[21] Letter of 30 November 1899, in Buckle, *Third Series*, vol iii, p 313.

[22] Paoli, *My Royal Clients*, pp 331–2.

[23] Roberts, *Salisbury*, p 708.

[24] RA QVJ, 9 December 1898.

[25] Letter of 16 January 1899, in Buckle, *Third Series*, vol iii, pp 334–5.

[26] Letter of 8 January 1899, in Buckle, *Third Series*, vol iii, pp 333–4.

[27] Report by the Cabinet du Commissaire Central, Nice, to the Prefect of the Alpes-Maritimes, Nice, 25 February 1899, ADAM 04M102.

[28] *The Anglo-American*, 6 March 1899.

[29] Reports by the Ministry of the Interior Special Railway Police, Nice, to the Prefect of the Alpes-Maritimes, Nice, 2, 6 and 8 March 1899, ADAM, 4M102.

[30] *The Anglo-American*, 1 May 1899.

[31] *The Anglo-American*, 21 November 1899.

[32] *The Anglo-American*, 23 January 1899.

[33] *Ibid.*

[34] *The Anglo-American*, 1 May 1899.

[35] Mallet (ed), *Life with Queen Victoria*, p 151.

[36] £2728 at 1999 values.

[37] *The Times*, 11 March 1899.

[38] *Eclaireur de Nice*, 6 March 1899.

[39] *The Times*, 13 March 1899.

[40] Mallet (ed), *Life with Queen Victoria*, p 153.

[41] Weintraub, *Victoria: An Intimate Biography*, p 600.

[42] Mallet (ed), *Life with Queen Victoria*, p 159.

[43] *Ibid.*, pp 156–7.

[44] *Ibid.*, p 161.

[45] RA QVJ, 29 March 1899.

[46] RA QVJ, 25 April 1899.

[47] Reuters reports in *The Times*, 15 April 1899; Court Circular, 15 April 1899.

[48] Mallet (ed), *Life with Queen Victoria*, p 158.

[49] F. Marion Crawford, *Taquisara*, 2 vols (New York: Macmillan, 1896).

[50] Mallet (ed), *Life with Queen Victoria*, p 157.

[51] *Ibid.*, p 156.

[52] *Ibid.*, p 157.

[53] Interview by author with Rev. Kenneth Letts, Chaplain, Holy Trinity Church, Nice, 2 November 1999. The church is at 11 Rue de la Buffa.

[54] C.F.Pascoe, *Two Hundred Years of the SPG: An Historical Account of the Society for the Propagation of the Gospel in Foreign Parts* (London: SPG, 1901), pp 734–42.

[55] *Dictionary of National Biography on CD-ROM*, entry on William Boyd Carpenter.

[56] Longford, *Victoria R.I.*, p 572.

[57] RA QVJ, 26 March 1899.

[58] Yvan G. Paillard, *Expansion occidentale et dépendance mondiale* (Western Expansion and Worldwide Dependence) (Paris: Armand Colin, 1994), p 190.

[59] RA QVJ, 19 April 1899.

[60] Edwards, *The Grimaldis of Monaco*, pp 153, 159.

[61] RA QVJ, 27 April 1899.

[62] Reuters reports in *The Times*, 14 and 27 April 1899.

[63] Reuters report in *The Times*, 18 March 1899.

[64] £6548 at 1999 values.

[65] £8076 at 1999 values.

[66] £1091 at 1999 values.

[67] Reuters report in *The Times*, 28 April 1899.

[68] R.A. Geo.V, CC 6 95; Pope-Hennessy, *Queen Mary*, pp 345–6. Queen Mary seems to have mixed up the dates of the three incidents, putting them all in 1899. The correct dates, if Reid's diaries, which appear logical and reliable, are to be believed, are:
1897: Phipps ultimatum. Court Circular mentions the Munshi for the outward journey and for the return.
1898: Ahmed, not the Munshi, left behind on Salisbury's advice. Court Circular does not mention the Munshi for the outward journey, but on 22 March it announced his arrival at Cimiez. It announces his return to Windsor but does not say if he was in the royal party on the journey.
1899: Court Circular does not mention the Munshi for the outward journey, but on 1 April it said he had arrived in Cimiez the previous day. It announces his return to Windsor. Queen Mary says Salisbury told the Queen that the French were such odd people they might laugh at Her Majesty about the Munshi. The Queen would surely have answered that he had already been there four times and they had not laughed at him. The confusion is repeated in secondary sources.

[69] *The Times*, 3 May 1899.

[70] Anand, *Indian Sahib*, pp 96–104.

[71] The nearest competitor was Germany where she spent 264 nights. She spent 122 nights in Italy, 33 in Switzerland and 22 in Belgium.

[72] RA QVJ, 1 May 1899.

[73] RA QVJ, 2 May 1899.

Chapter 11. Epilogue (pages 147–150)

[1] *The Times*, 17 January 1899.

[2] Postcard, author's collection.

[3] *The Times*, 6 March 1900.

[4] Howarth, *When the Riviera Was Ours*, p 74.

[5] Letter of 1 October 1899, in Buckle, *Third Series*, vol iii, p 402.

[6] QVJ, 11 December 1899, in Buckle, *Third Series*, vol iii, p 402.

[7] *Petit Niçois*, 29 December 1899.

[8] *Petit Niçois*, 15 December 1899.

[9] Roberts, *Salisbury*, p 757.

[10] Donal Lowry, 'When the World Loved the Boers', *History Today*, May 1999, pp 46–9.

[11] Albert Grundlingh, 'The Bitter Legacy of the Boer War', *History Today*, May 1999, p 22.

[12] *Financial Times*, 11 October 1999.

[13] Ramm, *Beloved and Darling Child*, p 247.

[14] Michael Holroyd, *Lytton Strachey: A Critical Biography* (London: William Heinemann, 1967 and 1968, revised reprint in one volume, 1994), p 495.

[15] *Ibid.*, p 496.

[16] Anon. (Lady Ponsonby?), The Character of Queen Victoria, *The Quarterly Review*, April 1901, p 304.

[17] *Dictionary of National Biography on CD-ROM*, entry on Queen Victoria.

Note on the Queen's Journal (pages 151–152)

[1] Longford, *Victoria R.I.*, p 42.

[2] Buckle, *First Series*, vol i, p 40.

[3] Buckle, *Second Series*, vol ii, p vi.

[4] Viscount Esher, *The Girlhood of Queen Victoria: A Selection from Her Majesty's Diaries between the Years 1832 and 1840*, 2 vols (London: John Murray, 1912).

[5] Queen Victoria, *Leaves from the Journal of Our Life in the Highlands from 1848 to 1861* (London: Smith Elder, 1868).

[6] Queen Victoria, *More Leaves from the Journal of a Life in the Highlands from 1862 to 1882* (London: Smith Elder, 1884).

[7] Queen Victoria, *Leaves from a Journal: A Record of the Visit of the Emperor and Empress of the French to the Queen and of the Visit of the Queen and HRH the Prince Consort to the Emperor of the French, 1855* (London: André Deutsch, 1961).

Chronology

1819	24 May	Victoria born
1834	28 December	Lord Brougham arrives in Cannes, which leads to the founding of a British colony
1837	20 June	Victoria succeeds to the throne
1840	10 February	Victoria marries Prince Albert of Saxe-Coburg-Gotha
1841	9 November	Prince Albert Edward, later Prince of Wales and King Edward VII, born
1860	24 March	France acquires Nice from Sardinia
1861	14 December	Victoria's Consort, Prince Albert, dies
1863	10 April	Railway reaches Cannes
1882	16 March–12 April	Queen at Menton – Chalet des Rosiers
1883	27 March	John Brown, the Queen's ghillie, dies
1884	28 March	Prince Leopold, the Queen's youngest son, dies in Cannes
1887	1–5 April	Queen at Cannes – Villa Edelweiss
	23 June	Abdul Karim starts to work for the Queen
1891	25 March–28 April	Queen at Grasse – Grand Hôtel
	31 March	Maharajah Duleep Singh confesses his misdeeds to the Queen
1892	14 January	Prince Albert Victor, son of the Prince of Wales, dies
	21 March–25 April	Queen at Hyères – Hôtel Costebelle
1895	15 March–23 April	Queen at Nice – Grand Hôtel, Cimiez
	21 March	Queen enjoys the Battle of the Flowers in Nice
	3 April	Queen calls on Lord Salisbury, the first of many meetings on the Riviera
1896	20 January	Prince Henry of Battenberg, husband of the Queen's youngest daughter, Beatrice, dies
	11 March–29 April	Queen at Nice – Grand Hôtel, Cimiez
1897	10 March	Abdul Karim on the royal train, despite the courtiers' threat of revolt if he came to Nice
	12 March–28 April	Queen at Nice – Excelsior Hôtel Régina, Cimiez
1898	13 March–28 April	Queen at Nice – Excelsior Hôtel Régina, Cimiez
	13 April	President Faure calls on the Queen
	10 July	Frenchmen arrive at Fashoda, Sudan, thus creating the Fashoda Incident
1899	12 March–2 May	Queen at Nice – Excelsior Hôtel Régina, Cimiez
	5 May	Queen departs from Cherbourg, her last time in France
	11 October	Anglo-Boer war starts. Queen's visit to the Riviera later cancelled
1901	22 January	Queen Victoria dies

179

Selected Dramatis Personae

The names and titles are those by which the persons were generally known in Britain.

Children of Queen Victoria and Prince Albert

VICTORIA (Vicky), Princess Royal, Empress of Germany and Queen of Prussia, 1840–1901.

ALBERT EDWARD (Bertie), Prince of Wales and later King Edward VII, 1841–1910.

ALICE, Grand Duchess of Hesse and the Rhine, 1843–78.

ALFRED (Affie), Duke of Edinburgh and Saxe-Coburg-Gotha, 1844–1900.

HELENA, (Lenchen), Princess Christian of Schleswig-Holstein, 1846–1923.

LOUISE, Duchess of Argyll, 1848–1939.

ARTHUR, Duke of Connaught, 1850–1942.

LEOPOLD, Duke of Albany, 1853–84.

BEATRICE, Princess Henry of Battenberg, 1857–1944.

ALBERT, King of Saxony, 1828–1902; married Caroline Wasa, daughter of Prince Gustav of Sweden; reigned 1873–1902.

ALBERT, Prince Consort of England, 1819–61; younger son of Ernst I, Duke of Saxe-Coburg-Gotha, and Louise, daughter of Augustus, Duke of Saxe-Coburg-Altenburg; married Queen Victoria 1840.

ALBERT, Prince of Prussia, 1837–1906; son of Albert Prince of Prussia, who was son of Friedrich Wilhelm III, King of Prussia; married Marie Frederike of Sachsen-Altenburg.

ALBERT I, Prince of Monaco, 1848–1922; son of Charles III; married firstly, Mary-Victoria Douglas-Hamilton, divorced 1880; secondly, Marie-Alice Heine, Duchess of Richelieu, widow of the Duke of Richelieu; reigned 1889–1922.

ALBERT EDWARD (Bertie), Prince of Wales and later King Edward VII), 1841–1910; married Alexandra, Princess of Denmark; reigned 1901–10.

ALBERT VICTOR (Eddy), Prince, Duke of Clarence, 1864–92; elder son of Prince of Wales; engaged to Princess Victoria Mary of Teck in December 1891 and the wedding was planned for 27 February 1892, but he died on 14 January. Princess Victoria Mary married Prince George, who later became King George V, and she chose to be known as Queen Mary.

ALEXANDRA (Alix), Queen, 1844–1925; eldest daughter of Christian IX, King of Denmark; wife of Prince Albert Edward, Prince of Wales, who later became King Edward VII.

ALEXANDRA FEODOROVNA (Alicky), Tsarina of Russia, 1872–1918; daughter of Alice, Grand Duchess of Hesse and the Rhine, who was daughter of Queen Victoria, and Louis IV, Grand Duke of Hesse and the Rhine; wife of Tsar Nicholas II of Russia.

ALEXANDRA FEODOROVNA (Charlotte), Tsarina of Russia, 1798–1860; daughter of Friedrich Wilhelm III, King of Prussia; wife of Tsar Nicholas I of Russia, who died in 1855.

ALFRED (Affie), Prince, Duke of Edinburgh and Saxe-Coburg-Gotha, 1844–1900; son of Queen Victoria; married Grand Duchess Marie Alexandrovna of Russia; created Duke of Edinburgh 1863; succeeded as Duke of Saxe-Coburg-Gotha 1893.

ALICE, Princess, Grand Duchess of Hesse and the Rhine, 1843–78; daughter of Queen Victoria, wife of Louis IV, Grand Duke of Hesse and the Rhine.

ALICE, Princess of Albany, later Princess Alexander of Teck and Countess of Athlone, 1883–1981; daughter of Prince Leopold, Duke of Albany, who was youngest son of Queen Victoria; wife of Alexander, Prince of Teck, youngest brother of the future Queen Mary, who renounced his German title in 1917 and was created Earl of Athlone.

ANASTASIA, Grand Duchess of Mecklenburg-Schwerin, 1860–1922; daughter of Grand Duke Michael Nicolaievich of Russia, who was son of Tsar Nicholas I; wife of Frederick Francis, Grand Duke of Mecklenburg-Schwerin.

ARGYLL, John Campbell Douglas, Duke of, 1845–1914; previously Marquess of Lorne; son of George Douglas Campbell, 8th Duke of Argyll; married Princess Louise, daughter of Queen Victoria; succeeded as 9th Duke of Argyll 1900.

ARTHUR, Duke of Connaught, 1850–1942; son of Queen Victoria; married Louise Margaret (Louischen), Princess of Prussia; created Duke of Connaught 1874.

BEATRICE, Princess Henry of Battenberg, 1857–1944; youngest daughter of Queen Victoria; wife of Prince Henry of Battenberg (Liko).

BRAZIL, Emperor of *see* Pedro II.

CAROLINE, Princess of Monaco, 1793–1879; née Marie Louise Caroline de Lametz, wife of Florestan I, Prince of Monaco; mother of Charles III of Monaco.

CHARLES III, Prince of Monaco, 1818–89; son of Florestan I; married Antoinette-Ghislaine de Mérode; reigned 1856–89.

CHRISTIAN, Prince of Schleswig-Holstein, 1831–1917; youngest son of Prince Christian, Duke of Schleswig-Holstein; married Helena, daughter of Queen Victoria.

CLÉMENTINE, Princess Bonaparte, 1872–1955; daughter of Leopold II, King of the Belgians, wife of Victor Napoleon, Prince Bonaparte.

EDWARD VII, King *see* Albert Edward.

ELIZABETH AMALIE (Sisi), Empress of Austria and Queen of Hungary, 1837–98; daughter of Maximilian Joseph, Duke in Bavaria; wife of Francis Joseph, Emperor of Austria and King of Hungary.

ERNST II, Duke of Saxe-Coburg-Gotha, 1818–93; son of Ernst I and elder brother of Albert, the Prince Consort, husband of Queen Victoria; married Alexandrine, daughter of Grand Duke Leopold of Baden; succeeded 1844.

EUGÉNIE, Empress of the French, 1826–1920; Countess of Montijo; daughter of Manuel Count of Montijo and Duke of Penaranda and Maria Manuela, née Kirkpatrick; wife of Napoleon III, Emperor of the French.

FRANCIS JOSEPH, Emperor of Austria and King of Hungary, 1830–1916; married Duchess Elizabeth Amalie of Bavaria; reigned 1848–1916; crowned King of Hungary 1867.

FRANCIS, Duke of Teck, 1837–1900; married Mary Adelaide, Princess of Cambridge; father of Victoria Mary, who married the future George V; succeeded 1871.

FREDERICK FRANCIS III, Grand Duke of Mecklenburg-Schwerin, 1851–97; son of Frederick Francis II; married Anastasia, daughter of Grand Duke Michael Nicolaievich of Russia, who was son of Tsar Nicholas I; succeeded 1883.

FRIEDRICH III (Fritz), German Kaiser and King of Prussia, 1831–88; son of Wilhelm I; until he became Kaiser he was Crown Prince; married Princess Victoria (Vicky), eldest daughter of Queen Victoria, Princess Royal; reigned for 99 days from 9 March 1888 until his death on 15 June; father of Kaiser Wilhelm II.

GEORGE, Prince, Duke of York and later King George V (Georgie), 1865–1936; second son of Prince of Wales; married Princess Victoria Mary of Teck; reigned 1910–36.

GEORGE I (Willy), King of Greece, 1845–1913; William, son of Christian IX, King of Denmark; brother of Alexandra, Princess of Wales and later Queen of England; married Grand Duchess Olga Constantinovna of Russia; elected King of Greece 1863.

HANOVER, Queen of see Marie.

HELENA (Lenchen), Princess Christian of Schleswig-Holstein, 1846–1923; daughter of Queen Victoria; wife of Prince Christian of Schleswig-Holstein.

HELENA, Duchess of Albany, 1861–1922; daughter of Prince Georg Viktor of Waldeck-Pyrmont; wife of Prince Leopold, Duke of Albany.

HELENA VICTORIA (Thora), Princess of Schleswig-Holstein, 1870–1948; daughter of Helena, Princess Christian of Schleswig-Holstein, who was daughter of Queen Victoria; unmarried.

HENRY (Liko), Prince of Battenberg, 1858–96; son of Prince Alexander of Hesse and the Rhine; married Princess Beatrice, youngest daughter of Queen Victoria.

HENRY, Prince of Prussia, 1862–1929; son of Friedrich III, German Kaiser and King of Prussia, and Victoria, daughter of Queen Victoria; younger brother of Kaiser Wilhelm II; married Irene of Hesse and the Rhine.

LEOPOLD, Prince of Battenberg, 1889–1922; son of Princess Beatrice, who was daughter of Queen Victoria; became Lord Leopold Mountbatten in 1917; unmarried.

LEOPOLD, Prince, Duke of Albany, 1853–84; youngest son of Queen Victoria; married Princess Helena of Waldeck-Pyrmont; created Duke of Albany 1881.

LEOPOLD II, King of the Belgians, 1835–1909; son of Leopold I; married firstly Archduchess Marie-Henriette, daughter of Archduke Joseph, Prince of Hungary and Bohemia; secondly Blanche Delacroix; reigned 1865–1909.

LORNE see Argyll.

LOUIS, Prince of Battenberg and Marquess of Milford Haven, 1854–1921; son of Prince Alexander of Hesse and the Rhine; married Victoria, Princess of Hesse and the Rhine, daughter of Princess Alice, Grand Duchess of Hesse and the Rhine, who was a daughter of Queen Victoria.

LOUIS IV, Grand Duke of Hesse and the Rhine, 1837–92; married Princess Alice, daughter of Queen Victoria, who died in 1878; succeeded 1877.

LOUIS NAPOLEON, Prince Imperial, 1853–79; son of Emperor Napoleon III and Empress Eugénie. Unmarried.

LOUIS PHILIPPE, King of the French, 1773–1850; son of Louis Philippe, Duke of Orleans, and Adelaide de Penthievre; married Marie Amelie, Princess of Bourbon-Sicily; reigned 1830–48, when he abdicated.

LOUIS PHILIPPE, Comte de Paris, 1838–94; son of Ferdinand, Duke of Orleans, Crown Prince of France, who was son of Louis Philippe, King of the French; married Marie Isabella, Infanta of Spain.

LOUISE, Marchioness of Lorne and later Duchess of Argyll, 1848–1939; daughter of Queen Victoria; wife of the Marquess of Lorne, later Duke of Argyll.

LOUISE, Princess of Saxe-Coburg-Gotha, 1858–1924; daughter of Leopold II, King of the Belgians; married Prince Philip of Saxe-Coburg-Gotha; divorced 1906.

LOUISE MARGARET (Louischen), Princess of Prussia, 1860–1917; daughter of Friedrich Karl, Prince of Prussia; wife of Prince Arthur, Duke of Connaught.

MARIA CHRISTINA, Queen Regent of Spain, 1858–1929; daughter of Archduke Karl Ferdinand of Austria; wife of King Alfonso XII of Spain, who died in 1885; mother of King Alfonso XIII; Queen Regent 1885–1902.

MARIE (Missy), Crown Princess and later Queen of Romania, 1875–1938; daughter of Prince Alfred, Duke of Edinburgh and Saxe-Coburg-Gotha; wife of Crown Prince, later King, Ferdinand of Romania.

MARIE, Duchess of Edinburgh and Saxe-Coburg-Gotha, 1853–1920; daughter of Tsar Alexander II of Russia; wife of Prince Alfred, Duke of Edinburgh and Saxe-Coburg-Gotha.

MARIE, Queen of Hanover, 1818–1907; daughter of Joseph George, Duke of Saxe-Altenburg; wife of George V, Duke of Cumberland and King of Hanover, who died in 1878; the kingdom was annexed to Prussia in 1866.

MARIE FEODOROVNA, Tsarina of Russia, 1847–1928; daughter of Christian IX, King of Denmark; married Alexander III, Tsar of Russia, who died in 1894.

MARIE-HENRIETTE, Queen of the Belgians, 1836–1902; daughter of Archduke Joseph, Prince of Hungary and Bohemia; wife of Leopold II, King of the Belgians.

MARY VICTORIA, Princess of Monaco, 1850–1922; daughter of William Archibald, 11th Duke of Hamilton and 8th Duke of Brandon, and Marie Amelie, Princess of Baden; wife of Prince Albert I of Monaco; marriage annulled 1880.

MARY, Queen *see* Victoria Mary.

MARY ADELAIDE, Princess of Cambridge, Duchess of Teck, 1833–97; daughter of Adolphus Frederick, Duke of Cambridge, who was son of George III; wife of Duke Francis of Teck; mother of Princess Victoria Mary, who married the future George V.

MAUD, Princess, 1869–1938; daughter of Albert Edward, Prince of Wales; wife of King Haakon VII of Norway.

NAPOLEON III (Louis Napoleon), Emperor of the French, 1808–73; son of Louis Bonaparte and nephew of Napoleon I; married Eugénie, Countess of Montijo; President of France, 1848–52; Emperor of the French, 1852–70.

NICHOLAS II (Nicky), Tsar of Russia, 1868–1918; son of Tsar Alexander III; married Alix (Alicky), daughter of Princess Alice, who was a daughter of Queen Victoria, and Louis IV, Grand Duke of Hesse and the Rhine; reigned 1894–1917, when he abdicated.

PEDRO II, Emperor of Brazil, 1825–91; son of Pedro I and Maria Leopoldina, Arch-duchess of Austria; married Princess Teresa Cristina of Bourbon-Sicily; reigned 1840–89, when he abdicated; his daughter, Princess Leopoldina, married Prince Ludwig August of Saxe-Coburg-Gotha, which was his connection with Queen Victoria.

PHILIP, Prince of Saxe-Coburg-Gotha, 1844–1921; son of Prince August Ludwig of Saxe-Coburg-Gotha and Marie Clémentine, Princess of Orleans; married Princess Louise, daughter of Leopold II, King of the Belgians; divorced 1906.

PRINCE IMPERIAL *see* Louis Napoleon.

PRINCE OF WALES *see* Albert Edward.

RUDOLF, Crown Prince of Austria, 1858–89; son of Emperor Francis Joseph; married Princess Stephanie, daughter of Leopold II, King of the Belgians.

SOPHIE, Crown Princess of Greece and later Queen of the Hellenes, 1870–1932; daughter of Victoria, German Empress, who was eldest daughter of Queen Victoria; wife of Constantine (Tino), Crown Prince of Greece and later King of the Hellenes.

STEPHANIE, Crown Princess of Austria, 1864–1945; daughter of Leopold II, King of the Belgians; wife firstly of Rudolf, Crown Prince of Austria; secondly Count Elmer Nagy Lonyay.

VICTOR, Prince Napoleon Bonaparte, 1862–1926; son of Prince Napoleon; married Clémentine, daughter of Leopold II, King of the Belgians.

VICTORIA, Queen of the United Kingdom of Great Britain and Ireland and Empress of India, 24 May 1819 – 22 January 1901; only child of Prince Edward, Duke of Kent, fourth son of King George III, and Princess Victoria Mary Louisa of Saxe-Coburg, widow of Emich Charles, Prince of Leiningen, and sister of Prince Leopold of Saxe-Coburg, who in 1831 became King of the Belgians; married Prince Albert of Saxe-Coburg-Gotha on 10 February 1840; reigned 20 June 1837 – 22 January 1901; proclaimed Empress of India 1 January 1877.

VICTORIA, German Empress and Queen of Prussia, 1840–1901; eldest daughter of Queen Victoria; Princess Royal; wife of Friedrich III (Fritz), German Kaiser and King of Prussia; until her husband ascended the throne in March 1888 she was Crown Princess of Germany; mother of Kaiser Wilhelm II.

VICTORIA EUGENIE (Ena), Queen of Spain, 1887–1969; daughter of Beatrice, Princess Henry of Battenberg, who was a daughter of Queen Victoria; wife of King Alfonso XIII of Spain.

VICTORIA MARY (May), Duchess of York and later Queen of England, 1867–1953; daughter of Francis, Duke of Teck; wife of Prince George, later King George V.

WILHELM II (Willy), German Kaiser, 1859–1941; son of Friedrich III and Empress Victoria, eldest daughter of Queen Victoria; married Princess Auguste Viktoria, daughter of the Prince Friedrich, Duke of Schleswig-Holstein; reigned 1888–1918, when he abdicated.

WILHELMINA, Queen of the Netherlands, 1880–1962; daughter of Willem III, King of the Netherlands; married Hendrik, Duke of Mecklenburg-Schwerin; reigned 1890–1948, when she abdicated voluntarily.

Bibliography

Archives

Bibliothèque du Chevalier Victor Spitalieri de Cessole, Nice
Departmental Archives of the Alpes-Maritimes (ADAM), Nice
Municipal Archives, Nice
Municipal Archives, Menton
Public Record Office (PRO), Kew
Royal Archives (RA), Windsor
St George's Church, Cannes

Books

Abdy, Jane, *The French Poster: Chéret to Capiello* (London: Studio Vista, 1969)

Aga Khan, *The Memoirs of the Aga Khan: World Enough and Time* (London: Cassell, 1954)

Alexander, Michael and Sushila Anand, *Queen Victoria's Maharajah: Duleep Singh, 1838–1893* (New York: Taplinger Publishing, 1980)

Allison, Ronald and Sarah Riddell (eds), *The Royal Encyclopedia* (London: Macmillan, 1991)

Anand, Sushila, *Indian Sahib: Queen Victoria's Dear Abdul* (London: Duckworth, 1996)

Andrews, Allen, *The Follies of King Edward VII* (London: Lexington Press, 1975)

Arengo-Jones, Peter, *Queen Victoria in Switzerland* (London: Robert Hale, 1995)

Aronson, Theo, *The Coburgs of Belgium* (London: Cassell, 1968)

——, *Grandmama of Europe: The Crowned Descendants of Queen Victoria* (London: John Murray, 1984)

——, *The King in Love: Edward VII's Mistresses* (London: John Murray, 1988)

——, *Heart of a Queen: Queen Victoria's Romantic Attachments* (London: John Murray, 1991)

Arthaud, Christian and Eric L. Paul, *La Côte d'Azur des écrivains* (The Writers' Côte d'Azur) (Aix-en-Provence: Edisud, 1999)

Ascherson, Neal, *The King Incorporated: Leopold II in the Age of Trusts* (London: George Allen & Unwin, 1963)

Ashdown, Dulcie M., *Queen Victoria's Family* (London: Robert Hale, 1975)

——, *Victoria and the Coburgs* (London: Robert Hale, 1981)

Aumann, Georg and Harald Bachmann, *Coburg und Europa: Die regierenden Fuersten der Ernestinischen und Coburger Wettiner seit 1353* (Coburg and Europe: The ruling Princes of the Ernestin and Coburg Branches of the Wettin Family since 1353) (Coburg: Historische Gesellschaft Coburg e. V., 1998)

Ayache, Georges, *Histoire des Niçois* (Paris: Editions Fernand Nathan, 1978)

Battersea, Constance, *Reminiscences* (London: Macmillan, 1922)

Baedeker, Karl, *South-Eastern France, including Corsica: Handbook for Travellers*, third edition (London: Dulau & Co., 1898)

——, *Southern France, including Corsica: Handbook for Travellers*, third edition (London: Dulau, 1902)

Bennet, James Henry, *Winter and Spring on the Shores of the Mediterranean*, fifth edition (London: J & A Churchill, 1875)

Bennett, Daphne, *Vicky: Princess Royal of England and German Empress* (London: Collins and Harvill Press, 1971)

Benson, A.C. and Viscount Esher (eds), *The Letters of Queen Victoria: A Selection of Her Majesty's Correspondence between the years 1837 and 1861*, 3 vols (London: John Murray, 1907)

Benson, E, *Queen Victoria* (London: Longmans, 1935)

Blake, Robert, *Gladstone, Disraeli and Queen Victoria* (Oxford: Clarendon Press, 1993)

Blume, Mary, *Côte d'Azur: Inventing the French Riviera* (London: Thames and Hudson, 1992)

Boorstin, Daniel J., *The Americans: The Democratic Experience* (New York: Vintage Books, 1974)

Bordes, Maurice, *Histoire de Nice et du pays niçois* (History of Nice and the Niçois Country) (Toulouse: Edouard Privat, 1976)

Boswell, James, *The Life of Samuel Johnson, LL.D.* (London: Charles Dilly, third edition, 1799. Reprint, London: Oxford University Press, 1938)

Bourne, Kenneth, *The Foreign Policy of Victorian England 1830–1902* (Oxford: Oxford University Press, 1970)

Braudel, Fernand, *The Mediterranean and the Mediterranean World in the Age of Philip II*, 2 vols (trans. Siân Reynolds) (London: Fontana/Collins, 1975)

Bresson, Jean, *La Fabuleuse Histoire de Cannes: Ces Demeures qui ont fait Cannes* (The Fabulous History of Cannes: The Residences Which Have Made Cannes) (Monte Carlo: Editions du Rocher, 1981)

Brewster, Margaret Maria, *Letters from Cannes and Nice* (Edinburgh: Thomas Constable, 1857)

Buckle, George Earle, *The Letters of Queen Victoria. Second Series 1862–1885*, 3 vols (London: John Murray, 1926–28)

——, *The Letters of Queen Victoria. Third Series 1886–1901*, 3 vols (London: John Murray, 1930–32)

Burkart, A.J. and S. Medlik, *Tourism* (London: Heinemann, 1974)

Burke, *Burke's Guide to the Royal Family* (London: Burke's Peerage, 1973)

——, *Burke's Royal Families of the World, vol I. Europe and Latin America* (London: Burke's Peerage, 1977)

Buzard, James, *The Beaten Track: European Tourism, Literature and the Ways to Culture, 1800–1918* (Oxford: Oxford University Press, 1993)

Campbell, Christy, *The Maharajah's Box: An Imperial Story of Conspiracy, Love and a Guru's Prophecy* (London: HarperCollins, 2000)

Cassarini, Jean, *Matisse à Nice 1916–1954* (Nice: Action Culturelle Municipale, Union Méditerranéenne pour l'art moderne, 1984)

Cecil, Algernon, *Queen Victoria and Her Prime Ministers* (London: Eyre & Spottiswode, 1953)

Cecil, Lady Gwendolen, *Life of Robert, Marquis of Salisbury*, 4 vols (London: Hodder and Stoughton, 1921–32)

Chadwick, Owen, *The Victorian Church*, 2 vols (London: SCM Press, 1987)

Charlot, Monica, *Victoria: The Young Queen* (Oxford: Blackwell, 1991)

Charlot, Monica and Roland Marks, *La Société Victorienne* (Victorian Society) (Paris: Armand Colin, 1978)

Colvin, Sidney (ed), *The Letters of Robert Louis Stevenson* (London: Methuen, 1899, new edition, 4 vols, 1911)

Conseil Général des Alpes-Maritimes, *Les Alpes-Maritimes à la Belle Epoque: un département en mutation (1880–1914). Catalogue de l'exposition* (The Alpes-Maritimes in the Belle Epoque: a Changing Department (1880–1914). Exhibition Catalogue (Nice: Archives départementales, 1991)

Cowles, Virginia, *Edward VII and His Circle* (London: Hamish Hamilton, 1956)

Crawford, F. Marion, *Taquisara*, 2 vols (New York: Macmillan, 1896)

Davidson, Angus, *Edward Lear: Landscape Painter and Nonsense Poet (1812–1888)* (London: John Murray, 1968)

De Châteauneuf, Charles Martini, *Affiches d'Azur: 100 ans d'affiches de la Côte d'Azur et de la Principauté de Monaco* (Posters Azur: 100 Years of Posters of the Côte d'Azur and the Principality of Monaco) (Nice: Editions Gilletta, 1992)

De Langlade, Jacques, *La Reine Victoria* (Queen Victoria) (Paris: Editions Perrin, 2000)

De Stoeckl, Agnes, *Not All Vanity*, George Kinnaird, ed (London: John Murray, 1950)

[Dempster?] *The Maritime Alps and their Seaboard* (London: Longmans, Green, 1885)

Denis, Alphonse, *Hyères ancien et moderne: Promenades pittoresques, scientifiques et littéraires sur son territoire, ses environs et ses îles* (Hyères Ancient and Modern: Picturesque, Scientific and Literary Walks on its Territory, Surroundings and Islands) (Hyères: c 1835. Reprint of 1910 edition, Marseilles: Laffite Reprints, 1995)

Département des Alpes-Maritimes, *Annuaire Administratif, statistique et historique* (Administrative, Statistical and Historic Annual) (Nice: Librarie Ch. Cauvin, 1861–1901)

Dessais, Joseph and Xavier Eyma, *Nice et Savoie: Sites pittoresques, monuments, description et histoire des départements de la Savoie, Haute-Savoie et des Alpes-Maritimes réunis à la France en 1860* (Nice and Savoy: Picturesque Sites, Monuments, Description and History of the Deparments of Savoie, Haute-Savoie and the Alpes-Maritimes reunited with France in 1860) (Paris: Henri Charpentier, 1864. Reprint, Peronnas, Ain: Les Editions de la Tour Gile, 1994)

Duff, David, *Eugénie and Napoleon III* (London: Collins, 1978)

——, *The Shy Princess: The Life of Her Royal Highness Princess Beatrice, the youngest daughter and constant companion of Queen Victoria* (London: Evans Brothers, 1958)

——, *Victoria Travels: Journeys of Queen Victoria between 1830 and 1900, with Extracts from Her Journal* (New York: Taplinger Publishing Company, 1971)

Editions Serre, *Nice 1900: La Légende du siècle* (Nice 1900: The Legend of the Century) (Nice: Editions Serre, 1996)

Edwards, Anne, *The Grimaldis of Monaco* (New York: William Morrow, 1992)

Ellis, Leroy, *Les Russes sur la Côte d'Azur: La colonie russe dans les Alpes-Maritimes des origines à 1939* (The Russians on the Côte d'Azur: The Russian Colony in the Alpes-Maritimes from the Origins to 1939) (Nice: Editions Serre, 1988)

Ensor, R.C.K., *England 1870–1914* (Oxford: Clarendon Press, 1936)

Epton, Nina, *Victoria and Her Daughters* (New York: W.W. Norton, 1971)

Escribe, Dominique, *La Côte d'Azur: Genèse d'un mythe* (The Côte d'Azur: Genesis of a Myth) (Nice: Gilbert Vitaloni et le Conseil Générale des Alpes-Maritimes (A.C.A.M.), 1988)

Esher, Viscount, *The Girlhood of Queen Victoria: A Selection from Her Majesty's Diaries between the Years 1832 and 1840*, 2 vols (London: John Murray, 1912)

Fulford, Roger (ed), *Dearest Child: Letters between Queen Victoria and the Princess Royal 1858–1861* (London: Evans, 1964)

——, *Dearest Mama: Private Correspondence of Queen Victoria and the Crown Princess of Prussia 1861–1864* (London: Evans Bros, 1968)

——, *Your Dear Letter: Private Correspondence of Queen Victoria and the German Crown Princess 1865–1871* (London: Evans Bros, 1971)

——, *Darling Child: Private Correspondence of Queen Victoria and the Crown Princess of Prussia 1871–1878* (London: Evans Bros, 1976)

——, *Beloved Mama: Private Correspondence of Queen Victoria and the German Crown Princess 1878–1885* (London: Evans Bros, 1981)

Gardiner, Juliet, *Queen Victoria* (London: Collins and Brown, 1997)

Gaucher, Marcel, *Les jardins de la fortune* (The Gardens of Fortune) (Paris: Hermé, 1985)

Girault, René, *Diplomatie européenne et imperialismes* (European Diplomacy and Imperialism), Histoire des relations internationales contemporaines, vol 1 1871–1914 (Paris: Masson, 1979)

Gladstone, W.E., *The Gladstone Diaries*, 14 vols (ed M.R.D. Foot and H.C.G. Matthew) (Oxford: Clarendon Press, 1986)

Gonnet, Paul, *Les Alpes-Maritimes autrefois: touristes et travailleurs* (The Alpes-Maritimes in Other Days: Tourists and Workers) (Lyons: Editions Horvath, 1993)

Graves, Charles, *Royal Riviera* (London: William Heinemann, 1957)

Gray, Jack, *Rebellions and Revolutions: China from the 1800s to the 1980s* (Oxford: Oxford University Press, 1990)

Green, J.R., *Stray Studies from England and Italy* (London: Macmillan, 1876)

Gregory, Alexis, *The Golden Age of Travel 1880–1939* (New York: Cassel, 1991)

Greville, Charles, *The Greville Memoirs: A Journal of the Reigns of King George IV, King William IV and Queen Victoria*, ed H. Reeve, 8 vols (London: Longmans, Green, 1888)

Grihangne, Roger, *Queen Victoria in Grasse* (trans and ed David Lockie) (Grasse: Ville de Grasse, 1991)

Guedella, Philip, *The Queen and Mr. Gladstone*, 2 vols (London: Hodder & Stoughton, 1933)

Gwynn, Stephen and Gertrude Tuckwell, *The Life of the Rt. Hon. Sir Charles W. Dilke Bart., M.P.*, 2 vols (London: John Murray, 1917)

Hardie, Frank, *The Political Influence of Queen Victoria 1861–1901* (Oxford: Oxford

University Press, 1935)

Hare, Augustus J.C., *South-Eastern France* (London: George Allen, 1890)

——, *The Rivieras* (London: George Allen, 1897)

Harris, Frank, *My Life and Loves*, ed John F. Gallagher (London: W.H. Allen, 1964)

Haug, James, *Leisure and Urbanism in Nineteenth Century Nice* (Lawrence, Kansas: The Regent Press of Kansas, 1982)

Hibbert, Christopher (ed), *Queen Victoria in Her Letters and Journals* (London: John Murray, 1984. Reprint, Harmondsworth, Middlesex: Penguin, 1985)

Hildesheimer, Ernest, *Guide des Archives de Alpes-Maritimes* (Guide to the Archives of the Alpes-Maritimes) (Nice: 1974)

Hindley, Geoffrey, *Tourists, Travellers and Pilgrims* (London: Hutchinson, 1983)

Hochschild, Adam, *King Leopold's Ghost: A Story of Greed, Terror and Heroism in Colonial Africa* (London: Macmillan, 1999)

Hodge, A. Trevor, *Ancient Greek France* (London: Duckworth, 1998)

Holroyd, Michael, *Lytton Strachey: A Critical Biography*, 2 vols (London: William Heinemann, 1967 and 1968, revised reprint in one volume, 1994)

Homans, Margaret, *Royal Representations: Queen Victoria and British Culture, 1837–1876* (Chicago: University of Chicago Press, 1998)

Homans, Margaret and Adrienne Munich (eds), *Remaking Queen Victoria* (Cambridge: Cambridge University Press, 1997)

Howarth, Patrick, *When the Riviera Was Ours* (London: Routledge & Kegan Paul, 1977. Reprint, London: Century, 1988)

Huberty, Michel, Alain Giraud and F. and B. Magdelaine, *L'Allemagne Dynastique* (Dynastic Germany), 7 vols (Le Perreux: Alain Giraud, 1976–94)

Jacobs, Michael, *A Guide to Provence* (London: Viking, 1988)

James, Henry, *Hawthorne* (New York: Collier Books, 1966; originally published 1879)

Jenkins, Roy, *Dilke: A Victorian Tragedy* (London: Macmillan, 1965; originally published 1958)

——, *Gladstone* (London: Macmillan, 1995; corrected edition, 1996)

Kingston, Patrick, *Royal Trains* (London: Spring Books, 1989)

Lamont-Brown, Raymond, *Edward VII's Last Loves: Alice Keppel & Agnes Keyser* (Stroud: Sutton Publishing, 1998)

Latouche, Robert, *Histoire de Nice*, 3 vols (Nice: Ville de Nice, 1951–65)

Leques, Paulette, *Tourisme hivernal et vie mondaine à Nice de 1860 à 1881: cercles et salons* (Winter tourism and the Life of Fashion in Nice from 1860 to 1881: Circles and Salons), in *Aspects de Nice du XVIIIe au XXe Siècles. Annales No. 19* (Nice: Faculté des Lettres et Sciences Humaines de Nice and Les Belles Lettres, 1973)

Letuaire, Henri, *Combat de Trafalgar* (The Battle of Trafalgar), pamphlet (Hyères: G. Bloch, 1891)

Levi, Peter, *Edward Lear: A Biography* (London: Macmillan, 1995)

Liautard, René, *Histoire du Pays Niçois: Des origines à l'epoque moderne* (History of the Country of Nice: From the Origins to the Present Day) (Nice: Editions du Rocher, 1991. Reprint, 1996)

Liégeard, Stéphen, *La Côte d'Azur* (Paris: Académie Francaise, 1887 & 1894. Reprint of 1894 edition, Nice: Serre, 1988)

Linn, Thomas, *The Health Resorts of Europe: A medical guide to the mineral springs, climatic mountain and seaside health resorts, milk, whey, grape, earth, mud, sand and air cures of Europe* (London: Henry Kimpton, 1899)

Login, Lena, *Sir John Login and Duleep Singh* (London: W.H. Allen, 1890)

Longford, Elizabeth, *Victoria R.I.* (London: Weidenfeld & Nicolson Ltd, 1964)

——, (ed), *The Oxford Book of Royal Anecdotes* (Oxford: Oxford University Press, 1989)

——, *Queen Victoria* (Stroud: Sutton Publishing, 1999)

Louise of Belgium, HRH Princess, *My Own Affairs* (trans Maude M.C. ffoulkes. London: Cassell, 1921)

Lutyens, Mary (ed), *Lady Lytton's Court Diary, 1895–1899* (London: Hart-Davis, 1961)

Magnus, Philip, *King Edward the Seventh* (London: John Murray, 1964)

Mallet, Victor (ed), *Life with Queen Victoria: Marie Mallet's Letters from Court 1887–1901* (London: John Murray, 1968)

McDonald, Ian, *The Boer War in Postcards* (Stroud: Alan Sutton Publishing, 1990)

Marx, Roland, *La Reine Victoria* (Queen Victoria) (Paris: Editions Fayard, 2000)

Millar, Delia, *The Victorian Watercolours and Drawings in the Collection of Her Majesty the Queen*, 2 vols (London: Philip Wilson, 1995)

Millar, Oliver, *Victorian Pictures in the Collection of Her Majesty the Queen* (Cambridge: Cambridge University Press, 1992)

Moore, Roy and Alma Moore, *Thomas Jefferson's Journey to the South of France* (New York: Stewart, Tabori & Chang, 1999)

More, Jasper, *The Mediterranean* (London: Batsford, 1956)

Moreau, Guy-Junien and Catherine Moreau, *Le Regina: De la Reine Victoria à nos jours, splendeurs et métamorphoses d'un palace, Nice 1897–1997* (The Regina: From Queen Victoria to Our Times, Splendours and Metamorphoses of a Palace, Nice 1897–1997) (Nice: Serre, 1996)

Morison, Samuel Eliot, *The Oxford History of the American People* (New York: Oxford University Press, 1965)

Mossop, J., *Thomas Robinson Woolfield's Life at Cannes and Lord Brougham's First Arrival* (London: Kegan Paul, Trench, Truebner, 1890)

Munich, Adrienne, *Queen Victoria's Secrets* (New York: Columbia University Press, 1996)

Murray, John, *A Handbook for Travellers in France*, 15th edition, 2 vols (London: John Murray, 1881)

Musée Masséna, *Les Anglais dans le Comté de Nice et en Provence depuis le XVIIIme siècle: L'Art Anglais au Musée Masséna* (The English in the County of Nice and in Provence since the XVIIIth Century: English Art at the Musée Masséna) (Nice: Editions des Amis du Musée Masséna, 1934)

Nevill, Barry St-John (ed), *Life at the Court of Queen Victoria 1861–1901* (Exeter, Devon: Webb & Bower, 1984)

Newsome, David, *The Victorian World Picture* (London: John Murray, 1997)

Noakes, Vivien, *Edward Lear: The Life of a Wanderer* (London: Collins, 1968)

Nock, O.S., *Railways of Western Europe* (London: Adam & Charles Black, 1977)

Office Intercommunal du Tourisme du Golfe des Iles d'Or, *Guide Touristique Hyères, les Palmiers et les Iles d'Or* (Hyères: Consultant Publicité Edition, n.d.)

Oxford University Press, *Dictionary of National Biography on CD-ROM* (Oxford, 1998)

Paget, Walpurga, *In My Tower*, 2 vols (London: Hutchinson, 1924)

Paillard, Yvan G., *Expansion occidentale et dépendance mondiale* (Western Expansion and Worldwide Dependence) (Paris: Armand Colin, 1994)

Pakenham, Thomas, *The Scramble for Africa, 1876–1912* (London: George Weidenfeld and Nicolson, 1991)

Pakula, Hannah, *An Uncommon Woman: The Empress Frederick, Daughter of Queen Victoria, Wife of the Crown Prince of Prussia, Mother of Kaiser Wilhelm* (London: Weidenfeld & Nicolson, 1996. Reprint, London: Phoenix, 1996)

Palmer, Alan, *Twilight of the Hapsburgs: The Life and Times of Emperor Francis Joseph* (London: Weidenfeld and Nicolson, 1994)

Paoli, Xavier, *My Royal Clients* (trans Alexander Teixeira de Mattos) (London: Hodder and Stoughton, 1911)

Pascoe, C.F., *Two Hundred Years of the SPG: An Historical Account of the Society for the Propagation of the Gospel in Foreign Parts* (London: SPG, 1901)

Pemble, John, *The Mediterranean Passion: Victorians and Edwardians in the South* (Oxford: Clarendon Press, 1987)

Plumptre, George, *Edward VII* (London: Pavilion Books, 1995)

Ponsonby, Arthur, *Henry Ponsonby, Queen Victoria's Private Secretary: His Life from His Letters* (London: Macmillan, 1942)

Ponsonby, Frederick, *Side Lights on Queen Victoria* (New York: Sears Publishing Company, 1930)

——, *Recollections of Three Reigns* (London: Eyre & Spottiswoode, 1957)

Pope-Hennessy, James, *Aspects of Provence* (London: Longmans, Green, 1952)

——, *Queen Mary, 1867–1953* (London: George Allen and Unwin, 1959)

——, *Robert Louis Stevenson* (London: Jonathan Cape, 1974)

Porter, Bernard, *Britain, Europe and the World 1850–1982: Delusions of Grandeur* (London: George Allen and Unwin, 1983)

Potts, D.M. and W.T.W. Potts, *Queen Victoria's Gene* (Stroud: Alan Sutton Publishing, 1995)

Quest-Ritson, Charles, *The English Garden Abroad* (London: Viking, 1992)

Ramm, Agatha (ed), *Beloved and Darling Child: Last Letters between Queen Victoria and Her Eldest Daughter 1886–1901* (Stroud: Alan Sutton Publishing, 1990)

Read, Donald, *England 1868–1914: The Age of Urban Democracy* (London: Longman, 1979)

Reid, Michaela, *Ask Sir James: The Life of Sir James Reid, Personal Physician to Queen Victoria* (London: Viking, 1987)

Robert, Jean, *Les Tramways de Nice et de la Côte d'Azur* (The Tramways of Nice and the Côte d'Azur) (Neuilly-sur-Seine: J. Robert, 1988)

Roberts, Andrew, *Salisbury: Victorian Titan* (London: Weidenfeld and Nicolson, 1999)

Roehl, John C.G., *Young Wilhelm: The Kaiser's Early Life, 1859–1888* (trans Jeremy Gaines and Rebecca Wallach) (Cambridge: Cambridge University Press, 1998)

Rothschild, Miriam and others, *The Rothschild Gardens* (London: Gaia Books, 1996)

Russell, Vivian, *Gardens of the Riviera* (London: Little Brown, 1993)

St Aubyn, Giles, *Queen Victoria: A Portrait* (London: Sinclair-Stevenson, 1991)

Saudan, Michel, Yolande Blanc and Sylvia Saudan-Skira, *De l'Hotel-Palais en Riviera* (The Hotel Palace on the Riviera) (Geneva: Atelier d'edition 'Le Septième Fou', 1985)

Sencourt, Robert, *The Life of Empress Eugénie* (London: Ernest Benn, 1931)

Sewell, J.P.C., *Personal Letters of King Edward VII: Together with Extracts from the Correspondence of Queen Alexandra, the Duke of Albany and General Sir Arthur and Lady Paget* (London: Hutchinson, 1931)

Sigaux, Gilbert, *History of Tourism* (trans Joan White) (London: Leisure Arts, 1966)

Sillitoe, Alan, *Leading the Blind: A Century of Guide Book Travel 1815–1914* (London: Macmillan, 1995)

Smollett, Tobias, *Travels through France and Italy, Containing Observations on Character, Customs, Religion, Government, Police, Commerce, Arts and Antiquities. With a particular Description of the Town, Territory and Climate of Nice, to which is added a Register of the Weather, kept during a residence of Eighteen Months in that city* (London: R. Baldwin, 1766. Reprint, Fontwell, Sussex: Centaur Press, 1969)

Souhami, Diana, *Mrs. Keppel and Her Daughters* (London: Harper Collins, 1996)

Steele, David, *Lord Salisbury: A Political Biography* (London: UCL Press, 1999)

Stephanie of Belgium, HRH Princess, *I Was To Be Empress* (London: Ivor Nicholson & Watson, 1937)

Stewart, Robert, *Henry Brougham 1778–1868: His Public Career* (London: The Bodley Head, 1986)

Stoney, Benita and Heinrich C. Weltzein (eds), *My Mistress the Queen: The Letters of Frieda Arnold, Dresser to Queen Victoria 1854–9* (trans Sheila de Bellaigue) (London: Weidenfeld and Nicolson, 1994)

Stowe, William W., *Going Abroad: European Travel in Nineteenth-Century American Culture* (Princeton: Princeton University Press, 1994)

Stoye, John Walter, *English Travellers Abroad, 1604–1667: Their Influence in English Society and Politics* (London: Jonathan Cape, 1952)

Strachey, Lytton, *Eminent Victorians* (London: Chatto & Windus, 1918)

——, *Queen Victoria* (London: Chatto and Windus, 1921)

Taylor, A.J.P., *British Prime Ministers and Other Essays* (ed Chris Wrigley) (London: Allen Lane, the Penguin Press, 1999)

——, *The Struggle for Mastery in Europe 1848–1918* (Oxford: Clarendon Press, 1954, reprint 1971)

Thomas, Keith, *Man and the Natural World: Changing Attitudes in England 1500–1800* (London: Allen Lane, 1983)

Thompson, H.P., *Into All Lands: The History of the Society for the Propagation of the Gospel in Foreign Parts 1701–1950* (London: SPCK, 1951)

Turner, Louis and John Ash, *The Golden Hordes: International Tourism and the Pleasure Periphery* (London: Constable, 1975)

Underwood, Peter, *Queen Victoria's Other World* (London: Harrap, 1986)

Van der Kiste, *Queen Victoria's Children* (Gloucester: Alan Sutton, 1986)

Victoria, Queen, *Leaves from the Journal of Our Life in the Highlands from 1848 to 1861* (London: Smith Elder, 1868)

——, *More Leaves from the Journal of a Life in the Highlands from 1862 to 1882* (London: Smith Elder, 1884)

——, *Leaves from a Journal: A Record of the Visit of the Emperor and Empress of the French to the Queen and of the Visit of the Queen and HRH the Prince Consort to the Emperor of the French, 1855* (London: André Deutsch, 1961)

Von Isenburg, Prince Wilhelm Karl, *Stammtafeln zur Geschichte der Europaeischen Staaten* (Genealogical Tables of European States), (Marburg: J.A. Stargardt, 1953)

Warner, Marina, *Queen Victoria's Sketchbook* (New York: Crown Publishers, 1979)

Watelet, Jean, *Bibliographie de la presse francaise et politique et de l'information générale. 1865–1944: 6 Alpes-Maritimes et Principauté de Monaco* (Bibliography of the French Press, both Political and General Information. 1865–1944: 6 Alpes-Maritimes and the Principality of Monaco) (Paris: Bibliothèque Nationale, 1972)

Watson, Alfred E.T., *King Edward VII as a Sportsman* (London: Longmans Green, 1911)

Watson, Vera, *A Queen at Home: An Intimate Account of the Social and Domestic Life of Queen Victoria's Court* (London: W.H. Allen, 1952)

Weintraub, Stanley, *Victoria: An Intimate Biography* (New York: Truman Talley Books/Dutton, 1987. Reprint, New York: Truman Talley/Plume, 1992)

Wharton, Edith, *A Backward Glance* (London: J.M. Dent, 1993; originally published 1934)

Withey, Lynne, *Grand Tours and Cook's Tours: A History of Leisure Travel, 1750–1915* (London: Aurum Press, 1998)

Wocker, Karl Heinz, *Koenigin Victoria: Eine Biographie* (Queen Victoria: A Biography) (Duesseldorf: Claassen, 1978)

York, HRH Duchess of and Benita Stoney, *Travels with Queen Victoria* (London: Weidenfeld and Nicolson, 1993)

Young, Arthur, *Travels in France and Italy* (London: 1792. Dent reprint, 1976)

Zeepvat, Charlotte, *Prince Leopold: The Untold Story of Queen Victoria's Youngest Son* (Stroud: Sutton Publishing, 1998)

zu Erbach-Schoenberg, Princess Marie (Princess of Battenberg), *Reminiscences* (London: George Allen & Unwin, 1925)

Articles

Adams, Jad, 'Was "K" Gay?', *History Today*, November 1999, pp 26–7

Anon., (Lady Ponsonby?), 'The Character of Queen Victoria', *The Quarterly Review*, April 1901, pp 301–37

Cane, André, 'Dans le Sillage de la Reine Victoria Lord Salisbury à Villefranche-sur-Mer' (In the Wake of Queen Victoria and Lord Salisbury at Villefrance-sur-Mer) *Nice Historique*, No 2, April–June 1984, pp 47–52

Caronia, Claire, 'La Communauté Protestante à Hyères de 1800 à 1945' (The Protestant Community in Hyères from 1800 to 1945), summary of a Master's thesis at the University of Nice, *Recherches Régionales Alpes-Maritimes et contrées limitrophes,* Archives Départementales, Conseil Géneral des Alpes-Maritimes, No 143, 1998, pp 35–61

Delormeau, Charles and Robin Avillach, 'Les Cimetières Anglais à Nice.' (The English cemeteries in Nice.) *Nice Historique*, No 4, 1991, pp 167–76

Dyer, Colin, 'Hivernants et habitants sur la Riviéra Francaise: Nice et Cannes jusqu'à l'arrivée du chemin de fer' (Winter Visitors and Inhabitants on the French Riviera: Nice and Cannes up to the Arrival of the Railway), *Recherches Régionales Alpes-Maritimes et contrées limitrophes,* Archives Départementales, Conseil Géneral des Alpes-Maritimes, No 143, 1998, pp 17–32

Grundlingh, Albert, 'The Bitter Legacy of the Boer War', *History Today*, May 1999, pp

21–7

Lowry, Donal, 'When the World Loved the Boers', *History Today*, May 1999, pp 43–9

Millar, Delia, 'Queen Victoria Goes South', *Country Life*, 26 September 1985, pp 860–2

Sainz de Medrano, Ricardo Mateos, 'A Child of the Caucasus', *Royalty Digest*, July 1993, pp 12–15

Sappia, Henri, 'Les Anglais sur la Côte d'Azur' (The English on the Côte d'Azur), *Nice Historique*, No 6, March 1899, pp 81–4

Searight, Sarah, 'Steaming Through Africa', *History Today*, July 1998, pp 12–19

Zeepvat, Charlotte, 'In Royal Footsteps', *Royalty Digest*, June 1998, pp 359–63

Index